PIMLICO

495

THE DEVIL'S GARDENS

Lydia Monin was born and educated in New Zealand. She holds a degree in Political Studies from the University of Otago and a postgraduate Diploma in Journalism from the University of Canterbury. She worked on a variety of documentaries for independent television company First Hand, before becoming a network news reporter for Radio New Zealand. She then joined Television New Zealand as a reporter and producer for regional news and current affairs. In 1997 she was awarded a Chevening David Low Fellowship to attend the Reuter Foundation Programme, Green College, University of Oxford. After joining Concordia she produced *The Devil's Gardens* television documentary series.

Andrew Gallimore was born and educated in Wales. He is a graduate in Industrial Relations from the University of Wales College of Cardiff, where he also attained a master's degree in journalism. A former print journalist, he began his television career at HTV's current affairs department before joining the original production team at the evening news magazine programme, *Heno*, for S4C in 1990. He then established Concordia, an independent television production company specialising in international documentary co-production. In 1997–98 he held a fellowship at the Reuter Foundation Programme, Green College, University of Oxford. He directed *The Devil's Gardens* television documentary series.

THE DEVIL'S GARDENS
A History of Landmines

LYDIA MONIN and ANDREW GALLIMORE

PIMLICO

Published by Pimlico 2002

2 4 6 8 10 9 7 5 3 1

Copyright © Lydia Monin and Andrew Gallimore 2002
Foreword copyright © Martin Bell 2002

First published in Great Britain by
Pimlico 2002

Pimlico
Random House, 20 Vauxhall Bridge Road,
London SW1V 2SA

Random House Australia (Pty) Limited
20 Alfred Street, Milsons Point, Sydney
New South Wales 2061, Australia

Random House New Zealand Limited
18 Poland Road, Glenfield,
Auckland 10, New Zealand

Random House South Africa (Pty) Limited
Endulini, 5A Jubilee Road, Parktown 2193, South Africa

The Random House Group Limited Reg. No. 954009
www.randomhouse.co.uk

A CIP catalogue record for this book
is available from the British Library

ISBN 0-7126-6859-4

Typeset in Bembo 11½/13pt by SX Composing DTP, Rayleigh, Essex
Printed and bound in Great Britain by Biddles Ltd, Guildford

Contents

Acknowledgements

In the process of producing *The Devil's Gardens* we filmed in eleven countries and travelled through many more to get to our destinations. This has been an ambitious project, which could only have been realised with the invaluable help of those already working in landmine-affected countries.

We would like to thank the following organisations for their logistical help, field support and expert knowledge: Mines Advisory Group, Handicap International, International Committee of the Red Cross, United Nations, the Cambodia Trust, the HALO Trust, Landmines Struggle Centre and FMAC.

We would like to acknowledge Bob Collins and Cenwyn Edwards of RTE in Ireland and S4C in Wales respectively, who had enough faith in the concept to ensure the project got off the ground in the first place. Geraint Stanley Jones, Giles Davies, Rebecca Jarrad and Godfrey Hodgson were all instrumental at various stages in the production.

Special thanks must go to friends and family for their support throughout this project, especially Nanette Monin, for her invaluable assistance during the final stages of writing this book.

The maps are taken from International Campaign to Ban Landmines, *Landmine Monitor Report 2001: Toward a Mine-Free World* (New York: Human Rights Watch, 2001; ISBN 1-56432-262-9) and are reproduced by kind permission of Human Rights Watch.

Finally, *The Devil's Gardens* owes much to the patience and generosity of the huge number of people who have agreed to be interviewed over the past couple of years. Unless indicated by reference numbers, quotes throughout the book are taken from interviews for the television series.

1997 Convention on the Prohibition of the Use, Stockpiling, Production and Transfer of Antipersonnel Mines and on their Destruction

ICELAND

NORWAY

CANADA

UNITED KINGDOM   DENMARK
IRELAND   NETHERLANDS   Po
                GERMANY   S
        BELGIUM   CZECH
        LUXEMBOURG   REP.
        LIECHTENSTEIN   AUSTRIA
        SWITZERLAND   SLOVENIA
    FRANCE   CROATIA
            SAN MARINO   BOSNIA
        MONACO   HERZEGOVIN
        ANDORRA   ALBANI
            HOLY SEE
PORTUGAL   SPAIN   ITALY   G

Atlantic
Ocean   TUNISIA   'MALT

        Morocco   Algeria   Libya

United States

                            •MAURITANIA   MALI   NIGER
BAHAMAS   DOMINICAN REP. •   •CAPE VERDE   CH
Cuba   ST. KITTS AND NEVIS   •SENEGAL
MEXICO   ANTIGUA AND BARBUDA   Gambia•
    JAMAICA   •ST. LUCIA   •GUINEA-BISSAU   BURKINA   BENIN
GUATEMALA   BELIZE   DOMINICA   ST. VINCENT AND THE GRENADINES•   GUINEA   FASO
EL SALVADOR   HONDURAS   Haiti   GRENADA   BARBADOS   •SIERRA LEONE   Nigeria
    NICARAGUA   TRINIDAD AND TOBAGO   LIBERIA   GHANA•   TOGO   Cameroo
COSTA RICA   VENEZUELA   Guyana   •COTE D'IVOIRE   C
PANAMA   Suriname   •IBRA
    COLOMBIA •   EQUATORIAL GUINEA •   GABON •
ECUADOR   Sao Tome
Equator   •   and Principe

Pacific   PERU   BRAZIL   Angc
Ocean   Z

        BOLIVIA   Atlantic   NAMIBIA
                    Ocean   BO
        PARAGUAY   SW
Tropic of Capricorn   S
                                A

                URUGUAY •
    ARGENTINA

    Chile

ICELAND

SIERRA LEONE

© **Landmine Monitor Report 2001** – Jasmine Desclaux-Salachas

Russia

EN

and

stonia
atvia
ania

Belarus

Ukraine
MOLDOVA•
Y
NIA•

BULGARIA   Kazakhstan   Mongolia
ONIA FYR   Georgia
              Azerbaijan–   Uzbekistan Kyrgyzstan
Turkey   **TURKMENISTAN**   North
yprus   Armenia   **TAJIKISTAN**   Korea
Lebanon– Syria   China   South
Israel   Iraq   Iran   Afghanistan   Nepal   Korea   **JAPAN**
JORDAN   Pakistan   Bhutan
         Kuwait   Pacific
Egypt   Bahrain **QATAR**   **BANGLADESH**•   Ocean
         Saudi   United Oman   India   Tropic of Cancer
         Arabia   Arab Emirates   Burma   Laos
Eritrea   **THAILAND** Vietnam
udan   **YEMEN**   Sri Lanka   **CAMBODIA**   **PHILIPPINES**   Marshall
ican   **DJIBOUTI**   Brunei   Islands   Micronesia
         Somalia   Palau
Ethiopia   **MALDIVES** •   **MALAYSIA**
LE) **UGANDA**   Singapore   **NAURU** • **KIRIBATI** •
     KENYA •   **SEYCHELLES** •   Papua–   Tuvalu
ep. Burundi   Indonesia   New Guinea   **SOLOMON**
?0   **ISLANDS**
TANZANIA •
         Comoros   Vanuatu   **SAMOA**
NA•   **MALAWI**   Indian   **FIJI**   Cook
                                       Ocean   Islands
ABWE   **MADAGASCAR**   **AUSTRALIA**   Tonga
NA   • **MAURITIUS**   **NIUE**
AND
         MOZAMBIQUE
| **LESOTHO**
A
                                                                    NEW
                                                                    ZEALAND

YEMEN	**118 STATES PARTIES (Signed and Ratified or Acceded).**
•**RWANDA** **RWANDA**•	**States that have joined the Treaty since 31 March 2000.**
Haiti	**22 Signatories (Signed but not Ratified).**
United States	*53 Non-Signatories (Not yet Acceded).*

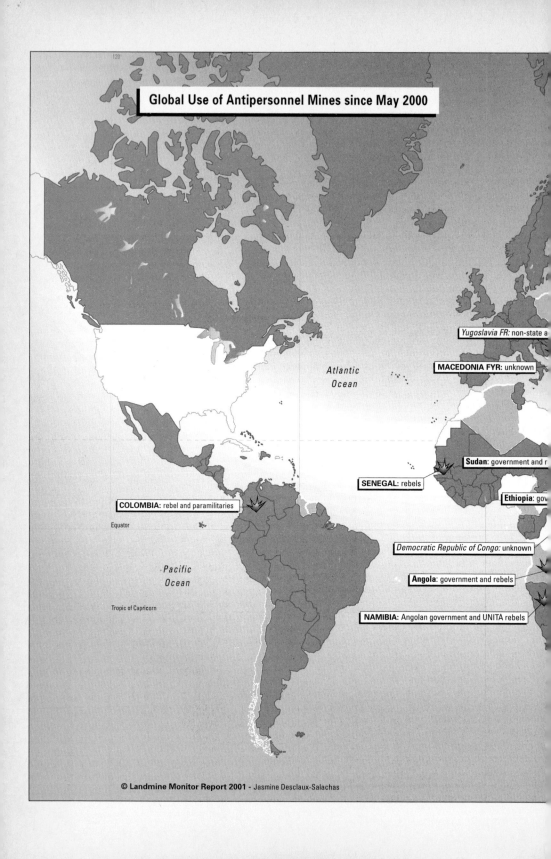

Global Use of Antipersonnel Mines since May 2000

Atlantic Ocean

Pacific Ocean

Equator

Tropic of Capricorn

Yugoslavia FR: non-state a

MACEDONIA FYR: unknown

Sudan: government and r

SENEGAL: rebels

Ethiopia: gov

COLOMBIA: rebel and paramilitaries

Democratic Republic of Congo: unknown

Angola: government and rebels

NAMIBIA: Angolan government and UNITA rebels

© Landmine Monitor Report 2001 - Jasmine Desclaux-Salachas

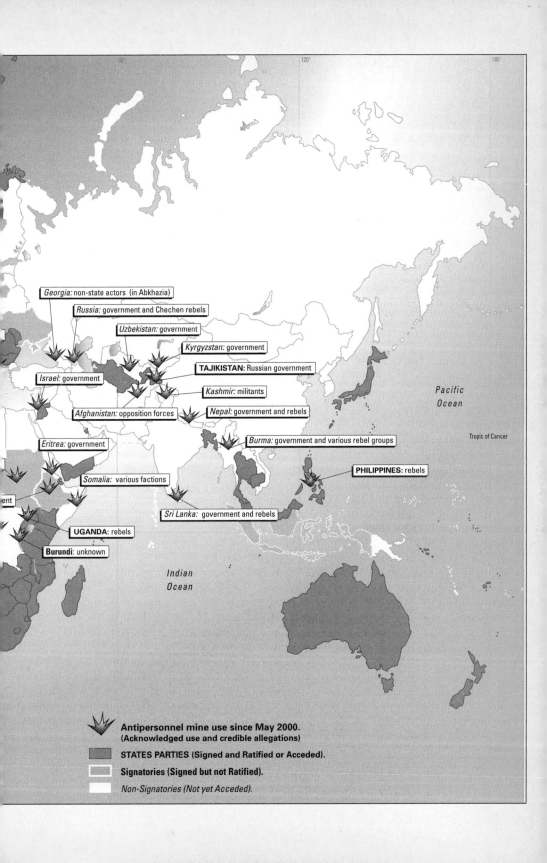

Georgia: non-state actors (in Abkhazia)

Russia: government and Chechen rebels

Uzbekistan: government

Kyrgyzstan: government

TAJIKISTAN: Russian government

Israel: government

Kashmir: militants

Afghanistan: opposition forces

Nepal: government and rebels

Eritrea: government

Burma: government and various rebel groups

PHILIPPINES: rebels

Somalia: various factions

ent

Sri Lanka: government and rebels

UGANDA: rebels

Burundi: unknown

Pacific
Ocean

Tropic of Cancer

Indian
Ocean

Antipersonnel mine use since May 2000.
(Acknowledged use and credible allegations)

STATES PARTIES (Signed and Ratified or Acceded).

Signatories (Signed but not Ratified).

Non-Signatories (Not yet Acceded).

Foreword
by Martin Bell

This is not a book which I wish had not been written, but it is certainly a book which I wish had not been necessary. In a safer, saner world, it would not have been. But technology has advanced and human nature remains obstinately the same. The world we live in is neither safe nor sane. It suffers from a great proliferation of weapons of war – one of which, a relative newcomer, claims lives and limbs with a quite unique ferocity. That weapon is the landmine. This book is its life story. Perhaps death story would be a better phrase – except that the landmine is, alas, very much alive.

I try not to have enemies. But the landmine, and especially the anti-personnel mine with the devil's ingenuity that goes into the making of it, is one of the few I allow. I encountered it regularly during that part of my life which was spent in the world's war zones – from Vietnam to Angola and from Nicaragua to Bosnia. The Bosnian experience was perhaps the sharpest of all. For the mines used there were home-made. The former Yugoslavia, manufacturer and exporter of landmines, combined a high-minded Third World diplomacy with intense and parallel activity in the international arms market. By a cruel irony, the engines of death used in Bosnia from 1992 to 1995 were in large measure made in Bosnia, the centre of the Yugoslav arms industry.

The landmine is cheap to make and easy to deploy. It claims lives without exposing troops to counter-fire, and is attractive to a military commander whose forces are outnumbered. It substitutes for infantry. It doesn't need to be watered or fed or disciplined. Although it dates back to the nineteenth century, it is characteristically a weapon of the civil wars of the post-colonial era in the twentieth century, and now the twenty-first. For regular armies it has outlived its usefulness – except perhaps for the Americans in Korea, and even there for political rather than military reasons. The Gulf War in 1991 showed that a well-equipped main force army in high-intensity warfare can circumvent a minefield, or blast a way through it, with relative ease. A guerrilla force, or ill-equipped government formation, cannot.

The landmine has two characteristics which distinguish it from other weapons of war. One is that it knows no ceasefire. Long after a peace treaty is signed and a ceasefire takes hold, it will continue to maim and kill its victims yet unborn. The other is that it has the effect of targeting civilians. Among those civilians two groups are specially vulnerable – children because of their curiosity and energy, and farmers because of their need to reclaim and work their land. The landmine is a weapon of denial.

Its stigmatisation has been well earned. Yet the campaign against anti-personnel mines is still in its early years. It has not yet recovered the impetus it lost with the death of its most charismatic champion, Diana, Princess of Wales. Its objectives are divided between the political and diplomatic side of the movement, which seeks to ban landmines, and the soldierly and practical which seeks to destroy them. The principal British demining agencies, the Mines Advisory Group and the HALO Trust, remain chronically underfunded. The anti-personnel mine is still *de facto* a legitimate weapon of war. The cluster bombs dropped by NATO on Kosovo in 1999 had the function of aerially sown landmines, yet were not covered by the Ottawa Treaty banning anti-personnel mines.

It is in this setting, of slow achievement against great odds, that *The Devil's Gardens* makes its timely appearance. Together with the television series of the same name, it tells the grim and compelling story of the most pernicious weapon of our time. It is a story that reflects no credit on anyone, except those who risk their lives to destroy landmines around the world.

Introduction

The events in this paragraph take no more than one hundredth of a second to unfold. The sudden exertion of pressure detonates a low explosive that in turn detonates a high explosive charge. The blast sends a violent wave of energy through human tissue that carries with it shattered fragments of metal, plastic, earth, vegetation, bone, flesh, clothing and footwear. The remains of the limb are now connected to the body by slivers of flesh. The wound is saturated with a cocktail of particles delivered at speeds of thousands of miles an hour by the blast wave.

The events in this paragraph take a few seconds to unfold. The victim is calm. It is quiet as the dust settles. Then, very gradually, there's a growing realisation that a truly terrible event has taken place. There's no immediate pain, but panic begins to set in.

The events in this paragraph take a lifetime to unfold. The pain is now unbearable. It's several hours since the explosion and the victim has yet to reach a hospital. When medical help arrives a surgical amputation is required to cut away the flesh that's inundated with debris. Eventually the wound has healed sufficiently for a prosthesis to be fitted. The patient learns how to walk again – taking the first steps towards a future of poverty, deprivation and prejudice.

In the time it takes to read this book, it's likely that this chain of events will have been triggered again by another unsuspecting victim. Based on the television documentary series of the same name, *The Devil's Gardens* is the story of how a weapon of war caused a humanitarian crisis. The landmine will serve as a legacy of twentieth-century evil long into this millennium. It kills and cripples civilians. It paralyses economies. The Devil's Gardens are sown by rich countries selling cheap weapons to poor countries. The crop reaped is human misery on an unimaginable scale.

The history of the landmine mirrors a century of social and military history: from its development by imperialist forces for the Great War to its distribution by superpowers throughout the developing world to the post-Cold War humanitarian crusade that was the Ottawa Process. When a conflict ends, the minefields ensure that the ravages of war hang around civilian activity for decades. After the guns fall silent, the buried killers take over – cutting off towns and villages, schools and hospitals, keeping people and food away from each other.

The public at large first became aware of the plight of the landmine victim when the late Diana, Princess of Wales, was photographed walking through an Angolan minefield in January 1997. But the campaign for a worldwide ban began long before Diana's involvement. The road to the Ottawa Treaty (on the prohibition of the production, transfer, stockpiling and use of anti-personnel landmines and on their destruction) has been globally divisive but also intriguing and colourful.

The origin of the landmine according to some commentators can be traced back three thousand years, making it one of the oldest weapons in existence. Others argue that weapons resembling the modern landmine were first used in the American Civil War. What is beyond doubt is that the widespread use of today's landmine, which is killing and maiming innocent people across seventy-one countries world-wide,[1] is a direct legacy of the Great War. What started as little more than a humble trap quickly became a weapon of mass destruction. The movement to ban landmines emerged after half a century of devastation caused by a weapon that had become commonplace in world wars, civil wars, tribal battles and sometimes even civilian disputes.

The laying of landmines caused a humanitarian crisis. The crisis began as the primitive landmine was adapted and refined, and as military strategists drew on past wars to see how they could cause even more damage to the enemy in future conflicts. Lessons learned during the Great War led to huge strides in landmine development. By the time the world was at war again, a generation later, the landmine was an essential part of every army's arsenal. The deserts of North Africa became the world's first massive minefield and people are still being killed and maimed there by sixty-year-old mines. The superpowers that emerged from the carnage of World War II fought each other on foreign soil and Southeast Asia became the first front line of the Cold

War. Korea, Vietnam and Cambodia became playgrounds for Soviet and American military boffins to try out ever more sophisticated landmines. It wasn't long before the manufacturers of these silent killers found a new market for their wares opening up on the Dark Continent. The flame of independence burned through Africa in the 1970s, igniting bloody civil wars, some of which, such as in Angola, are still raging. The focus of the Cold War shifted dramatically in 1979 when the Soviet Union invaded Afghanistan, and yet more mines were buried. The subsequent break-up of the Soviet Union and the Eastern bloc resulted in mainland Europe's first war in half a century: in the Balkans landmines were used as a weapon of terror between people who had once been neighbours and friends.

The *Devil's Gardens* project has involved four years of research culminating in a television documentary series and this book. It was started after the frenzy of media attention surrounding Diana, the Nobel Peace Prize (jointly awarded to the International Campaign to Ban Landmines and its leader, Jody Williams) and the Ottawa Treaty subsided. During the research period it became obvious that, outside the 'landmine fraternity', there was a perception that the issue could safely be filed away in the 'problem solved' folder. News media had moved on to other dramas, other crises. The *cause célèbre* was suffering from donor fatigue. If this book has one overriding purpose, it is to serve as a reminder that the landmine crisis is not over. In every country visited during the filming of the television series or research for the book, landmine casualties still arrive in far-flung hospitals, primitive factories still painstakingly produce prostheses by the thousands, and legions of protective-suited deminers still prod away remorselessly at the world's minefields.

There are thousands of innocent victims around the world who have fallen prey to the landmine, many of them children not even born when the weapon that ruined their lives was buried. But it hasn't always been the 'baddies' using the landmine. A cursory glance at the recent history of two countries, Cambodia and Bosnia-Herzegovina, provokes uncomfortable ethical questions. Civilians used mines to keep out both the Khmer Rouge and Serbian ethnic cleansers. They were prepared to trade the risk of landmine injuries in the future for the protection landmines offered them against the risk of torture and murder at the hands of would-be persecutors. A subsequent Cambodian government, installed after the Khmer Rouge had been driven into the jungles on the Thai border, used mines against the rebels. Without the government's use of mines, some say the Khmer Rouge would have taken over the country for a second time.

A complete ban on the use of landmines is a long way off. Campaigners claim that the Ottawa Treaty will eventually be strong enough to ensure the complete elimination of landmines and an end to the suffering the weapon has caused. However, the realisation of that vision doesn't seem likely. There are still many obstacles to overcome. The world's most powerful armies are not subject to the treaty, including the former Cold War powers, the United States, Russia and China. Landmines are still being used in current wars. They still serve a purpose as substitute soldiers, and they still allow poor armies or insurgents to lay claim to vast areas of land cheaply.

The arguments about how to solve the worldwide problem of landmines provoke more questions than answers: what effect is the Ottawa Treaty having? Can the use of the landmine be controlled through stigmatisation alone? Can landmines ever be eliminated when the technology to make them is so simple and so readily available? What happens to governments who join the Ottawa Treaty and then contravene it? There is also a great deal of debate about how global demining is funded and carried out. Why haven't mine-affected countries in the developing world been cleared of mines at the same rate as Europe was after World War II, or Kuwait after the Gulf War? Can demining operations be completed faster without cutting corners? Can they attract more money? This book attempts to answer these searching questions and many more, drawing on the knowledge and expertise of people who deal with the landmine problem on a daily basis around the world. The book also provides a global picture of the misery the landmine will continue to cause for a long time. The landmine crisis is far from over.

Lydia Monin
Andrew Gallimore
August 2001

I

'No Exceptions, No Reservations, No Loopholes'

THIS is a post-Cold War tale of intrigue and suspense. A story with a president, a princess and a pop star. It has heroes and villains, good guys and bad guys and a disparate group of campaigners who upstaged the governments of the world. The story begins in the unspeakable horror of the Vietnam War and ends with an international treaty, a Nobel Peace Prize, and one of the most remarkable feats of global diplomacy and political manoeuvrings of recent times.

The roots of what has come to be known as the International Campaign to Ban Landmines (ICBL) can be traced back to the Vietnam War. Defeated US military officers came back from Southeast Asia arguing that not only were the mines ineffective against the Viet Cong, but that American-laid landmines contributed greatly to the American casualty count. According to a declassified US Defense Intelligence Agency report, landmines and booby traps accounted for 65–70 per cent of Marine Corps casualties in Vietnam during 1965.[1] Other statistics claim that between a third and a fifth of all US deaths during the whole of the Vietnam War were caused by landmines.[2]

While the Vietnam War was a watershed in the history of the landmine it was also a landmark in the history of war reporting. By 1970 colour television was becoming commonplace and the swarms of largely unrestrained camera teams were supplying the networks with graphic images of civilians and soldiers killed and mutilated by an array of weaponry. There's no doubt that these pictures served to strengthen the anti-war movement in the USA during the conflict but they also had a lasting impact on the world's consciousness. The horrors engendered by these terrifying new weapons of war were the catalyst for a host of pressure groups and non-governmental organisations (NGOs) to take up the cause against the carnage. The International Committee of the Red Cross (ICRC) drew particular attention to the landmine due to its inherent failure to discriminate between combatant and civilian. The ICRC had expressed concerns about the landmine as long ago as the early 1950s when it published *Draft Rules for the Protection of the Civilian Population*, which called for the military to record and map minefields during times of war. At the same time it also required post-conflict exchange of information to ensure rapid clearance of mine-contaminated ground. However, this was a time when Cold War paranoia was at its height, and for states fighting proxy wars across the globe, the adoption of new international regulations on the use of landmines came, in terms of priority, a distant second.

Two decades of fighting in Southeast Asia prompted the ICRC into another attempt to apply international humanitarian law to the use of landmines. In 1973 it published *Weapons That May Cause Unnecessary Suffering or Have Indiscriminate Effects*. The main focus of this work was incendiary weapons such as napalm but the study also identified mines as a particular danger to civilians. The following year the ICRC convened a Conference of Governmental Experts on the Use of Certain Conventional Weapons. Landmines were on the agenda but many of the experts present argued that a ban was both impracticable and unjustified. A second session of this conference was held two years later at Lugano where draft proposals were discussed for the deployment of manually laid and remotely delivered landmines, the mapping of minefields, and the use of mines and booby traps in civilian areas. Much of what was proposed in Lugano ultimately became the basis of Protocol II to the 1980 UN Convention regulating the use of certain conventional weapons. The main thrust of Protocol II was that mines should not be directed against civilians. In practice, however, the Protocol was useless: it applied only to international arms conflicts at a time when landmines were widely used in bloody civil wars, and it did not provide any mechanism for policing its provisions. The 1980 Convention on Certain Conventional Weapons (CCW) may have had little practical effect but it did at least provide a basis for further debate.

The use of anti-personnel landmines escalated rapidly during the 1980s. International law was having no effect in checking the rapid proliferation of landmines especially in countries like Afghanistan,

Angola, Cambodia and Mozambique. By the 1990s the plague had reached Europe and Central Asia with the outbreak of conflicts in the former Yugoslavia and the former Soviet Union. The dramatic increase in the number of landmine casualties treated by their field surgeons prompted the ICRC to take action. In 1992 it published *Mines: A Perverse Use of Technology*, in essence a barrage of shocking images of mine victims from ICRC clinics. Robin Coupland, one of the ICRC's leading war surgeons, who had operated on hundreds of mine victims in Cambodia and Afghanistan, was one of the first medics to draw attention to what was becoming an epidemic of mine injuries:

> If you're going to run a campaign on an issue like this and influence policy makers you have to have four elements on which to base a campaign. Firstly, you have to provide reliable data. Secondly, you have to provide images. Thirdly, you have to be credible and, fourthly, you have to make it a public concern. Our hospitals provided most of the data about injuries in the early days of the campaign. And we also provided the images, what mines did to people. I think these images that came out of our hospitals and our rehabilitation centres were an essential component [of the campaign].

The impetus for a landmine ban came from several non-governmental organisations working in war-torn areas. One country which appeared to have a particularly acute landmine problem was Cambodia. Statistics were produced which showed the country to have the highest percentage of physically disabled inhabitants in the world and so a delegation was assembled by the Asia Division of Human Rights Watch & Physicians for Human Rights to investigate the use of landmines in Cambodia and their effect on the civilian population. The report of the visit became one of the seminal works on the issue. *Landmines in Cambodia: The Coward's War* was published in September 1991. It not only called for immediate action to abate the suffering of the Cambodian people but also openly derided the impact of landmine protocol in the 1980 Convention on Certain Conventional Weapons. 'It has been nearly ten years since these protocols were adopted, and there is very little to show for it', claimed the report. Citing the ineffectiveness of the protocol in any internal conflict, the authors concluded that the convention failed to address the reality of warfare. The final paragraph of *Landmines in Cambodia* was in essence a mission statement for what became a global campaign:

3

The United Nations and the International Committee of the Red Cross should consider an unconditional ban on the manufacture, possession, transfer, sale and use of landmines and other devices that detonate on contact in all international and internal conflicts. While such a law might not entirely eliminate the use of mines, it would stigmatise them in much the same way that chemical weapons are now vilified.[3]

The report was presented by Rae McGrath of the Mines Advisory Group and Eric Stover of Physicians for Human Rights at a conference in May 1992, which was organised by Handicap International and staged at the Senate Palace in Paris. The conference received limited publicity but, crucially, the report was distributed to all members of the European Parliament as well as to French and Belgian legislators. Within seven months the European Parliament had passed a resolution calling for a ban on the export of landmines. Within three years Belgium had passed a law banning landmines.

Coinciding with the publication of *Landmines in Cambodia* another group that had a unique insight into the terror wreaked by the landmine became increasingly proactive on the issue – the Vietnam Veterans of America Foundation (VVAF). Established by former Marine Lieutenant turned anti-war activist Bobby Muller, the VVAF fought not only for the needs of veterans but also for reconciliation with Vietnam. Muller led the first delegation of American veterans back to Vietnam in 1981 before returning to Southeast Asia three years later for a visit that would become integral to the formation of an international campaign to ban landmines. This time, Muller visited Cambodia and saw first-hand the sheer number of amputees in the country and the lack of any real provision for them. The plight of the landmine victim became a VVAF crusade and in the summer of 1991 it opened a prosthetics clinic in Cambodia. Muller soon realised that supplying new limbs merely addressed the symptoms and that the only way to deal with the disease was a widespread campaign to ban landmines. In November 1991, Muller met with Thomas Gebauer, head of the German-based Medico International, an aid organisation with which the VVAF had worked extensively on several other programmes, to discuss the possibility of orchestrating a landmine campaign. Aware of the need to secure political backing from the outset, the VVAF approached Vermont Democratic Senator Patrick Leahy. The senator had established the War Victims Fund to assist landmine victims and was a more than willing ally for the VVAF's campaign. Bobby Muller also found a supporter in Congress – Lane Evans, a Vietnam veteran from Illinois. The Leahy–Evans partnership in conjunction with the VVAF and other Washington-based non-governmental organisations ultimately led to the world's first unilateral moratorium on anti-personnel landmine exports. The ban was to last for one year but was subsequently extended several times until President Clinton announced a permanent export ban in 1997. The United States had taken the lead in the crusade against the landmine.

The International Campaign to Ban Landmines

On 2 October 1992, the Vietnam Veterans of America Foundation–Medico International partnership and the Human Rights Watch & Physicians for Human Rights partnership, together with Handicap International and British-based demining organisation the Mines Advisory Group (MAG) met in New York. It was at this meeting that the International Campaign to Ban Landmines (ICBL) was born. These organisations became the steering committee of the ICBL with the VVAF's Jody Williams appointed as the coordinator. From the outset, the ICBL operated with 'no central office or bureaucracy – member organisations were free to pursue the achievement of the campaign's goals as best fit their own mandate'.[4] The ICBL became a broad church with a membership that boasted more than 1,200 non-governmental organisations from over sixty countries around the world. Jody Williams attributes much of the success of the ICBL in attracting such widespread support to a matter of timing:

> We were the first concrete thing that people in the peace movement could concentrate on after the end of the Cold War. When the Berlin Wall came down people didn't think we were going to die in a nuclear conflagration anymore, and peace activists were lost. The landmine problem was very concrete and it didn't take much to explain it to people. It's pretty black and white that it's a bad weapon so we got popular support.

The idea of a ban on a particular type of weapon is not new. Informal customs such as the prohibition on the use of poison in war had held firm for many centuries before any attempt was made to draw up a code of conduct for warfare. However, there was a very real sense that this was a new type of international campaign working in a new environment. The Professor of International Relations at Oxford University, Adam Roberts, believes the whole campaign was very much a product of its time:

> The end of the Cold War had one very big effect on Western public consciousness in which a large number of issues came to be judged in what one might loosely describe as humanitarian terms. In other words, putting it simply, people were less concerned at defining which were the goodies and which were the baddies – which were the communists, and which were those fighting for freedom, or whatever crude categories there had been before – and more concerned with the issue of the humanitarian consequences of war and alleviating them. It was almost as if humanitarian standards had become the criteria by which to judge how one should respond to a conflict – and of course by humanitarian standards landmines are absolutely out of the picture as something that ought to be prohibited because of the hideous effects on all and sundry.

The International Campaign to Ban Landmines got off to a spectacular start. Forty NGOs turned up to its first conference in London in 1993. The number of participants doubled for its second conference in Geneva a year later. The ICBL's idea of non-governmental organisations operating in tandem with governments also appeared to be working. The only existing international agreement that attempted to restrict the use of landmines was the 1980 Convention on Certain Conventional Weapons. Such conventions can be reviewed after a ten-year period of the treaty becoming operational providing a signatory state calls for such a reappraisal. Although the review in itself was unlikely to achieve a worldwide landmine ban, the ICBL was aware that the process could be useful in raising the profile of the campaign.

Handicap International succeeded in putting enough pressure on the French President François Mitterrand to call for a Review Conference of the CCW, which began in Vienna on 25 September 1995. While expectations were low, the outcome of the negotiations were far worse than the ICBL had expected. The initial agreement imposed limited restrictions on landmine deployment with a requirement for carefully recording where they were laid and a warning system to stop civilians from accidentally wandering into a minefield. Its major weakness, however, was that like most such treaties governing the laws of war it was mainly applied to international conflicts and during the 1980s and 1990s the proliferation of the landmine problem was mainly associated with civil wars. After a few aborted attempts the review process was finally completed with no significant advances in implementing a ban but with one clause that was a setback to the campaign. The new protocol narrowed the definition of what constituted an anti-personnel landmine and also legalised the use of self-destructing, or 'smart' mines. If the review process was a setback, by now it became apparent that there was opposition to a ban even within the ever-expanding group of non-governmental organisations and demining agencies.

Humanitarian demining had grown almost in parallel with the political campaign since the late eighties and early nineties. One of the biggest humanitarian demining groups, the Mines Advisory Group, had been part of the ICBL since its inception and continued as a staunch supporter of the campaign. The other major British demining group, the HALO Trust, refused to be a part of the ICBL from the outset. HALO (Hazardous Areas Life-Support Organisation) director Guy Willoughby saw the campaign as a diversion from mine clearance that his organisation couldn't afford in terms of time or money: 'We took the view that lots of people and agencies were getting involved with the ICBL and our involvement would not help particularly. But it would be a distraction for us as an organisation with a tiny headquarters and low audited administration costs. We wanted to continue to concentrate on mine clearance.'[5]

One of the loudest of the dissenting voices is Paul Jefferson who set up HALO's first mine-clearance operation in Afghanistan. According to Jefferson the campaign has diverted funds from the real issue:

> It enables governments to claim that they are spending money on dealing with the problem of landmines, whereas in fact they are spending money on discussing the problem, on hosting conferences, on carrying out 'assessment missions', on promoting 'mines awareness' campaigns – on almost anything, in fact, other than the messy business of actually getting the mines out of the ground.[6]

One of the major bones of contention which divides the two camps is the actual number of mines currently buried around the world. Jefferson argues that the commonly quoted figure of 110 million landmines is a gross overestimation. It is a distortion in which he admits to having unwittingly played a central role. The story dates back to his time with the HALO programme in Afghanistan and a United Nations report which stated that there were thirty-five million mines buried in the country. Together with a colleague he calculated that for this figure to be correct, the Soviet army would have had to deploy 10,000 mines for every day of occupation in Afghanistan. Jefferson argued that this was not possible and that the maximum number of mines laid was likely to be less than a third of this figure. His calculations were subsequently presented to the United Nations which revised its Afghanistan estimate to ten million mines. This figure was then used as a benchmark – other mined countries such as Angola and Cambodia were assessed as having more or fewer mines than Afghanistan based on criteria such as hospital records, population numbers and length of conflict. A combination of all these figures produced a grand total of around 110 million mines.

According to Jefferson:

The general public and the politicians have been taken for a ride. You people out there, you have been misled by the ICBL, well meaningly, no doubt, but in the process they have presented the world with an oversimplified view of the landmine problem. What is even more sinister is they're holding out to the world that a ban can and is addressing the landmines problem. It cannot address the landmines problem and it will not address the landmines problem. In the eight years of its existence the ICBL has not reduced the casualty count by one leg. It has not returned one acre of land to a population of a contaminated country. The only thing that has done that is mine clearance. The mines problem is a practical problem and it screams out for two practical disciplines – the discipline of the medic for the landmine casualty, and it screams out for the discipline of the mine clearer to get mines out of the ground – in one of two ways. You either tread on it and detonate it or you clear it; it's as simple as that.

One of the founder members of the ICBL, Rae McGrath, calls the argument surrounding the figures 'ridiculous'. 'I wish we had been able to avoid it, but because we have to operate with the media we can't avoid the issue of how many mines there are, because the news media in particular need statistics . . . Why waste time arguing about how many mines there are. Let's just get on and clear the mines we find.'

Jefferson argues that:

the real, insidious damage being done by the ban-the-mines lobby is this: by distorting the figures, they imply that mine clearers are fighting a losing battle, that they cannot solve the problem . . . Most mine clearers see the political lobbying effort, the International Campaign to Ban Landmines, as having distorted the shape and size of the issue. In their rush to generate public outrage and political consciousness of the issue the ICBL has gone ahead with distorting statistics, presenting the image and shape of a problem which just doesn't exist.

Dissenting voices were of little concern to the ICBL at a time when it seemed that the most powerful man on earth was firmly on its side. When President Clinton addressed the United Nations' General Assembly on 26 September 1994 and pledged to fight for a worldwide agreement to end the use of anti-personnel mines the campaign took on even greater momentum. But while the President's words were an undoubted boost, seasoned campaigners in America knew that the real challenge was turning the promise into policy; or, as the ICBL said, turning 'rhetoric into reality'. The VVAF tried to provide Clinton with the military and political support he would need to fulfil his commitment to ban anti-personnel mines. In early 1996 the organisation set about courting retired three- and four-star generals to dispute the need for landmines in modern-day warfare. A full-page advertisement was placed in the *New York Times,* entitled 'An Open Letter to President Clinton'. Signed by fifteen retired senior US military officers, including the commander of Operation Desert Storm, General Norman Schwarzkopf, the letter stated that an anti-personnel mine ban was both 'humane' and 'militarily responsible'.[7] The advertisement became international news and considerably raised hopes that a forthcoming US military review on anti-personnel landmines would come out in favour of a total ban. However, the ICBL was about to experience another setback.

On 10 May 1996, the Chairman of the Joint Chiefs of Staff, General John Shalikashvili, took the conclusions of the review to the White House. Within an hour details of the findings had been released to the dismay of pro-ban campaigners. The commander-in-chief responsible for Korea had argued forcefully for the retention of anti-personnel mines. Six days later President Clinton announced a policy which adhered to the review. It contained four main elements. Firstly, the United States pledged to take a leading role in the international negotiations on a landmine ban. Secondly, an immediate ban would come into effect on non-self-destructing anti-personnel mines, except in Korea. Thirdly, the United States was reserving the right to use 'smart' mines in any conflict until any international ban took effect and, finally, that Korea would be an exception in any negotiation on a ban until alternatives became available or the risk of aggression had been removed. The campaign for an international ban had been dealt a serious blow. Reacting to the news Bobby Muller said, 'last week the President stressed his personal concern over landmines by describing the hours he has committed to addressing this problem, and by noting that he keeps an anti-personnel mine on his desk in the Oval Office. This proposal would make a mockery of the President's concern, and would run a dagger through the heart of our international campaign to ban this weapon.'[8]

Enter Canada

The Review Conference of the 1980 Convention on Certain Conventional Weapons had struggled on from the opening session in Geneva in September 1995, through various adjournments, and through to the publication of the new protocol in Vienna in May the following year. Delegates returned resigned to a world that would be awash with landmines for decades to come. A senior US State Department negotiator claimed that 'the Chinese have told us flat out that they'll give up nukes before they give up anti-personnel mines'.[9] The failure to reach any form of consensus, however, provoked many states to take unilateral action. During the course of the CCW negotiations a whole series of announcements were made from governments all over the world declaring anti-personnel export and deployment bans and stockpile destruction. Realising the need to coordinate these initiatives, the Canadian government invited all states that actively supported a landmine ban together with the non-governmental organisations to a meeting in Ottawa in October 1996.

In the build-up to the Ottawa conference, Canadian officials and the International Campaign to Ban Landmines were locked in discussions as to how to identify which states were likely to be genuinely supportive and which would use the meeting to scupper any progress. It became known as the 'good list'. The first step was to introduce a self-selection process to participation. The Canadian government asked those interested in attending the meeting to sign a declaration stating their intention to ban the use, production, stockpiling and sale of anti-personnel mines by the year 2000. State participation at the meeting would therefore divide into full status for signatories and observer status for nations who declined to endorse the declaration but who wished to attend the meeting. The United States agreed to sign the declaration on condition that the Canadians withdrew the timescale. The Canadians agreed and the United States attended but the affair had created bad blood. The United States had long considered itself to be the leading light in the campaign to ban landmines – yet it struggled to make Canada's 'good list'. Canadian-born journalist and author Michael Ignatieff expressed sympathy for the United States:

> Canada's not a big mine producer, if it's a mine producer at all, and it doesn't have any strategic reason to use mines and so it's very easy to be the good guy. That's the cynical reason. The deeper reason is that Canada has a long tradition going back to Lester Pearson, the Foreign Minister who invented peacekeeping as we know it. Canada has a long association with that kind of international humanitarian action so the Ottawa Treaty fitted right into a tradition of Canadian action as a kind of middle power, one of the good guys. But let's be clear about what it means to be a good guy; I mean, it's one thing to be a good guy about mines if you don't have some strategic interest that requires mines to defend.

After all the horse trading fifty countries attended the Ottawa conference as full participants, with a further twenty-four states present as observers. To gel the pro-ban forces the ICBL and the ICRC along with other prominent campaigners were totally integrated with state representatives at the conference. The opportunity to expose diplomats to the full force of the pro-ban campaign was too good an opportunity to miss.

The first three days of the meeting passed without major incident. Discussions proceeded at a theoretical level with everybody in agreement that landmines were fundamentally evil and that a global ban was undoubtedly a good idea. Nobody, however, was prepared for the drama that would unfold as the meeting drew to an end. In his closing address Canada's Foreign Minister Lloyd Axworthy, announced that his government would stage a treaty signing conference for a total ban in December 1997 and that Canada would sign it irrespective of how many other states supported the treaty. It was one of the defining moments of the entire campaign. The ICBL and its supporters were ecstatic – many of the diplomats, however, were furious. Several members of the US delegation had already left that morning, content with the outcome and oblivious to the sensational events developing in Ottawa. Some states that had supported an anti-personnel mine ban were also openly critical of the way in which the Canadian government announced their initiative, as indeed was one of the key men in the entire history of the campaign, Rae McGrath: 'It placed the United States in an embarrassing position. They didn't know it was coming and they were caught on the hop. Now that may have been very satisfying for the Canadians to embarrass their neighbours, but the fact is that it was very stupid, because at the very time you need the United States on board, they did the opposite.'

The United States, France and the United Kingdom argued that this 'coalition of the angels'[10] would not only have no real effect but they were also highly suspicious of the Ottawa Process and its strategic alliances with non-governmental organisations. The three countries much preferred to follow the path of the Conference of Disarmament in Geneva which effectively gave them the power of veto to control the rate of progress on any ban.

Within a few months the White House announced that the United States would not be supporting the Ottawa Process. In January 1997 President Clinton announced a permanent ban on US mine exports and pledged that his country would destroy its stockpile of non-self-destructing mines. Crucially, he also committed the United States to support efforts to enforce a global ban through the UN Conference on Disarmament. Critics argued that this was no more than a stalling tactic. The UN process was likely to take many years before reaching any agreement on a ban.

The positions of the United Kingdom and France mirrored each other very closely throughout the Ottawa Process. Both countries were initially sceptical and both reacted angrily to Axworthy's speech at the conclusion of the Ottawa meeting in October 1996. The basis for a shift in policy was also similar; election victories for the Labour Party in the UK and Lionel Jospin's socialists in France during 1997 paved the way for a change of emphasis on the landmine issue. Tony Blair swept into government in May 1997, and in his first month in office Foreign Secretary Robin Cook announced that the United Kingdom was to ban the import and export, transfer and manufacture of anti-personnel mines. More importantly he also announced that Britain would be in the 'fast track'[11] of the Ottawa Process. The Labour Party had promised to bring an ethical dimension to foreign policy. The Ottawa Process appeared to fit this ethos perfectly. On the other hand, Labour's love of 'Ottawa' may have had something to do with a certain princess.

Enter the Princess

Throughout its short history the ICBL has made no secret of the fact that generating public outrage and political consciousness of the issue have been the key strategies. And when, one morning in January 1997, the world's most photographed woman walked through a minefield, the campaign was about to receive publicity on an unimagined scale. Pictures of Diana, Princess of Wales, in protective clothing and visor walking through the minefields of Angola took the issue from the foreign pages of the serious newspapers to the front pages of tabloids and glossy magazines around the world. Derided by critics as a publicity stunt, the Princess's motives for participation were largely irrelevant. She moved the landmine issue several notches up the global political agenda.

'I thought it was terrific,' said Michael Ignatieff.

I thought the sight of her in Angola with all the demining stuff did more to publicise this issue than anything else. Cynics say it diverted attention from more worthy and earnest efforts but I thought this is the way the modern world works, you have to turn things into moral fashions. There are fashions in ethical issues the way there are fashions in skirts; and if you want an issue to become fashionable you have to associate it with a top model. She was the top model of the world, it's as simple as that. It produces a kind of shallow awareness. People thought mines are bad and Diana's good.

People may have thought that 'Diana's good' but the British government of the day certainly didn't. The Conservatives, in power at the time, shared the American stance on landmines – anti-ban and eager to develop ever more sophisticated mines. Diana's emotive call from Angola for a complete ban on landmines pitched her directly against Britain's elected government. Junior defence minister Earl Howe criticised Diana as a 'loose cannon'. He added that 'Britain is one of the goodies on landmines and we are helping to draw up a sensible worldwide compromise package'.[12] Even his wife agreed. From their country house in Buckinghamshire, Lady Elizabeth said, 'I think it's easy for the uninformed or the not very adequately informed to take it on an emotional level.'[13] A Tory backbench MP, Peter Viggers, claimed 'she was not up to understanding an important, sophisticated argument'. He added that 'the parallel that comes to mind is Brigitte Bardot and cats'. In a scathing article in the *Spectator*, Bruce Anderson wrote:

> She should have called for more mine exports. Instead, she used Angola as a catwalk . . . To begin with, and even in the children's wards, the Princess would regularly emit a light giggle, at once nervous and insincere, while her eyes flickered constantly towards the photographers. The first emotion came when she was told that she had been described as a 'loose cannon'. That makes me want to burst into tears, she replied. Can they not see that I am a humanitarian; always was, always will be? So she will, at the drop of a camera shutter.[14]

Welsh MP Anne Clwyd was invited to Kensington Palace in February 1997. In the course of her discussions with the Princess, Clwyd said Diana had described the Foreign Office's briefing prior to her visit to Angola as 'useless', while also claiming that the FO had stopped her visiting Cambodia. Mrs Clwyd received the invitation to Kensington Palace following her motion, signed by seventy-three MPs including Ken Livingstone, congratulating Diana 'for effectively highlighting the tragic humanitarian consequences' of the Conservative government's refusal to ban the production and use of landmines. The backlash against Diana backfired on her detractors. She had succeeded in capturing the public's imagination for an issue of which it was previously unaware. The Princess is reported as retorting, 'I am not a political figure. I'd like to reiterate now, my intentions are humanitarian. That is why I felt drawn to this human tragedy.' Sensing that Diana could provide the impetus required to make a global ban a real possibility, the Landmine Survivors Network and Rae McGrath invited Diana to deliver the keynote address at a seminar at the Royal Geographic Society on 12 June 1997. McGrath recalls, 'I always had this real frustration that we could always get stories in the *Guardian*, but you were preaching to the converted. We wanted to have stories on the front page of the *Sun*, the *Mirror* and the *Mail*. But [before Diana] we didn't have a hope in hell.'

Whatever her motives, there's no doubting the impact Diana had on the landmine campaign. Shortly before the British General Election of May 1997, she remarked that the Labour Party's stance on landmines was more sensible than the Conservative viewpoint. Her remarks prompted a very public debate on the political role of the royal family. In August 1997 it appeared that Diana had succeeded in changing the position of the world's richest and most powerful country on the issue of a landmine ban. Just a week after her return from Bosnia-Herzegovina, President Clinton, in what was interpreted at the time as a reversal of policy, announced that the United States would now participate in the Ottawa Process. A statement was issued by the White House, the full meaning of which would only become clear in Oslo a month later, that read: 'The United States will work with the other participating nations to secure an agreement that achieves our humanitarian goals while protecting our security interests.'[15]

The Landmine Survivors Network had taken Diana to Bosnia in August 1997. According to the network's co-founder Jerry White, she had insisted that this visit should be as private as possible. Her wish was to visit survivors in their homes as opposed to undertaking high profile photocalls in minefields. The visit to Bosnia was to be Diana's last public act of charity. She died in the now infamous car accident in a Parisian underpass on 31 August 1997. The landmine issue had a martyr.

In her death the 'People's Princess' had turned the landmine issue into the 'People's Crusade'. The timing of her death seemed to add to the general air of surrealism. Diana died two days before historic negotiations on a ban were due to start in Oslo. Addressing the Oslo conference, the UN Secretary General Kofi Annan said, 'The tragic accident that last Sunday took her life has robbed our global cause of one of its most compelling voices.' He added, 'I urge you to pursue with even greater determination this people's crusade that Princess Diana did so much to promote. She showed the world that one voice speaking as part of a global grass-roots movement can truly make a difference.'

Many of the seasoned campaigners who had been sceptical about Diana's involvement came to view her role as the final, crucial push towards a ban. Robin Coupland of the ICRC explained:

In 1995 the British Red Cross told us they would like to get Princess Diana involved in the campaign. We [the ICRC] had some reservations about this but when she went to Angola in 1997 the campaign was already rolling very fast and her going to Angola raised awareness about the mine problem. The fact that she died just before the Oslo conference at the end of August meant that everyone in the world had heard of the anti-personnel mine problem and was aware that governments were trying to work their way towards a prohibition and that was an enormous boost. There is no doubt that Princess Diana had an enormous impact on public opinion, it came very late in the campaign, it was if you like, the icing on the cake – necessary to get through to the prohibition.

The death of Diana, Princess of Wales, didn't signal an end to celebrity involvement in the landmine ban campaign. Diana's legacy will undoubtedly outshine that of any of her successors, but attempts have been made by landmine campaigners to bring on board other famous faces. French footballer David Ginola volunteered to be a Red Cross spokesman and has travelled to mine-affected countries. At the time of Ginola's recruitment, the Red Cross maintained that he did not see himself as a replacement for the late Princess. More recently, Paul McCartney has been a very visible supporter of the landmine cause. He appeared at a States Parties meeting in Geneva in September 2000 with his girlfriend and disability rights campaigner Heather Mills, who became an amputee herself in 1993 after a road accident. McCartney and Mills also went to Washington in 2001 to lobby US Secretary of State Colin Powell about the worldwide eradication of landmines. At least one demining agency is known to be thinking about trying to bring on board a new world-famous celebrity to draw people's attention to the mines issue. Critics of the landmine campaign in general, such as Paul Jefferson, are similarly critical of the participation of celebrities. Jefferson, who believes the only solution to the mine problem is demining, describes the involvement of celebrities as an 'indulgence' we can afford to foster because the mine problem is largely one that exists in the developing world, and not in our own 'backyard'.

All aboard?

The dramatic events in Ottawa had split the movement to ban landmines in two. On the one side there was the International Campaign to Ban Landmines and the states that firmly supported the

Canadian initiative. The other side, led by the United States, adhered to the United Nations Convention on Conventional Weapons.

Supporters of the Ottawa Process described the differences between the camps using the metaphor of a train leaving a station. The first on board would be invited to steer the train while those who hesitated were forced to take the train to a destination chosen by those who were on board first. Professor Adam Roberts believes that the United States found itself increasingly isolated on the landmine issue almost by accident:

> They're always at risk of missing the bus because they haven't got to the bus stop in an organised fashion. They've been discussing among themselves what to do on an issue, they've been trying out an imperfect policy and they haven't been able to grasp the moment. The same embarrassing situation arose in 1988 with the establishment of the International Criminal Court where the United States got itself involved in a very complicated position. It's perfectly understandable when they explain it to you, but it led to the US voting against the court with a weird variety of allies including China, Syria and other unholy partners they had in that vote – to the embarrassment of US officials.

As the months passed in 1997 it became clear that the Convention on Conventional Weapons was achieving nothing in terms of an anti-personnel mine ban. By June, a special coordinator, Australian Ambassador John Campbell had been appointed to highlight the landmine issue with members of the Conference. Within eight weeks he reported that there was little point in the Conference proceeding any further with the landmine issue until the Ottawa Process had run its course. By the summer of 1997 the United States' position had become a personal embarrassment for the President. Clinton's pledges on a commitment to ban anti-personnel landmines were often used by the ICBL to highlight what they perceived as a shift in the United States' position. Princess Diana's campaign reached its zenith during this point and the only other nations using the Conference on Disarmament as a means of opposing a total ban on landmines were the likes of China, India, Iran, Libya, Russia, Syria, Cuba and South Korea. By the summer of 1997, it was clear that the President's stance on the issue of a global landmine ban was not only very different from that of supporters of the Canadian initiative but also different from his

Republican-controlled Senate. Legislation, co-sponsored by Senator Leahy and Senator Hagel, to ban the use of anti-personnel landmines by US forces, received bipartisan support. Clinton's backing of the Pentagon's position on a landmine ban made him an increasingly isolated figure. Adam Roberts explained:

> It is the job of the President of the United States to adjudicate and find a way of making a coherent common policy out of the different interests of different agencies in the US government; the State department, the Pentagon, the Congress . . . different parts of the United States government on the landmines issue have had different approaches. President Clinton has not been a strong enough or intellectually coherent enough a President to make a coherent policy of those different approaches and the result on this issue as on a number of other issues has been an element of drift and indecision.

Canadian officials had been quietly working away at the practical implication of Foreign Minister Lloyd Axworthy's dramatic announcement. They obviously needed help – and got it from what became known as the Ottawa Process core group. The origins of this assemblage date back to a small group of countries who met the ICRC and the ICBL as part of the Convention on Conventional Weapons process in 1996. The first formal meeting under the auspices of the core group convened in February 1997 and included representatives from Austria, Belgium, Canada, Germany, Ireland, Mexico, the Netherlands, Norway, the Philippines, South Africa and Switzerland. It proved to be a good combination. Various members of the group had affiliations with the European Union, the Organisation of American States, the Organisation of African Unity and the G8. Each of the countries was charged with the responsibility of generating support for the Ottawa Process within its own region, and so started a diplomatic whirl of meetings and conferences in a frenetic attempt to adhere to the one-year deadline.

The Ottawa Process developed into a diplomatic exercise fast-tracked on a wave of public and political support. Over a hundred states convened in Vienna in February 1997 and the same month the ICBL used its 4th International NGO Conference on Landmines in Maputo to commit its full support to the Ottawa Process. With the political momentum in place, what the Process required now was a treaty document and within the core group the Austrians were charged with the task of drawing up a draft convention which would form the basis of negotiation. The aim was to keep the text as short and as simple as possible in order to demonstrate that the issue was in essence a simple one – landmines had to be banned – and to expose anyone trying to amend or complicate the treaty as being hostile to its intent. The first draft therefore contained only thirteen articles which completely encompassed a total ban on anti-personnel mines. To give the document added legitimacy, the Austrians invited all states, the UN, the ICRC and the ICBL to attend the 'Experts Meeting on the Text of a Total Ban Convention' in Vienna during February 1997. The nations that were hostile to the Ottawa Process at this stage, including the United States, the United Kingdom and France, used the meeting to declare their support for the Conference on Disarmament and at the outset refused to participate in any discussion on the text. The Process was not to be side-tracked, however, and the conference produced a second and eventually a third and final draft of the declaration. The final draft was issued worldwide on 13 May 1997 and was welcomed not only by the states that had supported Ottawa from the outset but also by the two significant new converts, the newly elected governments of France and the United Kingdom.

Just over six months after the challenge to sign a worldwide ban was issued in Ottawa a treaty was in place. Now it was time to find out who was likely to sign it. The Ottawa Process bandwagon arrived in Belgium in June 1997 for what the ICBL described as a 'make-or-break'[16] conference. The key issue in Brussels was a declaration that committed states to the negotiations scheduled for Oslo in September with a view to signing the agreed treaty in Ottawa in December. The Norwegians had offered to stage the final treaty negotiations at the first Ottawa meeting in 1996. Norway seemed to be the ideal venue with all the positive connotations of the recently negotiated Oslo Middle East Accord.

The Brussels Declaration was an unambiguous statement of intent, making it clear that the objective of the forthcoming negotiations was a 'comprehensive ban on the use, stockpiling, production and transfer of anti-personnel mines'.[17] It became the entry ticket to the Oslo negotiations. A total of ninety-seven countries signed up, pledging their intention to participate in the Oslo negotiations and to be signatories of the treaty in Ottawa in December. Even countries that had previously waited to gauge the reaction of the United States for guidance on the landmine issue signed up regardless.

The United States abandons ship

It came as no surprise when the United States confirmed that they were refusing to sign the Brussels Declaration. The core group met in Geneva to finalise preparations for the Oslo summit. During this meeting the United States asked to meet with the group to voice its concerns in private before the main negotiations. US Secretary of State Madeleine Albright had circulated a letter to other governments in which she explained that they would be arguing for five substantive changes to the Austrian draft. The ICBL by this point were in no mood for compromise. During her speech in the Brussels conference, Jody Williams, the coordinator of the ICBL, coined the phrase that would become the campaign's mantra – 'no exceptions, no reservations, no loopholes'. Other key members of the campaign were not so critical of the Americans. It was just one illustration of the uneasy alliance that existed at the very top of the International Campaign to Ban Landmines.

There was also considerable sympathy for the American position in other quarters. Professor Adam Roberts said:

> There's a curious paradox regarding this treaty and several others, that sometimes non-parties, and this is especially true of the United States, take a treaty more seriously than some parties. There are some states that sign treaties, it sounds good, they're on television becoming a party to a treaty, then ratifying, but do they do anything about it? Do they tell their armed forces what it implies? In some cases, I'm sorry to say, they don't. The United States is the opposite. They frequently don't ratify treaties. There's quite a queue of treaties in this field waiting to be ratified by the US Senate but they do instruct their armed forces in the terms of the treaty, and if you have a choice to which approach you'd prefer, the country that signs and ratifies but doesn't take it seriously or the country which doesn't sign but takes it seriously, I know which I'd prefer!

However, by 18 August 1997 the United States' position on the Ottawa Process was untenable and it announced that it was going to participate in the Oslo negotiations despite its refusal to sign the Brussels Declaration. Landmine campaigners were quick to acknowledge Diana's role in what was seen as a key moment in the process. Jerry White of the Landmine Survivors Network said, 'I think it was the thing which pushed them over the edge. Her symbolic visit to Bosnia showed that Clinton was just sitting on the fence on this issue. The timing was perfect, August is a dead month in Washington and she forced their hand.'[18]

White, however, was well aware of the full implications of American participation in Oslo: 'On the one hand it is terrific news; on the other hand it is worrying. America wants flexibility and wants to force exceptions into the Ottawa treaty which will make it all the harder to negotiate. We must all be ready for tough talks.'[19] The belated acceptance of the invitation to attend the talks was interpreted as an attempt to weaken a treaty it could no longer prevent. The US delegation arrived in Oslo seeking compromises – but its timing was not good. The opening ceremony of the Oslo negotiations was staged less than forty-eight hours after the death of Diana. Her death galvanised the campaign's resolve. There would be 'no exceptions, no reservations, no loopholes'.

The main amendments sought by the United States included a narrowing of the definition of what constituted an anti-personnel landmine to allow the continued use of 'smart' mines and mixed canister mines which comprise combinations of anti-tank and anti-personnel mines. One of the jokes of the conference became, 'When is an anti-personnel mine not an anti-personnel mine? When it's American'. Other clauses included deferral periods and a get-out provision if national security was threatened. The other key demand was a geographical exception for the use of anti-personnel mines in Korea. The South Korean capital, Seoul, lies 43 kilometres south of the Demilitarised Zone (DMZ) that separates the country from its neighbour in the north. American generals argue that, in the face of North Korea's one-million-strong army, the only way to slow down an invasion long enough to reinforce South Korea is through the maintenance of an extensive minefield. 'There is no place like it in the world,'[20] argued a beleaguered President Clinton. 'There is a line that I simply cannot cross,' he explained, 'and that line is the safety and security of our men and women in uniform.' Michael Ignatieff agreed:

The Americans objected to the Ottawa Treaty and have had a lot of trouble with landmines legislation simply because they believe that you've got to have a lot of landmines to preserve the territorial integrity of one of their allies. Now that's a pretty good reason to have landmines, actually, because the alternative might be 100,000

US troops or more guarding that area. You can protect that area very effectively if you use landmines instead of people, and at a lower cost. So these are issues that have to be dealt with and I'm not sure I have an easy solution to them. It's clear that we ought to make landmine use absolutely the exception, we ought to get its use down, we ought to enforce international protocols about their construction so that if you have to use them they can be demined at not excessive cost. We've got to do stuff about the needless injuries they cause but I don't see a world where they can be abolished altogether because they serve these strategic purposes and we're not going to live in a world without war, we're not going to live in a world without borders that are contested and fought over, we're not going to live in a world where we don't have to keep people out by force. That's just the world we're going to live in and so, I'm an anti-mine guy but I don't want to be a Utopian anti-mine guy and that means you have to keep your eye on the ball as to why mines are strategically useful.

Stories were circulating in the United States that the President himself was no longer convinced of the merits of his own case. *Time* magazine reported in September 1997 that Clinton wanted to sign the treaty but decided against taking on his Joint Chiefs of Staff who were united in their opposition of the Ottawa Process. One of Clinton's former top aides, George Stephanopoulos, claimed, 'the President's silence is a surrender to the military,' and added, 'but their case is flawed, and Clinton should instead side with the bipartisan majorities in the House and Senate and one hundred nations that favour a ban'.

As it became apparent that the conference was going to stand firm in face of the US amendments President Clinton made personal telephone calls to President Nelson Mandela and Canadian Prime Minister Jean Chrétien urging a compromise. His efforts were to no avail. After two weeks of hard negotiation the Americans had succeeded in strengthening the verification and compliance measures in the treaty, but none of its other proposals. The US delegation asked for, and received, a twenty-four-hour adjournment to allow for further 'consultations'. President Clinton was caught in the middle. There were serious diplomatic and political consequences to holding out for the amendments against the overwhelming support from other nations for the treaty, while his own military were demanding that the United States had to stand firm. Experts on US foreign policy, such as Adam

Roberts, believe that the President lured himself into an impossible position due to lack of forethought:

> President Clinton has proclaimed support for laudable liberal internationalist goals, and then has got into frightful muddles. The same was true of his attitude towards the United Nations when initially campaigning to be President. You'd think he was going to put US security in a UN framework but he ends up being a President who's ended up having to act outside a UN framework on a number of occasions, including, most recently, in Kosovo.
>
> The gap between Clinton's aspirations and what he has actually done, especially in this field of liberal international goals, has been strikingly inconsistent and it may be that this failure arises from a lack of thinking through in detail of these policies. There's very little evidence that his initial liberal goals have been thought through in relation to the particular security responsibilities of the States and that seems to have been a problem throughout the landmines issue.

When the conference reconvened the Washington delegation withdrew, finally, over their failure to gain support for an amendment which would have exempted the latest generation of 'smart' mines, pioneered by the US, from the treaty, and a second amendment which would have delayed the removal of mines from the border between North and South Korea. The ICBL immediately branded the US withdrawal from the talks a 'publicity stunt', claiming that the US amendments would have made a mockery of the Ottawa Process.

'It is not a sincere desire on the part of the US to be a real leader in the eradication of anti-personnel mines. President Clinton should be ashamed that he is willing to kill this treaty simply to save face,' said ICBL coordinator Jody Williams. Within minutes of the chief US delegate Eric Newsome announcing that all efforts to find a compromise had failed, a proposal for a total and immediate ban was approved by the Oslo conference. The news was greeted by rapturous applause both inside and outside the chamber.

For one of the founding members of the International Campaign to Ban Landmines, the United States walk out of the Oslo Treaty negotiations was a bitter pill to swallow. Bobby Muller remarked: 'It's ironic and sad that this country, which played so important a part in getting this campaign off the ground, is, at the end of the day, a no-show.'[21] He added, 'This is Basic Politics 101. It's political strength. It's money.'[22]

Conspiracy theories that the entrenched position taken by the US on the Korean minefields had more to do with money than strategy gathered momentum. Newspaper articles were published alleging that the Americans had been prepared to compromise on the use of landmines in Korea but wanted to retain the use of 'smart' mines.[23]

Further damaging revelations emerged from within the US military. A former commander in South Korea, Lieutenant General James Hollingsworth, said 'to be blunt, if we are relying on these weapons to defend the Korean peninsula we are in big trouble'.[24] He endorsed a report by Demilitarisation for Democracy, which attacked the Pentagon 'war game' Janus, which was used to predict that the removal of the Korean minefield would result in tens of thousands of additional allied casualties. According to the report, the Pentagon programmers fed faulty data into the game which drastically distorted the conclusions. The report's writers point to a Pentagon estimate of a North Korean advance at twelve miles an hour – impossible, they claim, over terrain as mountainous as Korea. Lieutenant General Hollingsworth also accused the Pentagon of underestimating North Korea's ability to breach the minefields and the willingness of the Pyongyang regime to use human wave tactics to trigger the mines. 'North Korea's disciplined troops will be just as willing to move through minefields, despite taking casualties, as they and the Chinese troops frequently did during the Korean War.'[25]

The United States, the country that had done the most to initiate a landmine ban, now found itself in the company of Russia, China, Iran, Iraq and Libya, on the outside of the humanitarian bandwagon that was the Ottawa Process. It was a public relations disaster that was about to get even worse. On 10 October 1997 the Nobel Committee announced that the Peace Prize was being jointly awarded to the International Campaign to Ban Landmines and its coordinator, Jody Williams. The committee described the ICBL's efforts as 'a process which in the space of a few years changed a ban on anti-personnel mines from a vision into a feasible reality'. The committee added that 'as a model for similar processes in the future, it could prove of decisive importance to the international effort for disarmament and peace'. Diana, Princess of Wales, was also singled out for her role in the campaign to heighten awareness of the 'seeds of death'.

For two of the leading personalities within the ICBL, the Nobel Prize served only to highlight further the differences that had emerged between them. 'I thought we should have considered turning it down,' said Rae McGrath. 'You could see this as a stamp of official approval on a civil society campaign – and that could just take the sting out of it. I have to say I was pretty much alone in that.' Jody Williams, meanwhile, had no doubts about accepting the prize, or its beneficial effect:

> The Nobel Peace Prize has obviously been very important for the campaign. None of us in the campaign believed that the Peace Prize was what we were working towards – the most important thing to us was the treaty. The prize has allowed the campaign to speak with greater moral authority. It has given us access to governments on a level that we didn't have before. Before we met with lower level functionaries, now we meet with the defence minister or the prime minister.
>
> I think that for a couple of months people were irritated that an individual was named but I think overall it was very important. I think the Nobel committee has been doing this for a hundred years and they know what they're doing and why they do it. Quite frankly, I think that part of the reason I was named individually is that I'm an American, and because the United States has not signed it was partly a political manoeuvre, a political decision on behalf of the Nobel committee to name me, an American, to be able to harass the United States more openly – and it worked.

'Of course, a lot of people hated it when Jody got it [the Nobel Prize] but my regret about that is that it took attention away from the main issue. There were articles written in magazines about Jody Williams and the campaign that could have been written about the issue rather than the personalities,' said Rae McGrath. 'If it was going to be awarded to an individual I would have liked it to be awarded in a symbolic way, certainly not to an American . . . It would have been a much bigger statement to give it to a victim or a deminer,' he added. To which Jody Williams responded: 'Frankly, I haven't spent a lot of time worrying about that. I worry about making sure the treaty works and that people are paying attention both inside the campaign and outside . . . I don't worry about other stuff. I quote the Pope, you know. The Pope's an interesting fellow and I'm an ex-Catholic. He was interviewed . . . and people said to him, "you're a very controversial Pope" which he is, and he said "some people like me and some people don't and that's just the way it is". If people are irritated by what I do and how I do it, that's their problem – I don't mind.'

World leaders were quick to congratulate the campaign and declare public support for the cause. Tony Blair said 'it gives recognition to a campaign that is supported by many people, not just in Britain but around the world'. In Washington the reaction was very different. The United States had been upstaged by the International Campaign to Ban Landmines and its Nobel Peace Prize. The landmine issue, which was initially a cause in which the United States was a leader, had become an anti-American crusade. Amid all the euphoria surrounding the Nobel Prize and the Ottawa Treaty, there was much consternation in Washington about being tagged with the 'bad guy' label. American foreign policy expert Professor Adam Roberts described the backlash:

They'd say things like, what's the address of the campaign? What's its real organisation and what has it really in practical terms done that compares with the lead the United States gave with its moratorium on landmines? On a number of issues to do with the laws of armed conflict and treaties the United States does have serious problems that entitle it to have, at the very least, hesitations before joining treaties.

I think it is reasonable to require time to sort out an alternative means of securing the frontier with North Korea. There is a balancing process between the humanitarian requirements of the anti-mines convention and the defence requirements and responsibilities that the United States has. It's not as if the landmine area on the border between North and South Korea is an area into which large numbers of innocent people are likely to walk into and get killed. Everybody knows where that area is and it is extremely well marked, so there isn't that problem which is the classic problem which gave rise to the treaty. So I have some sympathy with the American view on this and do not think it should be dismissed, nor do I think the United States should be treated as irresponsible or callous because it is slow in coming on board the treaty.

Within weeks of the United States walk out of the Ottawa Process at Oslo, President Clinton was scheduled to appear at Vancouver with Prime Minister Jean Chrétien. The President had been warned by White House aides that he faced a rough ride on a stance on the Ottawa Treaty which he shared with Russia, China, Iran, Iraq and Libya. When the press questions came, Clinton immediately went on the offensive:

We should look at the evidence. What is your record on landmines? Which nation has destroyed the most landmines? Which nation is doing the most to promote demining? The answer to that is the United States . . . this is a question of the way the treaty was worded and the unwillingness of some people to entertain any change in the wording of it. I believe I was the first world leader at the United Nations to call for a total ban on landmine production and deployment.[26]

The Ottawa Treaty

The signing ceremony began in Ottawa on 3 December 1997. The slender document banned the use, production, transfer and stockpiling of anti-personnel landmines and committed signatories to destroying existing stocks within four years of its entry into force. Two-thirds of the countries in the world signed up in the first two days. But getting countries to sign the treaty was one thing; it wouldn't be legally effective until forty countries had ratified it. Then a further six months passes before the treaty becomes legally binding. With a solid core group of supportive states, the ratification requirement was achieved by September 1998 and the treaty became law on 1 March 1999. On many levels, the Ottawa Treaty was a remarkable achievement. It is certainly the first attempt at taking such a commonly used weapon out of commission and it has been claimed that it was 'the fastest entry into force of any major multilateral treaty ever.'[27] It was not, however, a treaty with no exceptions, no reservations and no loopholes. Members of the demining community in particular appeared to be far more reserved in their celebrations, as Lou McGrath of the Mines Advisory Group explained:

We are quite happy about the treaty, [but] many of those in the campaign were probably dancing and singing about what's been achieved. We argued that the treaty should be a lot stronger as we were at the sharp edge of things. Many of the things not included in the treaty are going to be a major problem for us in the future; for example, mines that have an anti-disturbance mechanism on them aren't banned under the treaty and that's of major importance to us as we're the ones who are going to have to clear them. So probably we were not singing and dancing as much as other people, like Jody Williams.

To which the Nobel co-laureate retorted:

> I think that our success has been so huge and so large that we are held to abnormal standards. This is a new treaty and there will be violations. That doesn't mean it's OK, but I think if you look at the course treaties take internationally it's been quite successful in a short space of time by taking away conventional weapons that have been used by the military for hundreds of years.

Divisions among the victors

Despite the media coverage that often portrayed the landmine issue as one big humanitarian campaign, this broad alliance of deminers, campaigners, politicians, medics and the military is by no means a monolithic block and in many ways the Ottawa Treaty has served to highlight many differing agendas. The various camps are divided along fundamental issues. The pro-ban lobby believes that the process of removing landmines currently buried in the ground should proceed in tandem with a political movement to stop the production, sale and deployment of the weapon. The anti-ban camp doesn't believe that demining and political campaigning are complementary. Former bomb disposal officer Paul Jefferson believes that the campaign has actually damaged the mine clearance work:

> My real problem with the landmine ban is that by persisting with the concept that a landmine ban can work, when even ban supporters accept there is a distinct possibility it might not work, is that what they're doing is distracting attention away from the one thing that can really address the issue, namely mine clearance. People think the problem's being addressed. There is only a certain amount of room for the public, political and media consciousness for an issue like landmines – and if you occupy part of that room with the concept of a ban it means there is less room for mine clearance and the only thing that's going to save lives is mine clearance. When Europe or an expensive piece of real estate has a landmine problem it gets the best treatment, it gets landmine clearance. But when it's the Third World it becomes a media and celebrity and lobbying issue that people can talk about and the hard work of doing mine clearance is left to one side.

The accusation that the campaign has in any way detracted attention, and especially money, from mine clearance is angrily refuted by campaigners. Responding to allegations about the money spent on the global circuit of conferences and meetings, the ICBL not only denies attracting money away from mine clearance but claims that its efforts in lobbying politicians are what actually sustain the demining effort. Jody Williams argued that 'without governments there would be no treaty and there would be no demining because there would be no money for demining. If it wasn't for us meeting them and keeping them focused there would be no money for demining so it's a spurious argument from my point of view.'

The world's first humanitarian demining organisation, the HALO Trust, has also expressed serious reservations about the effectiveness of the Ottawa Treaty. Citing its post-treaty experiences in conflict zones, HALO claims that parts of the treaty have already been ignored, even by countries that signed up to the Ottawa Process. Guy Willoughby explains:

> Some parts that we come across are entirely impractical, such as rules on minefield marking. These rules state that all mine-affected countries must mark all minefields in a certain way – pigs might fly first. As for the whole thing, the proof of the pudding is in the eating. How many conflicts have there been in the last three years [1998–2001] that used mines? Chechnya–Russia, Kosovo, Ethiopia–Eritrea, Angola, Sri Lanka, Afghanistan to name a few. How many of the players in these conflicts had signed Ottawa?[28]

Indeed, none of the countries mentioned by HALO has ratified the treaty. It's the list of non-signatories that presents most difficulty for Ottawa's supporters. Without the signatures of the United States, Russia and China the treaty looks weak. The Russians and Chinese have historically been prolific producers of landmines and the weapons have been integral to military doctrine in these countries simply because they have extensive borders to defend. The core group of states in the Ottawa Process – Austria, Belgium, Canada, Denmark, Ireland, Mexico, Norway and Switzerland – were never great producers or users of landmines.

'Their landmines never turned up in the Third World anyway. I've cleared landmines in many parts of the world and all the mines I've come across are mainly Chinese and Russian with some Eastern bloc and a few American mines and maybe some South African mines,' argued Paul Jefferson. He added that 'if you look at all the nations who've signed up to the ban, the vast majority are nations who are not faced with the possibility or imminent possibility of war. The nations who've not signed the ban are the major producers and user nations of the anti-personnel landmine and they are nations who face the imminent threat of hostilities.' Despite not signing the Ottawa Treaty, China, Russia and the United States have adhered to self-imposed anti-personnel mine export bans and many international relations experts believe the Ottawa Treaty is strong enough to survive the current non-participation of the three powers. Professor Adam Roberts explains:

The extent to which these moratoria are being observed in practice is certainly something that needs to be looked at very closely, especially in the cases of Russia and China, but it is not true that just because these three states are not yet parties to the Ottawa Convention that it is not worth the paper it is written on. There is a certain larger movement of opinion against landmines which goes beyond the Ottawa Convention, which involves a wide range of national moratoria and which operates to reinforce some of the provisions of the convention. So I think the prospects of the convention having a significant effect are there and people who know anything about this say the number of new landmines being planted in on-going conflicts is already showing signs of diminution compared to what was going on five years ago.

In the era of NATO and UN peacekeeping missions in conflict zones around the world the issue of non-signatories becomes a practical as well as political problem for the treaty. When Canada signed the Ottawa Convention it included an 'understanding' that the treaty did not prohibit joint operations with non-signatories that continued to use anti-personnel mines. In August 1998 the Labour government in the United Kingdom rushed through all four stages of the Landmines Bill in a matter of hours in order to ratify the Ottawa Treaty before the first anniversary of Diana's death. But Britain also included the clause for joint operations with non-signatories. 'What's really sad is that this was negotiated under a Labour government that was meant to be totally committed to getting rid of anti-personnel mines,' said Rae McGrath. 'The senior politicians involved in this, [Tony] Blair and his cabinet, should be ashamed. They've got children and that kind of neat legalese jargon will eventually cost people's lives.'

The 'smart' solution

One of the major issues that continues to divide the United States and the International Campaign to Ban Landmines, and one for which it is very difficult to see any compromise, is the use of 'smart' mines, so-called because the mines self-destruct after a set time, kill and maim combatants in war zones but become harmless when the fighting's over. The 'smart' mine, say its supporters, is a legitimate weapon of war – to its critics, it's a neat way of exploiting a loophole. This issue goes to the very heart of the more general debate as to whether it is possible to ban a weapon like the landmine. Pictures of children with missing limbs provoke outrage. The moral argument against a weapon which kills and maims civilians is straightforward and utterly convincing. The speed at which a group of non-governmental organisations was able to mobilise international support for a global ban on landmines is conclusive evidence of the legitimacy of the cause. But the nagging question remains, can a ban possibly work?

'The biggest difficulty about mines as an issue is that we're all against it. When you're all against something and it's just evil, your mind stops thinking about why mines were necessary in the first place,' said Michael Ignatieff, adding, 'and mines were necessary in the first place because they serve very clear military goals very effectively.' For the arms industry, a new treaty banning old weapons presents a new opportunity to serve an old need. And at the moment American companies are ahead of the field in developing new generations of landmines. According to the manufacturers self-destruct mines do not contribute to the humanitarian problem caused by 'dumb' mines. No surprise there, say the campaigners; after all, the United States leads the way in 'smart' mine technology. The ICBL did not and will not compromise on the 'smart' mine issue. Campaigners argue that these mines are designed to self-destruct not out of any humanitarian concern but as a consequence of strategic military problems incurred by the use of scatterable mine systems. Armies using remotely delivered devices often find themselves having to breach their own minefields, which makes a self-destructing mine very useful. Whatever the motive for their design, serious questions remain about just how smart these new systems are. The US military claims a 90–95 per cent reliability rate with mines programmed to self-destruct within fifteen days. The remaining 5–10 per cent deactivate due to battery exhaustion within ninety days. They claim an overall reliability figure of 99.9 per cent. These figures are disputed because many 'smart' mines are remotely delivered and so their deployment adds another variable. Unless the pilot delivers the mines from the right height and at the correct speed and trajectory the weapons do not arm. If they don't arm they don't self-destruct and just lie on the ground waiting for someone to disturb and possibly arm them. Indeed, an ICRC study concluded that the use of 'smart' mines increased the likelihood of civilian casualties.

To counter these arguments against its 'smart' mines the United States has proposed that the Convention on Certain Conventional Weapons specify acceptable reliability rates: 'We believe that these specifications can be improved,' said Edward Cummings, Head of the United States Delegation to the CCW. He added that 'we also believe they can be applied to all remotely delivered landmines without degrading legitimate military requirements and that they are technically realistic and practical.'[29] It's the relentless progress of technological advance that many critics of the Ottawa Treaty point to in arguing that attempts to ban landmines are futile. Paul Jefferson says:

> What you're actually trying to ban is not a weapon – it's a concept, a way of thinking. It's the concept of a victim-operated trap being used as a method of defence or early warning. A victim-operated trap – we use them in every aspect of our lives. Whenever you go into a shop and a bell rings as you go in the door, that is the principle of a victim-operated trap. You perform an action and an alarm or another action occurs. To deny that concept in the extremities of warfare is ridiculous. People's lives are at stake. Look at the defenders of Sarajevo or Srebrenica holding their cities against the Serb ethnic cleansers. What would you do? Would you turn around and say we'd rather you went to your graves with a conscience clear of not having used anti-personnel mines to defend yourself?
>
> To ban a weapon successfully you have to be able to deny the technology to make it. You can have a ban, but a ban won't work unless you can prevent people from making a weapon. Now, a ban on chemical and nuclear weapons can work because the technology to make those weapons is quite rare and can easily be identified, as we're doing in Iraq. The technology can be identified and monitored to make sure people don't misuse that technology. But the technology to produce an anti-personnel landmine is available on the outskirts of every Third World city or town. If you can make cheap plastic or wooden toys, you can make anti-personnel landmines in their thousands.

Cheap and simple to make they may be, but that becomes irrelevant in the face of a ban, according to the ICBL. Jody Williams believes the humanitarian crisis is caused by the production and sale of landmines from rich to poor, from north to south.

> The proliferation of landmines is the result of mass production in the North. They were produced like lipstick or like cans of Coca-Cola, without thought and in a great number. If you look at the problem in the world today almost all the mines that are in the ground or in stockpiles come from factories. They were not produced by the individual soldier. Yes, it can be done, yes it is easy to do, but it is not going to be the problem when we get rid of mass produced landmines. Yes, there'll be a mine or two but not like we know today.

Trains, stations, tortoises and hares

During the campaign the ICBL often referred to their already quoted metaphor of the train leaving the station but there is a strong body of opinion that believes that the analogy of the tortoise and the hare would be more appropriate. While the ICBL raced away on the road to Ottawa the American tortoise just plodded along the route marked CCW. Throughout the short history of the campaign to ban landmines the United States, initially the hero but latterly portrayed as the villain, has consistently argued its belief that the Convention on Certain Conventional Weapons is likely to be a better long-term solution to the landmine crisis than the Ottawa Treaty. Derided by members of the campaign as nothing more than a stalling technique, the Americans have continued to work within the CCW, calling for the protocol dealing with landmines to be strengthened and enhanced. One of its key proposals is that the rules and restrictions governing the use of landmines apply in civil wars and internal conflicts when previously they were only effective in international wars. Adam Roberts believes that the Convention on Certain Conventional Weapons may well be more effective than the Ottawa Treaty in the long term, but he also acknowledges that without the hare the tortoise might not have left the starting line: 'The good thing about the [Ottawa] treaty is it moved forward very fast and there was a big recognition that something was being done. Those treaties under the Geneva Convention, when they do work, although they take a long time, they're probably far more effective than this treaty will be.'

One thing that the ICBL has certainly achieved is the stigmatisation of the landmine. Prior to the campaign the weapon didn't have the evil connotations that now exist in the mind of the public. Landmines have been placed beyond the pale. Those charged with the role of taking landmines out of the ground may not have seen the benefits yet, but most commentators believe the Ottawa Treaty to be better than no treaty, as Robin Coupland of the ICRC explained:

> It's very difficult to say whether an instrument of international humanitarian law is going to be very effective. I think a better way to look at it is to ask, 'will the use of anti-personnel mines in war in the future be the norm or an exception?', and I think that the Ottawa Treaty will make it likely that the use of anti-personnel mines will be an exception in the future rather than a norm.

While it may be impossible to measure the short-term impact of the treaty in terms of numbers of lives or limbs saved, the real benefits of Ottawa may be far more intangible according to Michael Ignatieff:

> Most people sign up to treaties and then most people don't live up to them. I mean, the number of treaties on everything from human rights to mines that don't get fully taken up is huge. It doesn't mean the treaties are useless, it means you can hang people when they commit themselves to a certain kind of language if you catch them breaking the treaty. It's a more effective sanction than if they haven't signed.

The remaining chapters in this book trace the development of the landmine from underground mining in ancient Egypt to the smartest mines on the market today. Is it really going to be possible for the world to say stop? Has the final chapter in the history of the landmine really been written? Some say yes, some say no, some say maybe.

Jody Williams says:

> The way we have succeeded is by stigmatisation of the weapon. We have no police force that can enforce the treaty. It is by making people believe that it is beyond the pale: like chemical weapons, making

governments, soldiers and the international community at large not accept use of the weapon. There will be violations for a while, but I also believe we will eventually get rid of the weapon entirely.

Paul Jefferson says:

We would all ban war, wouldn't we, if we had the choice, but except for those of us who live in a Utopian paradise, we accept that sometimes, unfortunately war is going to happen. War necessarily involves the use of weapons. The function of weapons is to maim and kill people. There is no humane way of achieving that. War is the sickness of our species.

Michael Ignatieff says:

The longest unfortified border in the world runs between Canada and the United States – mines are unthinkable on that border. Mines are unthinkable on the border between Germany and France and yet only fifty years ago the place was covered with mines. You get rid of mines when you get rid of border conflict; you get rid of mines when states decide they're going to resolve their disputes peacefully, you get rid of mines when you have stable states that have legitimate central authorities which aren't divided by civil wars. In other words, mine treaties are a start and then you have to do an awful lot more if you're going to get to a world beyond mines and that means a world where we have a stable system of internationally recognised nation states that don't wage war across each other's borders. When you have that, which is very, very far away and not in my lifetime, you might get a world without mines, but not until then.

PMF 1 (commonly known as the 'Butterfly Mine'), a scatterable, anti-personnel blast mine, made in the USSR (*photograph by Stephen Hart*).

VIGNETTE 1: Types of Anti-Personnel Mines

More than 300 types of anti-personnel landmines are believed to have been produced. Many are activated by pressure from above. However, they can also be detonated by the disturbance of one or more attached tripwires, by the release of pressure, by a fuse designed to detonate the mine when someone passes near to it, or by remote firing. Some mines don't explode the first time they are disturbed, but explode after several disturbances. Some have a time-control mechanism. Mines have been buried stacked on top of one another. Others have 'protection mechanisms' designed to kill or injure deminers. Mines can be buried by hand, by machine or scattered over wide areas from the air. Mines range in size and colour. Future mine development centres around more self-destructing, remote control and remote delivery mines. There are many different types of anti-personnel mine found in the ground today, and a few of the most common varieties are listed below.*

Blast Mines

Blast mines are the most common mines of all. The former Soviet Union specialised in producing this mine. They can be as small as the top of a canned drink. Blast mines explode immediately they are stepped on or disturbed. The blast (a wave of air) is the main cause of injury. The detonation of a blast mine is more likely to result in the severing of a foot or leg than to result in death.

Fragmentation Mines

The former Soviet Union, the former Czechoslovakia, the former Yugoslavia, and China, Egypt and South Korea have all made versions of this mine. When fragmentation mines are stepped on or disturbed the force of the explosion disperses small metal fragments, such as steel ball bearings, that have been packed inside the mines. The shrapnel or metal fragments can be projected over 360 degrees. The fragments cause the injury, which usually kills whoever is close to the mines and anyone standing 30 metres away could still be injured.

Bounding Fragmentation Mines

Bounding fragmentation mines leap out of the ground to about chest height, before the main charge detonates, causing horrific injuries.

* For more technical information refer to Colin King (ed.), *Jane's Mines and Mine Clearance*, Jane's Information Group Ltd, Surrey, 1996.

Most are activated by tripwire. Italian manufacturers became expert at producing this mine. An initial charge shoots the mines 1 or 2 metres into the air before the main charge goes off, dispersing fragments over 360 degrees. Like basic fragmentation mines, the shrapnel or metal fragments cause the injury, which usually kills whoever is close to the mines, but anyone standing 40 metres away could still be injured.

Directional Fragmentation Mines

Directional fragmentation mines, as their name suggests, disperse fragments over a specific area. They can be set off by tripwires or by remote control. Versions were made during the Cold War in the factories of the former Soviet Union and in the United States. Shrapnel is projected in a horizontal fan or a narrow cone shape when the mines are activated. Once again, the shrapnel causes the injury, which usually kills whoever is close to the mines, but anyone standing 200 metres away could still be injured.

2

The Demon from the Trenches

A T 7.20 a.m. on 1 July 1916, a massive pillar of earth, chalk and debris rocketed into a cloudless, sunny blue sky and sent shock waves pulsing through the ground. The tremendous roar of the explosion was quickly eclipsed by a barrage of German artillery fire. The detonation of a huge underground mine had signalled the beginning of the bloodbath that was to be the Battle of the Somme.

Eight minutes after the first explosion a whole series of mines were detonated simultaneously, shooting yet more columns of earth skyward into the early morning sunshine while the ground below heaved. The mines were the culmination of hours of painstaking digging under German positions. One group of tunnellers had come perilously close to being discovered when they broke through into a German dugout. The preparation of the mines had been part of the detailed planning of the Anglo-French offensive on the Somme – designed to relieve the pressure on the defence of Verdun, which had almost broken the French army. At 7.30 a.m. everything suddenly went quiet. Zero hour had arrived. Lines of British soldiers began to make their way out of their trenches to march off into the sights of the German machine gunners. Before the end of the day 20,000 of them would die and another 40,000 would be wounded. As waves of men began to be cut down in their tracks, a last mine, which had not exploded at the planned time, went off with another thunderous roar. It obliterated a German machine-gun nest but it also sent a shower of rocks and debris over the advancing British soldiers. In all, twenty-one mine chambers were exploded to herald the commencement of one of the most appalling and violent battles of World War I.

The type of underground mine used in the Battle of the Somme is key to the development of the landmine. Underground mining, seen as a precursor of today's landmines, is a type of mine warfare that predates the invention of explosive. The Assyrians and even the ancient Egyptians of 2000 BC[1] would dig a mine under the corner of an enemy's fortification, fill the hole with flammable material and light it, in order to let the fire bring down the fortification and so allow troops to march through unhindered. The method was used throughout the following centuries, most notably in medieval siege warfare, and again in the American Civil War when gunpowder and explosives had replaced fire on the battlefield. The 'fougass', which was notable for its employment in Europe in the sixteenth century, is seen as a type of landmine. The fougass worked like an 'underground cannon'.[2] It was essentially a hole dug in the ground and filled with gunpowder, rocks and metal fragments. It was used as a method of defence, so that once the gunpowder was detonated, any approaching attackers would be showered with rocks and debris. The modern landmine came about when explosives were shaped into small containers and the devices were made to be victim-operated, so that they didn't need a third party to detonate them. However, all land-mines produced before the twentieth century were used in relatively small numbers. World War I indisputably signalled the beginning of the race to mass-produce the types of landmines which cause havoc throughout the world today.

The Great War: a new style of combat

The beginning of the twentieth century heralded a crucial turning point in the way conflict would occur throughout the world over the next hundred years. The landmine was developed against the backdrop of rapidly accelerating industrialisation. Technological advances allowed for momentous changes in weaponry. The use of bayonets and barbed wire gave way to nuclear weapons within decades, as the world developed the frightening ability to self-destruct. '. . . there were moments, in the course of the thirty-one years of world conflict, between the Austrian declaration of war on Serbia on 28 July 1914 and the unconditional surrender of Japan on 14 August 1945 – four days after the explosion of the first nuclear bomb – when the end of a considerable proportion of the human race did not look far off.'[3]

Before World War I there hadn't been a war involving the majority of the world's powers for a century, and any war which did involve a major power had been won or lost relatively quickly. Battles were generally fought above ground. They were visible and had constantly moving front lines. Armies relied heavily on the use of cavalry. Opposing soldiers would generally do battle with each other face to face, and commanders on horseback were able to make strategic decisions by simply surveying the scene in front of them. Firepower was limited, both in terms of strength and volume. During the American Civil War guns were still generally inaccurate, unwieldy, and, compared with the mechanised slaughter of twentieth-century conflicts, were relatively few in number.

Industrialisation, however, changed for ever the way wars between big powers would be fought. Weapons could suddenly be mass-produced with increasing sophistication and firepower. By the time the Great War broke out in 1914, cavalry was still being used but its days were clearly numbered. The introduction of the machine gun and the magazine rifle meant attacking over open ground resulted in carnage. The Great War had paved the way for the wholesale slaughter of troops. In the first year of fighting on the Western Front the Germans and the Allies found themselves in a stalemate. Neither side could outgun the other with their new, powerful weapons, and both had suffered horrific losses in the first Battle of Ypres. As a result, the opposing armies began to take up defensive, static positions, digging long lines of trenches. The era of trench warfare had arrived.

Although the trenches were initially considered to be a temporary solution, they soon became a permanent fixture as the opposing armies realised the extent of the deadlock they were in. In fact, there was little movement in the war on the Western Front in four years. Both sides continued to slog it out while remaining heavily defended. It wasn't long before a trench society developed. An intricate network of ditches sprang up on both sides, including supply and communication channels to sustain the men holed up in their defensive positions on the front line. Life was bleak. Soldiers described having to stand knee-deep in mud and water for hours, even days, on end. They were likened to rats, huddling together in the relative safety of their underground homes. Outside the trenches lay vast coils of barbed wire, 'no-mans land', and ground littered with corpses. The soldiers in the trenches knew that if they attempted to advance out of their trench and into the open they could be massacred in the thousands. So the soldiers turned to new methods of waging war, primarily at night. Snipers went out on patrol, while others concentrated on laying barbed wire and digging yet more trenches.

The most sophisticated weapons developed by the early stage of the war were designed to be effective in the old style of open warfare. As a result, the new trench systems were proving to be an effective barrier in the face of an onslaught of fire. War strategists attempted to design their way out of the trench stalemate by producing a new array of weapons, such as the trench mortar, grenades and more powerful, streamlined guns. There was one war in the field, and another in the arms factories. 'The war in the west would from now on be won not by superior strategy, not by movement and rapid encirclement, but by the slow process of attrition. The Great War had turned into the first "industrial war" to be won as decisively on the home front, producing ever vaster quantities of guns and munitions, as in the field.'[4]

Underground mining was introduced for trench warfare. Tunnelling in the Great War was a more sophisticated version of the technique used in the American Civil War, medieval siege warfare and earlier conflicts. World War I soldiers would gouge a tunnel out of the earth and stack a massive amount of explosive (hundreds of pounds, sometimes tons) at the end of it, before leaving the area and detonating the explosive. The blast would usually be set off just before an attack to open a gap through which troops could advance. In France in the spring of 1915, both the British and the Germans had begun to tunnel under each other's trenches to lay underground mines. This strategy was a traumatic business: sometimes the Germans would preempt an attack and detonate charges under British tunnels, causing those tunnels to collapse and the men to be buried alive. Just as frightening was the prospect that opposing miners would sometimes tunnel right into each other. If the men met face to face like this, a fight to the death was often the only way out.

On the British side, the tunnellers were primarily coal miners from South Wales and England, who used parties of infantrymen to bolster their numbers. There were tunnelling companies in every sector of a battlefield. Alfred William Lewis, believed to have been with the 6th Battalion Northampton Regiment in World War I, referred to tunnelling in his memoirs. He said the mines were sunk down like a shaft 80 to 150 feet under ground, before the miners would strike out into passages, moving firstly under the British front line, then under the German front line and finally well into German territory – all while the Germans were doing the same in the opposite direction. He described miners having to work by candlelight, sometimes taking eight hours to hack their way through a yard of chalk with only a miner's pick: 'A man's luck was very uncertain down under, and nobody knew if he was coming up again alive. Or if he would be blown to pieces, or buried under chalk, or even gassed by the fumes of the mine that has been blown up . . .'[5]

Hundreds of German soldiers were blown up as a result of the mines that were exploded at the start the Somme Offensive. The effectiveness of the mine attack is questionable though, as the Battle of the Somme turned into yet another protracted fight with both sides incurring hundreds of thousands of casualties in just a few months. Another infamous tunnelling explosion occurred on 7 June 1916 under the Wyteschaete-Messines ridge, following two years of planning. The British blew up nineteen individual mines simultaneously, containing nearly a million pounds of explosive material. They say that the sound of the explosion was heard as far away as across the Channel in the south of England. The ridge virtually disappeared and its defenders were stunned into defeat, but while the attack itself was judged to be effective the ensuing fight took the pattern of many before it: a long, drawn-out and demoralising battle of attrition.

Former deminer Rae McGrath argued that a similarity exists between tunnelling and modern portable landmines that calls into question the military effectiveness of both techniques. He claimed that their use has been justified by the military in terms of the effect of the weapon on enemy morale, rather than the material damage caused at the time of the explosion – despite the fact that enemy morale was rarely so damaged that it led the enemy to concede defeat. McGrath said the vested interests in maintaining any given military strategy are far wider than whether the strategy actually works.[6] In wars such as Vietnam, the American military continued to justify the use of the anti-personnel mine (which was keeping the landmine manufacturing industry healthy), despite evidence showing the mine was actually killing and maiming its *own* troops.

Breaking the stalemate

The single event that did most to trigger the proliferation of the landmine during the Great War was the invention of the tank. During 1915 and 1916 the British had been developing a new weapon: an armoured vehicle capable of driving through trenches and barbed wire, while providing protection for advancing infantry. The tank's inventors believed it would help bring back the open warfare that had been lost in the immovable trench systems. The French followed suit, developing their own tanks, as did the Germans. While the tank was primarily designed to be able to plough through trenches, it was also designed to terrify troops. As every new weapon is invented, so a new plan is hatched to counter it. It was the invention of tanks that resulted in landmines entering the 'sphere of military strategy', according to Rae McGrath.[7]

The first British tanks weren't very successful and their reputation remained poor until very late in the war. They didn't really come into their own until World War II. Early tanks got bogged down in the mud and fell victim to armour-piercing ammunition. They were generally slow and mechanically unreliable. Some of the first tanks introduced as part of an attempt to break through the Somme in 1916 were so difficult to manage that their crew even ended up accidentally firing on the wrong side.[8] Others just got bogged down in the mud. However, despite all their faults the British tanks succeeded in terrifying the German infantry. In July 1917, rapidly expanding British tank battalions were re-organised into the Tank Corps. However, in the third Battle of Ypres that same month, tanks took much of the blame for thousands of British deaths when many of the machines lasted barely a day on the battlefield.

Tanks continued to be developed and refined, however, and their reputation slowly improved. This new weapon would ultimately help the Allies to defeat the Germans. On 8 August 1917, when the British and French tanks overwhelmed the front at Amiens, General Erich Ludendorff described the event as the 'black day of the German army'.[9] In the Battle of Cambrai in November the same year, tanks were used *en masse* successfully to break through German lines. Victory at Cambrai signalled that tanks were here to stay. By autumn 1918, tank production was increasing rapidly and the Allies acquired a stock of many thousands, ranging from heavy vehicles to medium and newer light 'whippet' tanks.

The tank was proving to be resistant to small arms fire, so the hunt began almost immediately for an alternative. The Germans had developed a strong defensive mentality during the war and were the first to develop a weapon to use against tanks: this was the anti-tank mine. The anti-tank mine was essentially a container of explosive with a pressure switch which would detonate and explode when a tank drove over it. Using a blast effect the mines would either cut the tank's tracks or blow off the wheels. They required at least three kilograms of explosive each (but usually contained two to three times that amount) to damage a tank's running gear.[10]

History of the portable landmine

The invention of gunpowder and other explosives hugely increased the potential for carnage on the battlefield. When gunpowder first surfaced centuries ago, so did early portable mines, the relatives of World War I's anti-tank mines. Chinese archaeologists recently unearthed ancient landmines from the early Ming Dynasty of the fourteenth to seventeenth centuries. These were iron balls with a small hollow extension, probably used for loading and detonating powder.[11] The Chinese were considered to be quite advanced in mine warfare and they might have used landmines even earlier than the Ming Dynasty.

Some of the very early anti-tank mines were simply fashioned out of artillery shells with pressure fuses. That method was also used in the American Civil War, where shells with fuses were either buried or attached to tripwires. Anything that has the basic components of a container, explosive content, a fuse and a detonator can be loosely described as a landmine. When the mine is disturbed or activated the fuse is initiated, the detonator fires and the content explodes. Adapted shells do the same job as landmines and they have been used instead of landmines in many modern wars.

In the latter stages of World War I there were further developments in landmine design. The Germans devised patterned minefields, using rows of anti-tank mines to stop massed tank attacks. Such ordered minefields – or at least the concept behind them – were nothing new. Julius Caesar, for example, used a primitive type of minefield during the siege of Alesia in 52 BC. He laid deep rows of a variety of obstacles such as traps, spikes and other weapons. Caesar's minefields were designed to injure the legs or feet of soldiers or horses' hooves. The large, methodically laid German minefields posed a big problem for the British, who realised they would have to produce a countermeasure to enable them to breach the obstacles. They experimented with various clearance methods, beginning with a roller attached to a tank that detonated the mines in the ground in front of it. At the same time the British were also catching up with the Germans by developing their own mines and minefield strategies.

A smaller version of the anti-tank mine, designed to be detonated by the footstep of a soldier, made only a low-key appearance in World War I. Anti-personnel landmines ranged from primitive devices such as bombs, grenades or other weapons with tripwires or pressure devices attached to them, to more sophisticated designs. Some were made of wood; others were fashioned out of metal and glass.

As outlined in Chapter 1, the anti-personnel mine is described as a 'victim-operated trap', where the victim unwittingly activates the weapon by disturbing it. A former bomb disposal officer argued that the basic design of a landmine is similar to many gadgets we encounter on a daily basis in any country – devices that are used as a way of defending territory or for warning someone away, such as a burglar alarm or a hunting snare.

The Greeks and the Romans invented some of the earliest victim-operated traps. They used small objects to slow down their attackers, such as the caltrop, a piece of metal twisted to produce four spikes. Soldiers would lay a caltrop on the ground with one spike pointing up, ready to injure whoever stumbled on it. Similar weapons were also made of wood. The anti-personnel landmine and the caltrop are linked in another way. They have both been described in military terms as 'force multipliers', or 'substitute soldiers'. Weapons that lie hidden for days, weeks or years and can still cause damage to enemy soldiers during an attack are useful to armies short on personnel. These 'substitute soldiers' need neither food nor sleep and have none of the other needs of a human soldier. During the American Civil War Confederate soldiers invented a landmine with explosives in it that could unwittingly be detonated by its intended victim. Their invention brought us closer than ever to the landmines in existence today. They planted these victim-operated landmines in houses, along roads and in ditches. Mines were also booby-trapped: they were attached by strings or levers to innocent looking objects such as jackknives or barrels of food in a house. When the objects were disturbed by enemy soldiers, the mines would explode.

It is a common misperception that the anti-personnel mine was invented in World War I to stop troops lifting anti-tank mines without detonating them. The first anti-tank landmines were large and awkward. Because they were designed to explode under the weight of a vehicle, they could be removed by enemy troops without detonating and then used against their original owners. The widely held theory is that the solution to this lay in protecting anti-tank mines with anti-personnel mines, a method commonly used in World War II. Anyone who then attempted to lift the anti-tank mines had a good chance of being killed or injured first. Military historians disagree that the anti-personnel mine was invented solely to protect the anti-tank mine because, among other reasons, machine-gun fire would usually cover a minefield anyway and deter anyone from hand-clearing anti-tank mines. Another argument is that the American Civil War produced the first real anti-personnel mines. However, most concede that even if it wasn't invented in World War I, the anti-personnel mine was indeed very useful for protecting the bigger mines.

Whatever the motive, the anti-personnel mine had found its way on to the battlefields of World War I – and, although its use was limited, it was feared. Anti-personnel mines were used as defensive barriers and to close roads. They were also used for their nuisance value, scattered around abandoned areas as troops withdrew. When mines were laid sporadically, without markings, it was usually because departing troops wanted to set up lethal obstacles in an area they were not planning to retake. Both sides laid mines and booby traps in abandoned areas. In his memoirs Alfred Lewis described mines in as 'very troublesome' in trench warfare. He said the Germans laid mines on roads, in lanes, in houses and in minefields; in other words, 'in front of you and behind you and behind himself'.[12] In his account of service in the 8th Battalion Duke of Wellington's Regiment from 1914 to 1915, another soldier, G. A. Handford, described mines as a 'menace'. He likened them to concealed snipers, lying below soil that looked completely innocent: '. . . and before one had time to escape, the result was he was being hurled through space minus a limb, and in many cases, his life. So no wonder our progress was really of a slow nature.[13]

Between the wars

Considering the successes of the tank in the latter stages of World War I, there was surprisingly little mine warfare development in the inter-war years. After 1918, the Allies were more concerned with recon-structing their crippled nations than developing military technology. For the governments of democratic countries, it was clear that another bloodbath like the one just experienced had to be avoided at all costs. However, thanks to Hitler's emphasis on building a military machine, Germany led the way in technological advances and mine warfare strategy. Hitler was far from subdued by his experience in World War I – on the contrary, he was strengthened by it. Germany's military strategists believed that the Great War had been lost because their weapons were not good enough. The bitter experience of being pummelled by massed armoured attacks on all fronts spurred them on to develop, arguably, the most modern mines and mine-warfare techniques.[14]

The invention in the 1920s of trinitrotoluene, or TNT (a light-weight, easy-to-handle, powerful explosive), led to the development of more reliable anti-tank pressure mines. By 1929, Germany was mass-producing a type of anti-tank mine called the *Tellermine*, that contained 10 pounds of TNT, three fuses and three anti-handling fittings (small fuses screwed into the mine casing which ensured the mine would go off if an attempt was made to remove it).[15] When the world economy plunged into crisis and the opportunity for political extremism opened across Europe, Hitler made his bid for power and the countdown to another war began. According to Eric Hobsbawm, the rise of militarism and of the extreme right in Germany and Japan made another world war not only predictable, but also expected.[16] Against this frightening prospect the development of weapons, especially in Germany, took on an air of urgency. By 1935 Germany had made two more versions of the *Tellermine*. The Germans also had a keen eye on mine warfare in other conflicts. Both the Republican and the Nationalist forces in the Spanish Civil War (1936–39) used anti-tank mines. Despite advances in their design, though, anti-tank mines could still be lifted. The Republican forces lifted Nationalist mines to use them against their former owners, which the Germans duly noted and then made sure anti-handling devices were fitted to their anti-tank mines. The Germans decided anti-tank mines with anti-handling devices would be extra secure if they were surrounded by a scattering of anti-personnel mines.[17] The Germans were ready to commence hostilities at the beginning of World War II with two types of anti-tank mines and one anti-personnel mine, but by the end of the war they had developed sixteen anti-tank mines and ten anti-personnel mines.[18]

Britain and other countries were much slower off the mark than Germany. For at least a decade after World War I Britain made no significant developments in the landmine, and rearmament didn't begin again in earnest until the mid-1930s when war seemed likely. The country's economy, devastated by World War I, had taken another massive blow during the Depression. Besides, the emotional trauma of the war for Britain ran deep and it was judged to be inappropriate to rearm in earnest in such an environment. Mine warfare training was practised by Britain in the lead-up to war but the country was still slow to produce new mines. Italy had used the interwar period for research, and during the war produced one of the earliest scatterable mines. The Americans didn't do any significant mine warfare training. It has been reported, however, that the Germans, French, Russians and Italians all entered World War II with metallic mine detectors.[19]

The anti-personnel mine comes into its own

During the interwar years the world's armies gradually began to see anti-personnel mines as useful weapons in their own right and less often as merely as protectors against the removal of anti-tank mines. The first wide-scale use of anti-personnel mines in their own right was seen in the war between Russia and Finland in 1939–40. The Finnish forces made extensive use of 'cast-iron fragmentation mines', which were mounted on wooden stakes and attached to a hidden tripwire; similar mines have remained in use ever since.[20] Another mine whose general design is still copied extensively today by countries that continue to manufacture landmines is the German *S-Mine*, also known as the 'Jumping Jack' or the 'Bouncing Betty', which was designed with two charges. On the first explosion the mine jumped a metre or two into the air, and then the main explosion went off, discharging ball bearings and steel fragments at a ferocious speed to a range of up to 30 metres. The main explosion tended to occur at the very sensitive level of a soldier's abdomen. The Germans were ready to enter World War II with an *S-Mine*, which, thanks to its ingenious design, could be detonated in three different ways. It could be activated electrically, by the pressure of a footstep, or by connection to a tripwire. The *S-Mine* quickly earned a reputation for being the most feared device encountered by Allied troops, as borne out by the comments of one soldier after his first encounter with the weapon: 'By now I had gone through aerial bombing, artillery and mortar shelling, open combat, direct rifle and machine-gun firing, night patrolling and ambush. Against all of this we had some kind of chance; against mines we had none. The only defence was to not move at all.'[21]

Soldiers said the *S-mine* made them sick with fear and this was a problem for their superiors. Commander of the British Eighth Army in

North Africa, Field Marshal Montgomery, described how problematic the *S-Mine* was in North Africa in 1943:

> The mine is now a definite factor in war, and has come to stay. The anti-tank mine presents no difficulties that cannot be easily overcome, as infantry can walk over it. But the *S-Mine* (a German jumping fragmentation mine), and the booby trap are new problems that have got to be faced up to in no uncertain way and with a very robust mentality. If this is not done the troops will get nervous of this and mine-conscious, and then you are done.[22]

Rae McGrath believes the new value attributed to anti-personnel mines came about as one way to solve the problems of life in a battle zone. When he was a soldier a great deal of his time was spent trying to get some sleep and the theory was that a few anti-personnel mines buried around a soldier's camp would blow up anyone planning a surprise attack.

Many anti-personnel mines are designed to kill, but others, such as the most common variety of anti-personnel mine found today, the small blast mine, are designed specifically to injure rather than kill. Landmines such as the blast mine are the *only* conventional weapons designed to injure. The usual injury is a 'traumatic amputation' of a leg (where the force of the explosion itself is powerful enough to take off the limb). Pressure-operated landmines designed to be powerful enough to blow a limb off but not powerful enough to be fatal have been around since at least World War II, if not World War I.[23] We are used to seeing the devastating effects of the blast mine on civilians, but there are military reasons why this kind of weapon was originally regarded as useful. A wounded soldier is a much bigger drain on resources than a dead one. Other soldiers have to give him first aid and get him to a medical facility. In the middle of battle, losing several men like this can be disastrous. Also, the sight of a comrade screaming in pain with his leg blown off in the field has a terrible effect on the morale of other soldiers. They become scared of advancing in case they encounter the same fate. Oxford University Professor of the History of War, Robert O'Neill, who fought with the Fifth Battalion, the Royal Australian Regiment in Vietnam, explains:

> [Troops] were always afraid of a landmine because it was there until you lifted it, whereas enemy artillery or machine-gun fire was only a problem while it was aimed in your direction. When it was hitting you it was horrible but for the most part it would be aimed

somewhere else. A landmine was always there, waiting for you, so they were frightening things and they did make troops hesitate and go more carefully.

World War II's mine gardens

By the time World War II broke out, all armies saw the landmine as an important weapon. The vast majority of mines were laid in ordered minefields, often as a way of buying time by slowing down an enemy's advance. Some of the rows upon rows of mines that were laid are still buried in European and former Soviet soil. A much smaller number of mines were used in unmapped and unmarked 'nuisance mining', which is considered later in this chapter.

The Germans led the field in terms of technology and design of landmines during World War II, in part because the Allies had been slow to rearm in the pre-war years. The Germans had worked out an overall strategy for the landmine. They planned their minefields methodically, measuring the exact spaces between rows of anti-tank and anti-personnel mines. Most armies protected their anti-tank mine-fields with either a separate but adjacent anti-personnel minefield in front of it, or by layering rows of both within one minefield. The mixed minefield was commonly considered to be the most useful from a defensive point of view. According to American army engineer Major William C. Schneck, the Germans, the British and the Americans preferred to lay anti-tank mines and anti-personnel mines separately, for two reasons. Firstly, most armies developed anti-tank mines before anti-personnel mines so the minefields also evolved separately in military doctrine. Secondly, less well-trained troops found it easier to lay minefields incorporating one type of mine. The practice also made it easier to dig up and reuse anti-tank mines, which were seen as more valuable if they weren't mixed in with smaller mines.[24] After World War II deficiencies were recognised in separating different types of mines, and more complex mixed minefields were used involving clusters of anti-personnel mines around anti-tank mines.

Minefields could be both 'tactical' (deep and wide), which blocked an enemy's advance and channelled them into 'killing grounds', and 'protective', which were generally smaller minefields laid in front of a key defended position. Minefields would generally be covered by firing weapons for extra defence should troops attempt to breach the minefield. Sometimes a 'safe lane', or a gap, would be left through the minefield when it was being laid, so that troops and vehicles could cross it. The Germans also introduced the concept of 'dummy' or 'phoney' minefields, which were later used by both sides. If neither the time nor the resources was available, troops would buy themselves time by putting up minefield fences and markings to bluff the enemy into halting, or at least slowing, its advance.

The conventional method of laying minefields during World War I and World War II was ordered. The mines were usually recorded, mapped and fenced off. Sometimes the enemy side of a minefield wouldn't be marked, but often the enemy would be well aware that a minefield had been laid. It may seem at first as if the practice of marking minefields would be counterproductive (although the marking and fencing of minefields was generally part of an international code of military conduct). However, the purpose of a minefield was not to make the ground completely impassable. It was to provide an obstacle to slow down the enemy. If they wanted to pass it, they would still have to lift the mines and risk being caught by an exploding mine or by covering fire. Any gaps left in a minefield would generally be too narrow to launch a full-scale attack, especially with tanks and other armoured vehicles. Even if the troops suspected a dummy minefield, it's doubtful they would risk just ploughing straight through it. For these reasons, the minefield has been described as a 'stabilising force', limiting the possibility of surprise attack.

It wasn't long before each side tried to outdo the other with its use of mines. In 1943, in response to fears of an Allied invasion of northwest Europe, Hitler ordered the building of the Atlantic Wall. He put Rommel in command; Rommel then brought together reinforced concrete defences, thousands of obstacles and millions of mines as a defence along the coast of France and Holland. However, by this time the Allies' use of flails, rollers and ploughs to clear mines was a lot more advanced and the Atlantic Wall held up for just a few hours in the Allied invasion in June 1944. Robert O'Neill believes one reason that Germany made such use of mines, especially in the last stages of the war, was that the country was largely on the defensive with the Allies pressing in on it. During the Italian campaign, the Germans began to make more use of anti-personnel mines and booby traps as they faced withdrawal and ultimate defeat. The Japanese laid a considerable number of minefields against the

Allies, using them in the jungle, along beaches and anywhere they were short on manpower.

The Soviet influence on mine warfare

The Soviet Union was prolific in its use of massive minefields during World War II. It is estimated that Soviet forces laid up to 200 million mines (but this is likely to be a vast overestimation) during the war, mostly on their own land. Soviet mine warfare techniques developed during World War II have been used by generations of Russian soldiers and copied by other armies and insurgent groups in many subsequent conflicts.

The Soviets built heavily mined fortifications wherever they suspected the Germans would attack. In the years preceding the outbreak of World War II the Soviets placed a high priority on strong defences. In 1936, work began on a massive fortification system, the 'Stalin Line', which ran southwards along the western edge of the Soviet Union from the Baltic to the edge of the Pripet Marshes. It was based on the Maginot Line, a series of defensive fortifications that the French had begun to construct along France's eastern frontier, from Switzerland to Luxembourg, in 1929. According to French military theory defence would be key in the next war and strong fortifications would reduce the need for soldiers: 'The whole of military science [in the years leading up to World War II] was applied to the problems of devising and perfecting permanent defence systems against which the opponent would batter himself to exhaustion . . .'[25]

The landmine fits well into this military strategy because of its role as a 'force multiplier', or substitute soldier. The Soviet Union needed a way of defending and holding vast expanses of land. The Stalin Line consisted of, among other things, concrete, field works, artificial lakes, natural obstacles, pine trunks masking anti-tank ditches and landmines. The extensive range of obstacles, which was several miles deep, was carefully hidden so that the enemy had no idea what lay behind a standard line of defending soldiers. Although the Soviets used millions of mines in defensive belts, they also used mines offensively along roads to disrupt supply routes and to take unsuspecting soldiers by surprise.

During the battles on the Eastern Front the Soviets used many heavy fortifications, and minefields succeeded in either slowing or halting German attacks. Mine belts were sometimes laid behind the outermost row of deep anti-tank ditches, as an added hidden danger should the enemy manage to plough through all the other obstacles. Alternatively, thick belts of anti-tank mines were laid in front of and among the ditches. When wooden-cased mines were used the chances of the Germans being able to detect the mines with metal detectors were slim. The Germans advancing on Leningrad found these types of mines to be a major problem: 'A nasty surprise also was the wooden mines encountered here for the first time. Electrical mine detectors did not react to them. In some places the German sappers had to clear as many as 1,500 of these dangerous contraptions.[26]

Vast Soviet minefields were key in the biggest tank battle of all time, at Kursk in 1943. The Battle of Kursk was one of the turning points of the war and mines have been described as one of the 'decisive'[27] factors in the victory of the Soviet Union over Germany. The Red Army entered the battle extremely well prepared: it had spent three months building fortifications around Kursk before the Germans attacked in a pincer formation from the north and the south. The Soviets poured all their available resources into the battle, outnumbering thousands of German tanks, guns and aircraft. Soviet fortifications were carpeted with various barricades, ditches, traps, guns and mines. They laid a mixture of 3,000–4,000 anti-tank mines and anti-personnel mines per square mile.

> Close to the perimeter were five parallel lines of trenches, forming a defensive belt two to three miles deep. Seven miles back was a similar line, and yet another lay twenty-seven miles behind the first. In the weeks before the Germans attacked it was possible to lay very thick minefields with, in places, no fewer than 2,400 anti-tank mines per mile of front, with anti-personnel mines in addition.[28]

When they began their advance, the German tank regiments drove head-on into Soviet guns and minefields. One German soldier reported the 'Russian artillery ploughed the earth around us'.[29] Many tanks were stuck in the mud and 'hundreds were immobilised by mines'.[30] The tanks were disabled so close to their starting point that infantry soon caught up and overtook them. The Germans had attempted to use guns to detonate mines and clear paths through them, but to no avail. The Soviets covered their minefields with constant fire, so that any crews who remained in their disabled tanks became easy targets. Some Soviet soldiers were also strategically placed within minefields so that they could also attack the tanks that had been put out of action by the mines.

As described earlier, one of the purposes of minefields is to channel the enemy into 'killing fields' and the plan at Kursk is a classic example. The minefields had been laid in such a way as to steer tanks into the sights of carefully placed anti-tank gunners.

The Soviets proved adept at laying minefields during a German attack, as well as before it. During the Battle of Kursk the Soviets continued to lay mines and to take casualties, even in minefields that had already been cleared by the enemy. At times they found they got better results by responding to the changing circumstances of a battle: 'The Soviets discovered that it was far more efficient to lay several dozen mines hastily in the path of the approaching tanks, than to sow whole fields with hundreds of mines before the tanks actually arrived.'[31]

The Battle of Kursk lasted less than a fortnight, as the Germans were forced to retreat. They had battered themselves to exhaustion against such a massive barrage of Soviet weapons and obstacles. They had lost 70,000 men, 1,500 tanks (over half the number they started with) and most of their thousand-strong fleet of aircraft.[32] Mines had played a key part in the German defeat.

The Soviet Union relied heavily on landmines as a method of defence during World War II. So many mines were laid that clearance operations are still going on to this day, yet Russia continues to place a high priority on landmines, including anti-personnel mines. During the Cold War the Soviet Union became a major producer and exporter of mines, especially to regimes it supported in the developing world. Russia has not signed the Ottawa Treaty and it has used mines extensively in the recent conflicts in Dagestan and Chechnya. The Soviet design of minefields has also been copied in more recent conflicts, such as the Gulf War. The Iraqis under Saddam Hussein fought a defensive war from behind massive Soviet-style mine belts.

A testing ground for measure and countermeasure

World War II was a testing ground for developing new mines and new clearance methods. The Italians, who would later become one of the world's biggest producers and exporters of mines[33] invented an air-delivered scatterable mine for use against Australian troops in North Africa. The Germans also invented their own scatterable mines, but used them sparingly. Scatterable mines, which armed after they hit the ground, foreshadowed the use of the mine in wars to come. Air-dropped mines were used extensively by the Americans during the Vietnam War and by the Russians when they invaded Afghanistan. The Soviets developed a remote-controlled mine during the war and along with the Germans and the British are reported to have experimented with versions of a 'flame' mine. Improvised explosive devices made to act like mines were used in World War I and they continued to be used in World War II. The Finns invented anti-tank mine substitutes called 'bunches of grapes.' Six or seven hand grenades were wired together before being thrown at a passing enemy tank. Any weapon buried or camouflaged with an attached fuse can pass as a type of landmine. Adapted artillery shells were common, but drums of petrol or even napalm could be made into landmines.[34] It is claimed that the Japanese converted torpedo warheads into huge landmines to deny the Americans access to island airstrips.

In response to the British use of effective electronic mine detectors in North Africa, the Germans used a wooden-cased mine, which was more difficult to detect, but it still included metal components and British advances in metal detectors meant they could still be located. As detection technology improved, mines were made out of materials that were harder to detect. The Italians were ahead in this field and made the casing of one of their mines from Bakelite. The Germans improvised with mines, continually trying to outwit the Allies' methods of detection, clearance and burial. Commanding the 7th Panzer Division on the Meuse in 1940 in the German breach through the Maginot Line, Erwin Rommel described the way he used his tanks to prevent Allied mine laying:

> I had already given orders, in the plan for the breakthrough, for the leading tanks to scatter the roads and the verges with machine and anti-tank gun fire at intervals during the drive to Avesnes, which I hoped would prevent the enemy from laying mines. The rest of the Panzer Regiment was to follow close behind the leading tanks and be ready at any time to fire salvoes to either flank.[35]

The British, in response to German mine laying, spent much time honing their clearance techniques. They began to breach the major German minefields, by firing explosive cables and 6-foot long torpedoes that blasted a huge hole in the minefield's wire fence and detonated any mines in the immediate area. The British also adapted tanks to make them into mine clearers by attaching huge threshers or flails on the front of them. The flails would strike the ground, detonating mines, in much the same way that today's mine-clearance vehicles do. This clearance technique was far from thorough, though. Soldiers on foot or in vehicles were still injured when they encountered mines on either side of a cleared path. Allied troops in Italy were known to use flocks of sheep as one way of trying to breach German minefields. Sometimes there wasn't time to clear a minefield before trying to advance through it. During one battle forty British light tanks hoped to breach a German minefield by driving straight through it but in the event every single tank was disabled. A British bomb disposal officer with the Royal Engineers in Holland lost a leg when he took a lightweight tank to scout for mines and triggered the explosions of three mines buried in a row. He knew he was in a mined area, but assumed the tank would protect him.

Manual clearance was also dangerous for troops who weren't cautious enough around mines. Richard J. Hutchings, who served with the Royal Corps of Signals from 1940 to 1945, described the tragedy that befell his party when one man took one risk too many. At Querqueville in July 1944 his party was crossing a path that first needed to be cleared of mines. The mines were collected and put in a pile. A few of them were so corroded that their detonators could not be removed. A sergeant, worried about the unexploded mines, tried to blow up the pile by shooting at it, but to no avail. Finally a signalman, to prove the sergeant was overly concerned about the danger of the mines, began tossing stones at the pile: 'The sergeant begins to speak, but I do not hear the words. A blast of air and sand hits me like a wall, lifts me bodily and drops me on my face. My ears ring with the explosion. Then silence followed by groans.'[36] One man was killed and two were badly injured as a result of the explosion.

Major Robin Williams, a lieutenant with the 69th Field Company Royal Engineers at the time, wrote about the unenviable nature of the job of a mine clearer, a science that was still crude in those days:

Mine clearance was a hazardous business; one had to be careful or one was liable to be blown to eternity. First a mine had to be located using a mine detector (equivalent to a modern mine detector) or a steel prodder. Then it had to be identified . . . If it could not be neutralised *in situ* a long piece of wire was attached to it and it was pulled from the ground, in which case it might or might not go off.[37]

One of the characteristics of a mine is its unreliability. Even modern mines are unreliable. Early landmines had even bigger rates of failure. Some early anti-personnel mines didn't go off when stepped on, and even the much-feared *S-Mine* sometimes didn't jump out of the ground as it was supposed to, in order to detonate the main explosion in midair. From a military point of view, the fact that a few mines may not have worked properly when they were part of a huge minefield wasn't considered a huge problem.

'Nuisance mining' and booby traps

In World War II individual anti-personnel mines were commonly scattered or buried as well as being laid alongside anti-tank mines as part of massive minefields. Rae McGrath claimed that, contrary to popular belief, minefields consisting entirely of anti-personnel mines were soon enshrined in military strategic thinking in World War II and were commonly laid for their nuisance value. They were actually referred to as 'nuisance minefields'.[38] Mines were scattered on roadside verges, in rubble, or in abandoned houses on both the Western and the Eastern Fronts. 'Nuisance mining' in World War II was a larger-scale practice of the method used in World War I and it often went hand in hand with booby trapping. The Germans mastered 'nuisance mining' as they withdrew through Italy, France and Holland. One story tells of a German army camp that was taken during the drive across northwest Europe in late 1944. The Allies sent in their mine and booby-trap experts, certain that the abandoned camp would be littered with mines. Not finding any, they assumed the Germans simply hadn't had the time to put any down. They encountered no problems until one of the soldiers urinated against a fence. An electrical connection made by the urine set off a mine and the massive explosion destroyed the camp.

World War II veteran Sir Patrick Nairne remembered that the Germans tossed mines on roads and paths in Holland. The relief of finding that the enemy had withdrawn was always tempered with caution about possible mines on the paths. Sir Patrick recalled having to be particularly careful about houses. Soldiers trod on mines looking for places to set up equipment such as machine guns. He also recalled that bayonets were used to prod the ground for mines, but soldiers sometimes got a feel for where mines had been laid, especially when they saw freshly turned earth, or divots taken out of the ground.

During the D-Day operation in 1944, Major Robin Williams remembered the Germans leaving anti-personnel mines hanging in trees, which often killed unsuspecting British infantrymen. For a while the Soviets even trained dogs to seek out the undercarriages of tanks, then fitted them with explosive devices and let them loose in the presence of enemy tanks. These so-called 'mine dogs' carried linen saddlebags on their backs filled with explosives or anti-tank mines and connected to a rod. When the rod was either bent or snapped, the charge went off. The practice was short-lived but while it lasted the sight of such a dog struck fear into many a tank crew. It is reported that a German SS recruit, as part of his training, actually had to dig himself into the ground, pull the pin out of a grenade and balance the grenade on his helmet while a tank drove over him and the grenade exploded.[39] The British used booby traps in North Africa. Japanese soldiers often booby-trapped everyday objects such as pipes, torches, radios and cans of fruit. They are even known to have booby-trapped the bodies of dead or wounded soldiers.

El Alamein: the enduring legacy of World War II landmines

The war in North Africa was a key development in the history of the landmine. Huge mixed-barrier minefields involving hundreds of thousands of anti-personnel and anti-tank mines were used in the desert. The North African campaign was fought on a coastal strip about fifty miles wide, which ran along the only main road. Mines were initially used to protect strong points in the fighting between British and Italian forces on the Egyptian–Libyan border. The British halted an Italian attack on Egypt in 1940 by using large quantities of mines, as a consequence of which the Italians suffered a large and demoralising number of casualties. At the four-week Battle of Gazala in 1942 British forces laid more than half a million mines over a forty-mile front to defend the Libyan fortress of Tobruk and the nearby Gazala line.[40]

It was at El Alamein, however, that minefields became infamous for shaping a battle. In fact, it has been said that the Battle of El Alamein was fought in one huge minefield. Most of the mines were laid by the British Eighth Army before the battle, but both sides laid so many minefields that many German mines ended up as British ones and vice versa. El Alamein forms a natural bottleneck between the Mediterranean and the Qattara Depression. It was in this bottleneck that Field Marshal

Montgomery's Eighth Army stopped Rommel's Afrika Korps and, in October 1942, turned the tide of the North Africa campaign. The vast, flat terrain of the western desert was suitable for large, methodically laid minefields. Armies had few natural barriers such as ridges or mountains to assist in their defence so mines became extremely important. During the Battle of El Alamein there were only about 2,500 to 3,500 metres between the German and British front lines and minefields guarded both armies. The Germans and the British used mines as a 'force multiplier', but Rommel relied especially on mines to compensate for shortages of weapons and manpower. Around 300,000 mines used by Rommel – 80 per cent of the total – were recycled from old minefields.[41] He also lifted British, French, German and Italian mines to use against their former owners.

During the North Africa campaign, British patrols would venture out nightly to try to discover as much as they could about the German positions and their minefields. The patrols would creep forward, 20–30 yards at a time, trace the boundaries of minefields and scrape the sand away to reveal the mines, taking care not to disturb them, especially the anti-personnel mines. The operation was codenamed Operation Lightfoot. Rommel's mines slowed the Eighth Army down considerably, but Montgomery's soldiers were still able to clear and penetrate the German defences, using artillery fire to help detonate some of the mines. Rommel called the desert plateau 'the Devil's Garden'. He had become obsessed with using mines. His minefield at El Alamein was five miles deep, but he is even reported to have wanted to build a minefield using more than fifty million mines spanning the length of the French coast when he was in command of the Atlantic Wall.

The mines buried in the North African desert have outlived both Rommel and Montgomery. The weapons laid in a theatre of war have now become weapons capable of hurting innocent people who weren't even born during World War II. British and German anti-personnel landmines are still killing and maiming people at El Alamein, which is sometimes referred to as 'the village of the empty handshake' because of the number of locals who have lost hands or arms (as well as suffering other injuries) to mines. Many accidents happened soon after 1945, when it was common for whole herds of cattle and clans of camel-herders to fall victim to landmines. Ten men might leave to graze livestock and only one or two men would return alive.[42] Over the decades shifting sands and rain have moved some of the remaining mines and corroded the detonators, making them unstable. The people most affected by the mines nowadays are Bedouin herders, who live an impoverished existence in the sparsely populated desert.

Stories abound. Hamed Khalil Malouf was grazing his sheep one evening; he says he remembers hearing an explosion and later woke up in hospital. A landmine had blown off several of his fingers and generally disfigured one hand. He complained that when people shake his hand they make fun of him and treat him as if he is different. Sometimes entire families fall prey to the landmine. A Bedouin husband and wife both lost limbs in this way. Gomaa Yeosef was herding his cattle and preparing a fire to make tea when he heard a sudden explosion. He knew immediately that part of his left leg had been blown off. Eventually a passer-by carried him to hospital. He lost the rest of the leg in a high amputation and, as he didn't have the money to buy a prosthesis, has had to drag himself around on his stump ever since. His future wife lost a leg to a landmine when she was just twelve years old, while she herded cows. She was fortunate to be able to get an artificial leg, but described herself as 'very upset, nervous and angry'. Zenib Saad was fortunate to be able to get married at all after her accident. A disabled Bedouin woman is not seen as a good prospect for marriage, especially as women in Bedouin society traditionally carry the burden of childcare and all domestic duties.

Many mine incidents, especially among the Bedouin, go unreported. According to the Egyptian army, by April 2000 there had been 8,313 landmine victims in Egypt – most of them civilians.[43] This figure includes incidents in the eastern region, a result of the Egypt–Israel conflict in the past decades. However, minefields in the eastern region are at least more visibly marked than those in the western desert. In regions where the Bedouin live, there are few warnings of minefields. The Egyptian army is responsible for mine clearance in El Alamein, and open-air mine dumps by the sides of main roads are regularly topped up with corroded mines and unexploded ordnance (such as grenades, mortars and bombs).

The mine problem hampers new development. Newcomers arrive in El Alamein looking for jobs in the growing oil industry and for new areas in which to graze animals. Tourism is also increasing in the area. The Landmines Struggle Centre claimed a tenth of Egypt's agricultural land is rendered unusable because of landmines.[44] Health services are scarce in the mine-affected areas, and local hospitals are not equipped to deal with the traumatic nature of mine injuries. The state provides medical treatment and artificial limbs to mine victims, but much of the help available goes to the military rather than civilians. Many rehabilitation centres are run by military organisations and there is little financial compensation for victims. Families of the dead often receive nothing at all, partly because the police are frightened of wandering into the desert to collect evidence.[45]

The director of the Landmines Struggle Centre in Egypt, Ayman Sorour, worked in human rights before working with the Bedouin victims of landmines. He claimed the suffering caused by the landmine is worse than the legacy of other abuses because there is no one individual to blame. There is no resolution for the victims. Someone who has suffered a human rights violation can often name, or perhaps even put in jail, the person who abused him or her. The blame for laying landmines is much harder to pinpoint. The Egyptian government periodically asks the British and German governments for money to clear mines, but it is reluctant to invite international non-governmental organisations in to help demine its land. The military has always been quite secretive and protective. Egypt has itself been a producer of landmines in the past and it is unclear whether or not production has ceased. Egypt hasn't signed the Ottawa Treaty banning landmines, because it still sees landmines as militarily useful. The Middle East remains a volatile region and Egypt remains prepared for the possibility of renewed conflict with Israel. Sir Patrick Nairne, who was also a part of the British army which laid minefields at El Alamein, claimed the responsibility for clearing mines should lie with the country that has the mine problem – although he stressed that the victors and perhaps the losers, should provide technical expertise and aid. Whatever the answer, a solution seems some way off. The long-term cost of the El Alamein campaign is obviously the effect on the Bedouin, who became the unfortunate victims of someone else's war.

However, whether mines actually won the battle in the desert is debatable. Rae McGrath is certain mines were far from indispensable.

If those massive minefields had achieved their objective we'd still be fighting that war in the desert now, wouldn't we? I'm not sure that the military thinks so deeply about these things once they're at war. We all like to think that they are deep strategies. In my experience most wars are cock-ups and fast solutions . . . and that has to become strategy because nobody actually wants to say well, actually we didn't know what we were doing – we were lost – but we won. What they say is: this was our strategy all along. War isn't *that* organised.

By the end of World War II anti-personnel mines and anti-tank mines were firmly established as major weapons. The anti-personnel mine had developed from the Great War as a useful way of bolstering anti-tank mines, but by the time the world next went to war had become an indispensable weapon in its own right. The anti-personnel landmine stood apart as a weapon to be feared and hated. It inflicted horrific wounds, and dismembered limbs − not uncommon among weapons of war − but some types of anti-personnel landmines were, and still are, the only conventional weapons in the theatre of war designed to injure rather than to kill. The anti-personnel landmine was used for many reasons: to instil fear in soldiers, to protect anti-tank mines, as a general hindrance and to slow down attacks when laid as part of huge barrier minefields. Troops who knew landmines were buried in their path would have to think hard about how to approach them. The presence of just a handful of mines was enough to render a huge area unsafe. Landmines were a constant, unseen threat that could psychologically break a soldier.

The majority of landmines were deployed in a relatively controlled fashion right up to the end of World War II. There was some 'nuisance mining' but it didn't resemble anything like the widespread indiscriminate mining that is common today. However, the damage a landmine can inflict after a war has ended became apparent after World War II. A landmine remains active for decades, and it cannot discriminate between soldiers and innocent people. After the end of World War II, the accepted school of military thought was that mines were useful. The world's major armies were not using mines against civilians in the deliberate and widespread way some guerrilla armies do today. Up to 1945, landmines were used in a theatre of war where the front lines were populated only by soldiers. After World War II, front lines began to run through cities, and civilians became pawns in conflicts. The use of the landmine rapidly increased once poorly equipped armies realised how cheap, easy to obtain and easy to use landmines were. It is impossible to say who would have won and how World War II would have been played out if mines had never been invented. What is certain is that two world wars introduced the wide-scale use of the landmine and that it would be used in almost every subsequent conflict.

MCN 50 (Soviet equivalent of the Claymore), a directional fragmentation mine, made in the USSR (*photograph by Stephen Hart*).

VIGNETTE 2:
Stepping on a Landmine

Many people who trigger a landmine die immediately, or before they get to hospital. In fact, one estimate suggested that for every person who reaches hospital another dies in the field. The Landmine Survivors Network claims that around 300,000 people have been injured around the world and that less than 10 per cent have access to proper medical care. Those who do survive suffer crippling and painful injuries.

According to a leading ICRC surgeon there are three patterns of mine injury. The first is when someone stands on a mine and triggers it with the pressure of their foot. The foot is shattered and mud, grass, gravel and sometimes parts of the mine and of the foot itself are driven upwards into the remaining part of the limb. Usually the foot that came into contact with the mine is completely severed from the leg. Depending on the size of the explosion, the other foot or other parts of the body may also be injured. The problem for surgeons not familiar with these types of injuries is that a lot of dead and destroyed muscle gets driven up inside the leg. Pieces from plastic mines can also be difficult to locate on an X-ray. If a leg is amputated without catching this dead and damaged tissue, the area gets infected, resulting in yet higher amputations later on. It is a great temptation for surgeons to save as much of the limb as they can, especially a knee or elbow joint. In the worse case scenario someone whose foot is severed by a mine could end up with an amputation at thigh or even hip level as the surgeon works his way up the leg trying to keep ahead of the infection. This practice used to be referred to crudely as 'salami surgery'. One Red Cross surgeon says the term is really one of abuse – it indicates that doctors should have amputated correctly in the first place. Unfortunately, children may need later operations that have nothing to do with 'salami surgery'. As a child grows, the bone may just grow out of the skin, requiring further amputation.

The second type of injury results from a fragmentation mine, which is often triggered by a tripwire, so that the mine explodes a little distance away from the victim. In this case the victim is peppered with fragments, and injuries can occur to the head, chest and abdomen. The third pattern of injury occurs when someone, such as a child, picks up a mine or someone working in a field accidentally hits a mine with his or her hand. This can result in amputation of one or both hands as well as face and eye injuries.

Mine injuries are expensive. Victims require on average four times as much blood for transfusions as do other war-injured and they stay in hospital on average three times as long. They require more antibiotics, more dressings and the attentions of highly skilled surgeons. ICRC surgeons consider mine injuries to be among the worst of all war injuries and the most difficult to treat. Most developing countries don't have anything approaching the resources required to cope adequately with landmine victims. They need competent ambulance staff, surgeons, nurses, medicines and physical rehabilitation centres. International aid fills some of the gaps, but not all.

3

A New Front Line

Less than a decade after the end of World War II, Southeast Asia became the front line between the world's major powers. The Cold War arose from the embers of World War II, when wartime allies, the Soviet Union, Britain and the United States, became divided over the post-war future of Germany and Eastern Europe. Communism was spreading and in 1949 NATO was formed as a safeguard against a possible Soviet attack. The world was split into two main zones: capitalist and communist. The United States strongly believed in the 'domino theory' – that if one country fell into the grip of communism, other countries in the area would follow suit. The Cold War, which lasted from 1946 until 1989, ushered in a new style of warfare. It precipitated several conflicts where the superpowers fought proxy wars in foreign countries such as Korea and Vietnam, into which Cambodia and Laos were drawn. The wars fought over communism were seen by both sides as opportunities to suppress the enemy while flexing their military and political muscle: '. . . in Moscow, Beijing and Washington after 1950 the world was seen to be dividing into three blocs, the communist and capitalist locked in confrontation, with a weak, neutralist Third World which might be drawn to one side or the other.'[1]

The nuclear arms race intensified during the Cold War, but rapid technological advances in production techniques, materials and electronics also ushered in new developments in conventional weapons including more sophisticated landmines. The Vietnam War opened up an opportunity for a global landmine industry and subsequent regional conflicts in Southeast Asia and elsewhere kept the industry ticking over.

Millions of landmines manufactured in the world's richest countries eventually ended up in the soil of the world's poorest countries. Guerrilla armies and resistance groups similar to those in Vietnam and Cambodia began to use landmines indiscriminately – against civilians as well as soldiers. The landmine was cheap and easy to use: even badly trained fighters now had a weapon they could use to terrorise people. By the time it became apparent that the anti-personnel mine was wreaking havoc throughout the developing world, it was too late. The major powers and the landmine industry had unleashed millions of mines into the theatre of global conflict.

A warning from Korea

Korea became the first Cold War battleground. The Soviets and Americans had partitioned the country after World War II. Attempts to reunify Korea reached a stalemate after Stalin began building up the north as a communist state while the Americans remained staunchly in favour of a democratic Korea. The spark of war was ignited when North Korea suddenly invaded the South across the 38th parallel in 1950, in an attempt to remove what was seen as a Western puppet government and to restore the whole of Korea to the rule of Kim Il Sung. The war pitched the forces of the United Nations (mainly American but also British, Canadian, Turkish and others) and South Korea against the communist forces of North Korea and China. The United Nations initially fought back the North Koreans, before the Chinese invaded and the battle stabilised around the 38th parallel, a position similar to the Western Front of 1915–17 in the Great War.[2] The troops settled into a war fought behind barbed wire entanglements, in sandbagged trenches and deep dugouts. One major difference between the Great War and the Korean War, however, was the use of huge minefields.

The United Nations made extensive use of landmines in barrier minefields in front of the main allied lines, all along the 38th parallel. They had access to more mines than the Chinese and North Koreans but they were also looking to compensate for a shortage of troops in the face of a massive enemy force. The Chinese and North Koreans became experts at camouflage, so even the United Nations' superior weapons weren't enough to halt attacks. The UN forces needed a way of protecting their position that involved an element of surprise and landmines provided that. The Chinese and the North Koreans also used mines around the 38th parallel. The 151-mile Demilitarised Zone remains one of the most heavily mined areas in the world. The border minefield has stayed in place since the cease-fire was reached in June 1953. In fact, the continuing defence of South Korea with mines is cited by the United States as the major reason for their opposition to the Ottawa Treaty banning landmines, as discussed in Chapter 1. However, the value of the existing minefields in Korea is the subject of much debate, especially as political tension has been evaporating between North and South Korea. Rae McGrath has pointed out that barrier minefields in the Gulf War were breached in as little as twenty minutes when they weren't covered by airpower or ground fire: 'Militarily their arguments based on Korea would be thrown out by a first year class of military students and it should be kind of embarrassing for the Pentagon that they made the argument.'

A former Korean army general claims the DMZ is likely to remain a 'belt of death' even if Korea is reunified because of inadequate mapping and because a large number of the mines are difficult to detect.[3] It became apparent during the Korean War that anti-personnel mines could become a major hazard for the army using them. Even some military historians who argue that mines were useful in the two World Wars cannot say the same about Korea. The ground war in Korea was fought in mountainous terrain in an extreme climate. The environment did not suit mine warfare. Some of the minefields were sown along steeply sloping hillsides and when the spring thaw melted the snow, the wet ground shifted the mines down the hill and minefield fences and markers fell down. Wiring parties had to venture out under the cover of darkness to fix the fences. Professor Robert O'Neill explains:

You can imagine what that would've been like on a freezing precipice on a hillside, not knowing exactly where the outer edge of these mines was: it was terrifying, and the Chinese were aware that minefield fence repair parties would come out so they would ambush them. A few friends of mine spent a lot of time in Chinese prisons having been caught during minefield fencing operations.

The shifting of mines posed a problem for both sides and it was 'very easy', according to Professor O'Neill, for soldiers to be blown up on their own mines that had moved outside the original edges of a minefield. He recalled one platoon commander who was on patrol when he was blown up by one of his own mines that had been moved in that way. Mines came to be feared by the soldiers they were meant to be *protecting* in the Korean War. The threat that troops could be blown up by their own mines foreshadowed larger scale difficulties in the Vietnam War.

However, these problems weren't officially recognised at the time. After all, it is only relatively recently that the American military finally admitted publicly that mines were a problem for their own troops in Vietnam. Another warning from the Korean War was the Chinese troops lifting enemy mines and using them against their former owners. This practice was limited in Korea and didn't occur on anything like the scale it did in Vietnam. Perhaps even more significant in the debate about the usefulness of mines is the fact that the Chinese cleared corridors through minefields simply by moving troops through them.[4] Minefields have traditionally been used to channel an enemy attack into 'killing fields' – but if the enemy is prepared to go straight through a minefield then at least some of the intended effect is lost. It cannot be assumed that every country or every army places the same importance on minimising its own casualties. Cultural and societal attitudes have a big influence on the way wars are fought and lives are more expendable in some countries than they are in others.

Vietnam leads to a landmine industry

A little more than a decade after Korea, the continuing spread of communism led the Cold War powers to clash once again on Southeast Asian soil. The Vietnam War began to escalate in 1964, after years of simmering tension. Vietnam had been partitioned by the Geneva Agreements of 1954, which ended the colonial war with France. The north became a communist state and the south a non-communist state. The Geneva Agreements stipulated that elections should be held with a view to unification, but the South Vietnamese premier refused to take part. The United States sent military advisers to South Vietnam as early as 1954 amid fears of communist aggression. The Viet Cong (which evolved from the Viet Minh, a resistance group that had fought the French) increased its guerrilla activities and America responded by increasing its support for South Vietnam. After an alleged attack on a United States warship in 1964, Congress passed a resolution to take military action. By the time the United States made the commitment to escalate the war in Vietnam in 1965, it saw China as the biggest communist threat and justified its involvement in Vietnam by assuming the role of a global police force.

The Vietnam War was characterised by a massive display of airpower. In its efforts to stop the movement of weapons and troops from North to South Vietnam along the Ho Chi Minh trail, the United States dropped more bombs on Vietnam than were dropped during World War II. More than fifteen million tons of bombs, mines and shells were used in Vietnam between 1965 and 1975 – that is 280 kilograms of ordnance for each citizen of North and South Vietnam.[5] The campaign, against the activities along the Ho Chi Minh trail, is reported to have cost the US $2 million dollars per day.[6] Endless craters can still be seen along roadsides – one of the few visible reminders of the war. University of Florida History Professor Robert McMahon said the decision to wage war from the air was in line with the United States' traditional policy of attempting to keep the loss of its own troops to a minimum. He believes the US hoped to bomb the North Vietnamese and the Viet Cong to the negotiating table to get a better deal. It didn't work, so a decision was taken to commit ground troops. By 1966, the US had over half a million troops in Vietnam, and it was well and truly entrenched in a hugely controversial war.

Since World War II, methods of remotely delivering mines had become more sophisticated. When the Vietnam War broke out, military boffins found themselves with a massive testing ground. As part of its aerial bombardment, the United States unleashed remotely delivered landmines, carpeting Vietnam, Laos and Cambodia along the Ho Chi Minh trail. Pilots dropped so many mines they referred to them as 'garbage'. Also known as 'scatterbabies', they could be dropped from a great height without detonating. The barrier minefield concept was of no use in the Vietnam War because it wasn't fought along traditional 'fronts'. Battlefields constantly moved and changed. The Americans fought their ground war from fortified 'firebases'. They launched hit-and-run attacks from these firebases to capture or kill Viet Cong and North Vietnamese. Air-dropped minefields were very different from the traditional marked and mapped minefields deployed during the two World Wars. It was impossible to know the exact boundaries of areas scattered with mines. A frightening new era of unmapped mines had begun.

The Vietnam War was a turning point in the manufacture, supply and distribution of landmines. During and after the war some of the world's developed nations began manufacturing large quantities of landmines. A landmine industry got underway. According to Rae McGrath, commercial interests took over from military in pushing landmine development, as some big American companies began to see an opportunity to make big money out of manufacturing air-dropped weapons. McGrath claimed that by the 1960s the manufacture of mines was an industry driven process not a military driven one.

> The industry was selling things to the military and the military was saying 'wow they're shiny – we'll have a million of them' . . . and that's proved by the fact we ended up with millions of these weapons in stockpiles and yet the military, in the end, agreed they actually weren't any good. Well, why were they buying them? Very few military people could ever give you a really sensible strategy for their use of landmines and the reason was the arms industry drove the strategy from the 1970s onwards.

While the Americans were dropping high-tech mines and bombs from the air with the help of big companies, the Viet Cong relied chiefly on resourcefulness, cunning and terror in its offensive use of mines throughout the war. The Viet Cong fighters laid anti-tank and anti-personnel mines indiscriminately. They attempted to thwart every move the Americans made, including scattering metal fragments on roads to slow down mine detection teams. At other times they would wait until an area had been cleared, before replanting a mine, ready to explode when unsuspecting troops or vehicles attempted to pass. The terrain in Vietnam exacerbated the effects of indiscriminate mine-laying. Mines were much more difficult to map, mark or detect in a country made up of jungle, paddy fields, dykes and rivers than they had been in the North African desert thirty years earlier. The Viet Cong were very resilient – they did after all survive in vast networks of underground tunnels for the duration of the war. They were fearless and would detect and lift enemy mines expertly by poking the ground with a piece of wire.

The Viet Cong fighters became expert in – and notorious for – their use of indiscriminate mining, booby traps and surprise attacks. They would fashion improvised mines out of any explosive they could find, packing it into seemingly harmless objects. A coconut shell hanging from a tree; a pile of buffalo dung; a dead animal; an abandoned container – all of these could suddenly be transformed into a lethal weapon. This type of mine warfare had a terrible psychological effect.

Mine injuries are painful and they look horrific – severed limbs are common. It is extremely traumatic for other soldiers to witness one of their colleagues blown up on a mine. The Vietnam War was a particularly gruesome conflict in general, and many veterans suffered severe psychological problems when they tried to return to a normal life. During the war there were reports of atrocities, including the My Lai massacre in March 1968 where US troops slaughtered 200 Vietnamese civilians. The My Lai massacre was shrouded in mystery with allegations of a military cover-up, but according to military historian and defence analyst Charles Messenger it must be seen in a wider context. '. . . My Lai was a symptom of the nature of the war in Vietnam. US troops had seen their comrades blown to pieces on Viet Cong mines and booby traps. They knew the Vietnamese peasantry was aiding the communists, willingly or not, and the gulf between the American troops and the Vietnamese people was growing ever wider.'[7] The insidious cruelty of mine use, it seems, had helped to drive the Americans over the edge psychologically.

Landmines are a paradox. From the American military point of view, the Vietnam War is one of the best examples of how ineffective and even counterproductive mines can be. During the war Americans often fell victim to their own mines. This happened for several reasons. Firstly, American pilots dropped thousands of unmapped mines from the air. Secondly, the war had no static fronts and troops were constantly moving through different and unfamiliar territory – sometimes areas their own pilots had just mined. Finally, and perhaps most importantly, the Viet Cong had become expert at stealing enemy mines to bolster its own supplies. Professor Robert O'Neill recounted two incidents where troops were killed by their own mines over two days in Phuoc Tuy province towards the end of his tour.

His brigade commander needed a strategy to block the Viet Cong coming in from the east of the province, so he decided to use a barrier fence and minefield because it was easiest to patrol. A regular patrol system was then set up to check that no one had been into the minefield. However, a soldier on a routine morning patrol stumbled on one of his company's own mines. He was killed and two others were wounded. The mine was buried directly in line with the path that ran alongside the barbed wire fence protecting the minefield. It is thought the Viet Cong removed the mine and replanted it there on purpose. The next day the same company was working with a team of soldiers searching for mines with mine detectors. The platoon commander stood on a raised area of ground near the fence to explain to the troops which areas had been cleared. When he had finished talking he stepped off into the uncleared area and landed on another mine planted in line with the fence. He was killed – all because either he lost his balance or momentarily forgot where he was. It's estimated that between a third and a fifth and of all US deaths were caused by mines.[8] Professor O'Neill claimed the Viet Cong had been helping themselves to American mines for several years before the outbreak of full-blown war by stealing them from the South Vietnamese.

The fall of Saigon and the futility of landmines

On 30 April 1975, the North Vietnamese entered Saigon. After a decade of American involvement the war was over. Vietnam became a unified socialist republic and vast numbers of South Vietnamese fled their country, fearful for their lives. The catastrophic failure of the American military machine to pound the North Vietnamese into submission is still a bitter and torturous memory for America. The country struggled to come to terms with a devastating war so far from home. Huge amounts of money and weapons had proven to be no match for men and women with few resources but with a stubborn determination to win.

By 1975, millions of mines had been buried by American, South Vietnamese and North Vietnamese forces. The landmine had become the poor man's weapon, perfect for armies with limited resources such as the Viet Cong. It's now accepted that the landmine caused more harm than good to the American soldiers in Vietnam, but the killing and maiming didn't stop when the battlefields were deserted. Civilians are still falling victim to the landmine a quarter of a century after the end of the war. Chuck Searcy, a Vietnam veteran who felt compelled to return to Vietnam, worked until recently for the Vietnam Veterans of America Foundation in Hanoi. He regularly saw landmine victims come through the VVAF prosthetics clinic.

A landmine is a definite impediment to any activity, so the conventional military view is that you're limiting military options. The problem is that you limit every option – for military or civilians, for water buffalo or for children or for economic development . . . Landmines have never won a battle and I think it's unlikely

74

landmines have ever made a significant difference in either repelling an enemy attack or protecting soldiers and I think today the world is finally coming to that conclusion.

After the war, Vietnam became politically and economically isolated from the rest of the world. Now things have changed. The US lifted its economic embargo in 1994, and the Vietnamese government is inviting foreign investment into the country. After so much death and destruction Vietnam has abandoned strict communist ideology for market reform. Outside the international community for so long, Vietnam is being welcomed back into the fold. International non-governmental organisations are starting to clean up the pollution of mines and unexploded ordnance. However, because of the tensions of the past, demining aid has been slower to arrive in Vietnam than in many other mine-affected countries and that has adversely affected civilians living among landmines.

Quang Tri

One of the fiercest battlegrounds of the war, Quang Tri province, has one of the biggest problems with mines and unexploded bombs in the country today. It lies near the 17th parallel, or the former DMZ, and it was where more than 60 per cent of the fighting took place. Large numbers of mines were planted south of the DMZ as part of the 'MacNamara Line', a line of defence from the South China Sea to the mountains of the Annamite Chain. Over the course of the war, especially as the North Vietnamese began to advance into American-held territory, the areas immediately south of the 17th parallel were shelled, bombed and mined by both sides.

Since 1975 Quang Tri provincial authorities have reported more than 5,000 deaths and almost 7,000 injuries to mines or unexploded ordnance.[9] One man in Quang Tri lost both hands to an American bomblet in 1972 and he lost a foot to a mine a year later. Another man lost his leg to a mine, when he was looking after water buffalo in the fields. A two-year-old girl was killed and her three-year-old brother was injured when they played with a bomblet they found not far from their house. A teenager lost part of his arm when he handled a mine he found in the field. Handicap International has calculated that one out of every seven mine victims in Quang Tri wasn't even born at the time the Vietnam War ended. They're falling victim to weapons of a war that has little relevance to their lives in the twenty-first century.

Quang Tri has a big problem with 'unexploded ordnance', from old bombs, shells and mortars littering the ground. Unfortunately, this scrap metal – some of which still contains active explosive – is a valuable commodity in the Third World. The average income per capita per annum for the people living in Quang Tri province is about $130. For some people, landmines and unexploded bombs are just one more hazard in the daily battle to survive. Scrap metal can be traded for rice and other necessities. Poverty forces people into the minefields to search for bits of old bombs or mines. In 1995, in a small sub-district of Quang Tri, Tri Phong, around twenty scrap dealers along Highway One each moved around a hundred tons of scrap ordnance a year.[10] The British demining agency Mines Advisory Group, found 4,000 items of unexploded ordnance and ninety-one mines in their first sixty weeks of a clearance operation at Quan Ngang, the site of an old American firebase in Quang Tri. Once large amounts of scrap started coming to the surface, scrap metal collectors attempted to get on to the site. Over one weekend when the Vietnamese military set up an operation to stop the collection of scrap at Quan Ngang they cautioned more than 300 scrap dealers from three provinces. MAG leaves scrap metal that has been verified to be safe in piles for locals to pick up in the hope they won't take so many risks.

Cambodia Trust Founder trustee Dr Peter Carey described a 'cycle of conflict', relating to the collection of scrap metal. The weapons manufactured in Chicago and Detroit and dropped on Vietnam are recycled as scrap metal by peasants, sold by the peasants to wholesalers and sold by the wholesalers to the Japanese. The Japanese then refine the scrap into high grade steel and send it back in steel plates to the automobile industries of Detroit and Chicago, which results in people driving around in cars which have been produced through the cycle of the Vietnam War, even though they aren't aware of it.

Some residents aren't as willing as the scrap collectors to risk their lives. They abandon the land and fall into even deeper poverty. In the Gio Linh district in Quang Tri in 1995 between 3,000 and 4,000 hectares of farm land, mainly around former US military bases, uncultivated because of the presence of mines and ordnance.[11] Before international agencies started mine clearance in Vietnam a few years ago, the military used to carry out only limited mine clearance. In the past residents have waited as long as seven months for the military to arrive to clear mines or unexploded bombs. The residents, losing patience, then sometimes attempted to get rid of the items themselves.[12]

Cambodia: nearly thirty years of mine warfare

A tropical country of forests and meadows, Cambodia is blessed with rich natural resources including wood, gemstones and minerals. However, extensive mining over a quarter of a century has blighted Cambodia's Eden. The country has an extremely serious landmine problem. It's thought that the Cambodian conflict may have been the first in history in which mines have claimed more victims than any other weapon.[13] There is no doubt Cambodia is one of the world's most heavily mined countries. By the end of the Vietnam War huge shipments of landmines were ending up in the hands of Third World insurgent armies. They arrived as part of military aid packages from the big powers offering either overt or covert support to resistance fighters. Cambodia's mine problem began when it became drawn into the Vietnam War and worsened through mine laying by the Vietnamese, the Khmer Rouge and government troops during two subsequent decades of regional conflict.

Since the early 1990s many mines have crossed the borders of Cambodia but it's not known which mines were imported and which were brought in by foreign armies. Thirty-six different types of anti-personnel mine from about a dozen countries have been found in Cambodia.[14] A large number of Vietnamese mines have been used, but American, Soviet, Chinese, Israeli, Belgian, Yugoslav, Czech and German mines have also found their way into Cambodian soil at some stage. All parties in Cambodia's conflict used mines. Most were laid defensively but some were also laid offensively. The overall use was indiscriminate, unmapped and unmarked. The main purpose of mines in Cambodia was to deny the enemy access to strategic sites, bridges or roads, to protect and defend and to terrorise civilians and to control their movement. Mines were layered on top of each other over the years as the fighting advanced and retreated across the same ground.

Cambodia, as well as Laos, was bombed as part of the American offensive along the Ho Chi Minh trail in the Vietnam War, much of which went through Cambodia's mountains and jungles. The United States also bombed Cambodia in an attempt to destroy Viet Cong bases there. They dropped as many bombs over Cambodia as were dropped on Germany during World War II.[15] Disturbingly, declassified United States' government documents suggest that the carpet-bombing of Cambodia helped bring the brutal leader Pol Pot to power. The CIA director of operations reported in 1973 that Pol Pot and the Khmer Rouge were using the damage caused by B52 strikes as the main theme of their propaganda, resulting in the successful recruitment of a considerable number of young men to their cause.[16]

Cambodia was also drawn into the Vietnam ground war. Landmines were laid around North Vietnamese base camps in eastern Cambodia as early as 1967. When Cambodia's left-wing leader Prince Norodom Sihanouk was ousted by pro-American Cambodian Prime Minister Lon Nol in 1970, full-blown war broke out in Cambodia and Sihanouk became allied with the Khmer Rouge, as well as the Viet Cong and the North Vietnamese. War was to plague Cambodia for the next twenty years and all sides used landmines. By 1972 the North Vietnamese controlled much of eastern Cambodia while the Khmer Rouge had taken over the south. The Americans bombed both areas.

The peace agreement ending the Vietnam War cut the alliance between the North Vietnamese and the Khmer Rouge. By this stage half the population had fled to the cities to escape the fighting. The Khmer Rouge then set about advancing towards Phnom Penh, mining areas along the Mekong river in the process. In April 1975, the same month that Saigon fell to the North Vietnamese, the Khmer Rouge, led by Pol Pot, overthrew the Lon Nol military government and renamed Cambodia Kampuchea. Cambodia then fell into the grip of one of the most brutal regimes ever known. Over the next few years as many as one and a half million people lost their lives in what came to be known as 'the killing fields' as the educated and professional classes were singled out for torture and massacre. Thousands were taken to Tuol Sleng, a former Phnom Penh secondary school which was turned into a death camp. When the Vietnamese discovered the school they left it virtually untouched – its torture beds, barbed wire and oppressive atmosphere serve as a constant reminder of the horrors its prisoners were subjected to. The Khmer Rouge slogan was 'Preserve them – no profit. Exterminate them – no loss. We will burn the old grass and the new will grow.'[17]

Provocation by the Khmer Rouge led the Vietnamese to invade Cambodia in December 1978 and before long they occupied the whole country. Pol Pot withdrew his forces to the jungles on the Thai border and the Vietnamese installed a new government under former Khmer

Rouge leader, Heng Samrin. The Khmer Rouge continued its guerrilla war against the new Vietnamese-backed government. Both sides used landmines to control the movement of civilians. Large quantities of mines were used by the Vietnamese to protect their bases. The Khmer Rouge and Thai forces added to a growing border mine belt on their side to stop any enemy advances. By 1979 tens of thousands of civilians ended up on the mined Thai border as they sought refuge from the fighting as well as from famine. In 1984 the biggest minefield in Cambodia – 600 kilometres in extent – was laid by the Vietnamese along the Thai border after they had pushed more than 22,000 civilians and soldiers into Thailand.[18] The minefield effectively closed the border. Few refugees dared cross the minefields, although some offered to escort refugees across – for a hefty price. As well as laying large minefields, the Khmer Rouge, like the Viet Cong, became expert at using improvised mines. Grenades would be attached to ground level tripwires and hung in trees. Mines were also booby-trapped, or buried on top of each other in a stack.

As a result of international pressure and its desperate need for aid and foreign investment, Vietnam finally withdrew from Cambodia in 1989. Yet more mines were laid after the Vietnamese withdrawal. Fighting and mining moved backwards and forwards over the border area. The new state of Cambodia used mines to compensate for a shortage of resources and troops, especially between 1989 and 1992 when it was protecting provincial cities, towns and villages from the Khmer Rouge and Western-backed factions based in Thailand. Guy Willoughby of the HALO Trust said the Cambodian government, along with the Vietnamese, laid most of Cambodia's mines. However, he pointed out that if the state of Cambodia hadn't used a large number of mines for protection, the country could have fallen once more into the grip of the Khmer Rouge, an argument he suggested may make people a little uncomfortable. Government troops also laid anti-personnel mines randomly around towns and villages to stop any secret meetings between villagers and insurgents. A peace agreement over Cambodia was reached in 1991, but the use of mines continued and civilians were far from safe. In that same year the Khmer Rouge began the secret repatriation of hundreds of refugees as part of the supposed peace process, herding them through minefields at night, into 'zones of free Kampuchea' without UN protection.[19] In 1992 Khmer Rouge commanders laid minefields around villages to stop people leaving the areas they still controlled. Reports of mine use by the Cambodian army and the Khmer Rouge continued as late as 1995 and 1996, when there was a heavy spate of fighting in the northwest of the country. Over half of the wounded arriving at hospitals in the area were reported to be the victims of anti-personnel mines and one in four was a civilian.[20] Cambodia's King Sihanouk denounced the use and stockpiling of landmines in 1994, but the Royal Cambodian Armed Forces and the Khmer Rouge opposed his ban. Cambodia finally ratified the Ottawa Treaty in July 1999.

The new landmine industry made it possible for a host of foreign landmines to cross Cambodia's borders. One particular type of Russian anti-personnel mine often found by deminers, for example, had been used in Cambodia since the 1980s, a period that coincided with the growth of the Russian arms industry. However, there are suggestions of an even more direct connection between major powers and mine warfare in Cambodia. In 1991 Asia Watch reported that Chinese and British forces trained Cambodian resistance fighters in the use of mines, other explosives and booby traps against civilian as well as military targets.[21] War correspondent John Pilger wrote that a former SAS officer in Thailand told him that the SAS had trained the Khmer Rouge in the use of mines. That officer told Pilger: 'We used mines that came originally from Royal Ordnance in Britain, which we got by way of Egypt, with markings changed. They are the latest; one type goes up in a rocket and comes down on a parachute and hangs in the bushes until someone brushes it. Then it can blow their head off, or an arm.'[22] When John Pilger exposed his story of the SAS training Khmer Rouge forces, the British government responded with blanket denials.

A 'landmine culture'

Anti-personnel landmines became so much a part of daily life in Cambodia that a so-called 'landmine culture' developed. After decades of war people were so familiar with mines they would keep them to use around their property or to trade on the black market. Fishermen used TNT extracted from mines to stun fish. However, one of the most significant ways civilians used landmines was as a means of keeping out the Khmer Rouge during their reign of terror. If a village had only a few soldiers and a few guns at its disposal, mines were used as a very practical form of defence, in the same way other people lock and alarm their houses. They offered villagers protection against torture and possible death, even though the mines left in their garden might eventually injure a member of the household. In a similar way, the citizens of Sarajevo mined their property in the Bosnian war to keep out the Serbs. Former bomb disposal officer Paul Jefferson described how Cambodian civilians under threat were faced with a very stark choice: 'What would you do if the Khmer Rouge were cruising your neighbourhood and they got into your town? People would be bayoneted to death, if they were lucky. People use every measure possible to protect themselves and you trade off the risk of possible casualties tomorrow for the increased degree of certainty of safety tonight.'

Another example of Cambodia's landmine culture is illustrated by Dr Peter Carey, who claimed soldiers used mines in a blasé fashion, which exacerbated the dangers to civilians. He cited young soldiers who, too lazy to patrol at night would lay mines on the culverts and the paths leading to their encampment. The mines would then be left lying around as the soldiers were too drunk or could not be bothered to pick them up. Dr Carey talked of 'almost a nonchalance in which mines are used and abused'. During the Cambodian war landmines were available on the black market, and sometimes even in the city or town markets, for civilians to use to protect their property. It has been rumoured that on rare occasions landmines were used to settle personal disputes.

Although there is little evidence that mines continue to be traded and used in this way, one incident in 1999 suggested that civilians are still keeping mines in their houses. Six people were killed when an anti-personnel mine exploded in a private house in Tuol Kok, Phnom Penh. Mines also appear still to have some value as an item for trade. Researchers for the ICBL discovered evidence of three cases of people storing mines for possible cross-border trade. In one case, a demining agency found some villagers unwilling to hand over mines to be destroyed because they could sell them across the Thai border for about 50 US cents each.[23] Because Cambodia is a signatory of the Ottawa Treaty, it is now illegal to lay mines, even though the Cambodian legal system has some way to go before it reaches an 'acceptable standard of rule of law'.[24]

The endemic problem of mine injuries

One measure of the extent of Cambodia's landmine problem is the huge number of people injured by the weapon. Cambodia has one of the highest landmine injury rates in the world. The numbers run into tens of thousands. It is estimated that one in every 240–250 Cambodians has stepped on a landmine. In 1997, the Mines Advisory Group found that one in every two to three landmine and unexploded ordnance victims was injured as a result of someone else's accident. Consequently there is a steady stream of people lining up to be fitted with prostheses. In one of the main prosthetics clinics in Phnom Penh, landmine survivors – the young, the old, men, women, soldiers and civilians – all talked of their utter despondency. They said that even with prostheses they couldn't work or play sport as they used to and they couldn't visualise a future with their disabilities. One patient at the clinic, Sao Chamreun, a single amputee, said the constant support and reassurance of his friends and relatives offered his only hope of getting on with his life.

Losing a limb carries with it a huge stigma in Cambodia, where amputees are known as 'crocodile meat'. Many are forced to beg. One of the places they gather is the famous temple-city at Angkor Wat, which has now been opened to tourists. Beggars hope to cash in on the 'holiday in hell' trade, which sees tourists rushing to be the first into countries which have experienced a brutal past. Where elephants once transported Khmer Rouge landmines around the country, now they carry tourists up the hill behind the temples at sunset to view the ruins. On their way up the hillside tourists pass amputee beggars in varying states of disfigurement. One beggar at Angkor has lost both hands and both feet. She can't even hold the money people give her.

Amputee beggars also gather at the Phnom Penh market. Mike Boddington, chief executive of POWER (Prosthetic and Orthotic Worldwide Education and Relief) claimed there were a group of 'professional' beggars in the market, who, even though they had been fitted with prostheses, chose to pretend they were still amputees because it was their best chance of making enough money to survive. Boddington said the beggars would remove their prosthetic limb and leave it around the back of the stall so that they could attract sympathy as an amputee, before putting it back on to go home at the end of the day. Boddington believes a new limb still offers these beggars a better life. Whether amputees decided to continue begging or not, he said they could still have a wider range of opportunities and a greater degree of choice and of freedom with a prosthesis. Michael Ignatieff has seen many landmine victims in countries all around the world, and he has stressed that the effect of amputation is much worse in a poor community.

Amputation is just a very different thing in a poor and destitute culture than it is in a Western one . . . I'm very struck by the way in which injury to women ruins their lives to a degree that it doesn't ruin men's lives. A women without a leg is human refuse in patriarchal societies . . . and that's a differential that prosthetic limb fitting can only partially compensate for, but it's better than nothing.

The plight of returning refugees

Ironically, as Cambodia enters the most peaceful and stable era it has seen in forty years, its people are more at risk from landmines than ever. The former killing fields, the scene of so much butchery, are now a tourist attraction. They stand as a permanent reminder that a regime like Pol Pot's should never be allowed to happen again. But Cambodia is now being held hostage to a new type of killing field: the minefield. Refugees are returning from camps on the Thai border to land that has not yet been cleared because they are so desperate to reinhabit their old homes. In the early 1990s hundreds of thousands of refugees returned from Thailand. According to the World Food Program in 1998, there were still 110,000 internally displaced people either waiting to be resettled or just returned to their villages. Many of their villages were mined. In 1999, 37,000 refugees from camps in Thailand returned to heavily mine-infested areas in Samlot, Samrong and Anlong Veng.[25]

Battambang, in the northwest of the country, is another badly mined province. It bore the brunt of the civil war fought from 1979 onwards between the Vietnamese and their allies in Cambodia and the Khmer Rouge. Fighting has gone backwards and forwards throughout the province for the last fifteen to twenty years. Troops laid mines, then retreated through the mined areas and sometimes blew themselves up on their own mines. It's estimated that in some districts of Battambang the whole population has been displaced at some stage. Everywhere bright red skull and crossbones signs warn of mines. Deminers work metres away from houses where children play. Daily agricultural life goes on around the minefields. The landmine toll in Battambang has been described as 'carnage'. The local Emergency Centre for War Victims is brimming with amputees. Emergency is a privately funded Italian hospital with clean white buildings, set among manicured sub-tropical gardens. Many of the hospital's patients are children. They are 'lucky' to have access to good treatment, but they are sad and quiet. There is no laughter and there is none of the normal energy children display. While the overall number of mine casualties is dropping in Cambodia, the percentage of incidents involving children has been increasing over the past three years, from around one in six of the total number of casualties in 1998 to one in three to four in the first five months of 2000.[26]

Emergency's medical coordinator, Stefania Caratti, claimed there hasn't been enough attention given to the needs of Cambodia's landmine victims. She said the worst problems involved poor transportation and poor health facilities. Sometimes, patients were simply sent to the hospital nearest to the accident site – and poorly conducted amputations led to infection, requiring the patients to have more surgery at better equipped hospitals. Caratti said most mine victims that have come through her hospital have been young men, but there have also been many children. The children were injured when they either went with their parents into the bush or the fields, or when they picked up and played with mines or bombs. Stefania Caratti has also noticed seasonal trends. Three to four times the number of injuries happen during the dry season than they do in the rainy season, when fewer people are working the land.

One story that has shocked even the most hardened of soldiers and deminers is that of Lach Lorn, a thirteen-year-old boy whose parents abandoned him after he stepped on a mine. Lach Lorn lived with his mother, stepfather, six brothers and sister in a very remote village near the Thai border. He went with a brother to look for mushrooms, at his mother's request, when he stepped on a landmine and lost his left arm and leg. His parents then abandoned him. Soldiers took him to a hospital in Thailand where he underwent crude surgery. Lach Lorn was then returned to Cambodia and left to beg for food in a broken wheelchair. An ICRC expatriate found him and took him to Emergency in Battambang. Several attempts have been made to track down his parents, but to no avail. He still needs further surgery and after that it is likely he will be sent to an orphanage. When asked about his injuries, Lach Lorn repeated over and over that he had lost his mother. The reason this child was abandoned by his parents and left to face a horrific ordeal by himself – he is lucky to have survived at all – was because his parents couldn't afford to look after him. The psychological and social effects of landmines are devastating.

Denial of land

Blessed with fertile lands, Cambodia once produced a surplus of rice and fruit. In a country where 85 per cent of a population of 11.4 million are dependent on the land, the plague of landmines has destroyed Cambodia's economy and culture. Landmines prevent people from growing rice, from getting access to water and to community services. According to the government demining organisation, the Cambodia Mine Action Centre (CMAC), 644 square kilometres is still mined and a further 1,400 square kilometres is suspected of being mined.[27] Farmers have to enter fields and rice paddies, often when they know there is a danger of mines. Sometimes farmers attempt to clear the mines themselves, unable to wait for professional deminers. When one farmer is blown up on a mine it spreads fear and anxiety among a whole village, paralysing people who are too afraid to continue cultivating the land. It all depends how desperate they are for food: 'In Cambodia it is not unusual to encounter families who have lost several members to mine explosions but who still farm and graze the same land. When questioned regarding the inherent dangers in this lifestyle their answer is characteristically one of acceptance, a threat accepted because it is marginally the lesser risk when measured against total destitution.'[28]

Cambodia has many international aid agencies working to clear once productive land, but in 1999 the mine-clearing programme was rocked by a scandal involving the national demining agency which coordinates the work of the non-governmental demining organisations. The CMAC faced allegations of corruption and mismanagement. CMAC donors suspended funds and demanded an audit. The audit, while critical of management practices, found that only a small proportion of funds, mainly related to money allocated by the Cambodian government, couldn't be accounted for. Australia is the biggest cash donor to CMAC, and it was one of the first to restore funding to the organisation after the audit and a reform process had been set in place. Some donors who suspended funds to CMAC continued to fund mine clearance through other organisations. MAG programme manager Archie Law estimated that at least another decade of mine clearance is needed in Cambodia before the level of mine contamination is similar to that of the World War II mine contamination in Europe. He said the situation in Cambodia will be judged to be acceptable when there is a significant drop in casualty rates, when people have access to community services and agricultural land and when people can walk around without fear of mines.

Laos: the victim of de facto landmines

Laos, like Cambodia, became both a victim of the United States air-bombing campaign along the Ho Chi Minh trail, and a third party in the Vietnam ground war. Although the United States never officially declared war on Laos, it used it as a testing ground for all sorts of new weapons. Between 1964 and 1973 the United States flew more than 580,000 missions over Laos, dropping around two million tons of bombs.[29] It has been estimated to be the equivalent of one bombing mission every eight minutes for nine years. Parts of northern Laos were bombed to destroy anti-American, communist Pathet Lao bases and the south of the country was bombed as part of the Ho Chi Minh trail. It is estimated that up to a third of that ordnance quantity detonate on impact and a quarter of a century later Laos is still dealing with a huge quantity of unexploded bombs. Ten of the country's eighteen provinces are severely contaminated.[30] It is thought that, per capita, Laos is the most heavily bombed country on earth. A good indication of how contaminated the soil in Laos is is the number of potentially dangerous items found. The government demining organisation reported clearing almost 90,000 mines and items of unexploded ordnance in 1999 alone.[31] Many of the bombs American air crews dropped were cluster bombs, which opened in the air to release small bomblets, or 'bombies', over a wide area. One single bomblet, which breaks up as it explodes, can spread dangerous fragments over up to 150 metres. Bomblets, roughly the size of tennis balls, are considered to be *de facto* landmines because when they fail to explode as they were designed to they function in the same way anti-personnel mines do. In a controlled test of American bomblets in 1966, 26 per cent failed to explode.[32] There are also several reports of air crews simply hitting the wrong targets, killing innocent people and littering the ground with explosives.[33]

Laos also saw some heavy ground fighting. While America was carrying out its bombing missions the Pathet Lao guerrillas and the North Vietnamese fought the American-sponsored Royal Lao Army, the South Vietnamese and Hmong irregulars. The Pathet Lao facilitated the flow of supplies along the Ho Chi Minh trail, which made them a target of the American bombing campaigns. The Vietnam cease-fire in 1973 was quickly followed by a cease-fire in Laos, but violations of this led to the Americans attacking Pathet Lao positions at the request of the Laotian government, before all US air operations finally stopped. Like

Cambodia, Laos came under communist control in 1975.

Many of the landmine-related problems in Laos echo those in Vietnam and Cambodia. Two of the biggest issues according to the government are the denial of land, and the barriers to development. Mines and bombs prevent the rebuilding of infrastructure. The rate of injuries in Laos is not as catastrophic as in Cambodia, but people continue to be injured and killed there each year.

Like Cambodia, Laos has a something of a 'landmine culture'. Although the trade in scrap metal has been outlawed in Laos, military scrap has been put to all sorts of everyday use. Blacksmiths use the bases of artillery shells as anvils; cluster bomb casings are used as roof supports and as plant pots; boats are made out of fighter bomber fuel tanks and bomb casings; shells and cartridges have become cooking implements; lamps have been fashioned out of bomblets. In 1997, two men were killed and four other people seriously injured when an artillery shell being used as an anvil exploded. It had been repeatedly heated and cooled for several months without incident.[34] A lot of confusion exists among villagers as to when an item of ordnance is safe. Some mistakenly believe a bomb is less dangerous the more corroded it is. However, according to Lou McGrath many injuries are also caused by people taking risks, such as adults trying to extract explosive from bombs or children knowingly playing with bomblets: 'I think people become blasé. I know in Britain after World War II – and probably people have still got them somewhere in their house – people picked up incendiary devices or bits of shells and put them on the mantelpiece. It's very much the same thing . . . People get used to seeing it day in and day out so they become blasé just as people did here after World War II.'

By the 1990s the landmine had wreaked havoc across Southeast Asia. With an industry driving the development of weapons, the Vietnam War became a testing ground for air-dropped landmines and cluster bombs. The Viet Cong seized the opportunity to steal American mines, and all of a sudden the weapon that was once the preserve of big, powerful armies became the weapon of choice for guerrilla armies. The days of mapping and marking all mines were gone, and the landmine became a weapon of terror, used indiscriminately against civilians as well as soldiers and rebels. The landmine plague spread quickly from Vietnam to Cambodia, while Laos languished in the aftermath of American bombing raids. Landmines and unexploded bombs became a part of the daily life of civilians. Vietnam, Cambodia and Laos are now at peace, but the landmines laid during the years of hostilities are still creating bloodshed. Hospitals set up to treat the war injured haven't closed down because landmines have created an ongoing need for them. Landmines are also stalling the vital rebuilding process that should start as soon as peace is declared. Unfortunately, the countries in Southeast Asia were only the first of many stops as the landmine rampaged throughout the developing world.

VIGNETTE 3: Physical Rehabilitation

Surgery is only the beginning of the extensive treatment required to rehabilitate landmine victims. After a mine victim has surgery to amputate one or more limbs, he or she needs to get mobility back with the help of crutches and, if possible, to have immediate physiotherapy. A stiff joint may make it impossible to use a prosthesis. Some developing countries can't afford extensive physiotherapy services and rely more on channelling funds into providing prostheses. Weeks after surgery the patient will need a prosthesis to be fitted if they're to have any chance of living a normal and productive life. A prosthesis has three components: a socket, a replacement limb and an artificial joint if it is needed. For mine victims, learning to use a prosthesis can take months. Each artificial limb costs around US $120. Life-long medical care and prostheses in the developing world is estimated at US $10,000, where many people earn as little as US $1 a day. A child's prosthesis needs to be replaced every six months, an active young person's every two years and an adult's every three to five years. Some people can't use prostheses because the shape of their stump does not allow it. If a child has grown out of a prosthesis but continues to use it without getting it replaced, it can cause hip and back problems. In Kabul, Afghanistan, one mine victim who had lost both legs made himself a wheelchair out of a bedstead and some bicycle wheels. After pushing himself about on the contraption for some time he damaged his back. When he finally got to a prosthetics clinic he needed as much treatment for his back as he did for the fitting of his new limbs.

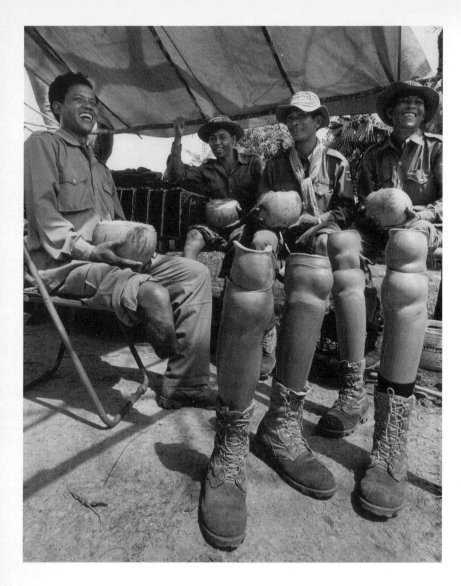

Cambodia, October 2000 (*photograph © Sean Sutton/MAG*).

4

The Age of the Guerrilla

T HE onset of the Cold War ushered in an era of peace in the First World and the Second World, while the Third World became a war zone. Very few of the world's poorest countries came through the second half of the twentieth century without some form of revolution and armed struggle. A very clear pattern emerged. The collapse of the colonial system produced a generation of leaders who had liberated their people and were now set upon programmes of Soviet Union-style social reform and modernisation. The United States, assuming its role as protector of the free world, set out to stop the spread of communism by supporting insurgent groups fighting to overthrow leftist regimes. The Western-backed guerrilla against the Soviet-backed government was the major form of conflict in the latter half of the twentieth century and the Third World became 'a worldwide zone of revolution – whether just achieved, impending or possible'.[1]

Nowhere was this more evident than in Latin America, parts of which have endured countless revolutions throughout their post-colonial history. It was in Cuba that guerrilla warfare first hit global headlines when Fidel Castro and his band of revolutionaries aided by Che Guevara overran the weak regime of President Fulgencio Batista in 1959. The Cuban revolution made guerrilla warfare glamorous. It inspired a generation of leftist revolutionaries to take up arms. Ironically, the landmine issue, and more specifically the Ottawa Treaty, is one issue that actually unites Cuba and the United States of America. They are the only two countries in the Americas that have refused to sign the treaty. This is no holy alliance, however. The Cubans refuse to sign because there are American landmines buried around the Guantanamo US naval base on the southeast corner of the island. Fidel Castro rejected a request from Canadian Prime Minister Jean Chrétien to sign up to the Ottawa convention. He said he had no plans to stop using landmines because of the military threat he perceived from the United States: 'Mines constitute for us a defensive weapon which we would not make the mistake of renouncing because Cuba has no nuclear weapons, bombs or guided missiles to defend itself against a United States' attack.'[2]

Castro and Che Guevara may have been the first 'superstar' guerrillas but the most important strategist on the art of insurgency was Mao Tse-tung. In 1937 Mao wrote his definitive text, called simply *Guerrilla Warfare*. The work would be massively influential, not only in the way the communist Chinese revolution would be fought, but also in shaping the next half-century of guerrilla warfare around the world. He believed that there were three basic steps to fighting a guerrilla war successfully. Firstly, to organise, consolidate and preserve an isolated settlement. With an established base the second step could begin: a campaign of sabotage and terrorism. Underpinning the first two steps Mao believed that a training programme for agitators and a widespread political crusade to indoctrinate the population was then required. This provided the guerrilla force with the platform to take the third step, an orthodox military campaign against the enemy.

Mao believed that guerrillas should be lightly equipped and highly mobile. Surprise and deception were the keys. He also stressed that one of the most important tasks for any guerrilla force was to hold on to any territory gained right up to the last stages of a campaign. Consequently, landmines became a key weapon in the guerrillas' arsenal. The defensive use of mines in conventional warfare was adapted for guerrilla warfare. Instead of building massive barrier minefields, mines were used in smaller numbers as perimeter defences for military installations, roads, bridges and supply lines. 'Mines are a prototypical weapon for guerrilla forces,' claims Human Rights Watch, 'serving to defend rural-based insurgents with the same specificity as government forces' aerial bombardments are designed to dislodge them.'[3] The *New York Times* published an interview with a leader of the El Salvadorian Farabundo Martí National Liberation Front (FMLN) guerrillas in which he defended their use of landmines:

A propaganda campaign has been launched because of the use of mines, trying to make it a human rights issue . . . This campaign is aimed at forcing us to renounce a weapon that has been very important to us.[4]

Counter-insurgency involves constant army foot patrols to wear down guerrilla forces. The guerrillas in turn anticipate the route of advancing patrols and mine the paths. In a document allegedly taken from an FMLN unit in San Agustin, Usulután, entitled *Armamento Popular*, the guerrillas talk of three categories of 'weapons of the people': contact bombs, Molotov cocktails and landmines. The document describes mines as 'what we use to wear down enemy forces in action, when they are dispatched on foot to their daily positions.'[5]

In a country like Colombia that has been subjected to a state of constant internal conflict for the past forty years, the landmine has become part of everyday life. Most of Colombia's major guerrilla groups admit to continued deployment and manufacture of landmines: 'The laying of mines has become an indiscriminate mechanism for both attack and defence. It has been used by all armed groups, both legal and subversive, to protect such things as power transmission line towers, oil pipelines, military bases, training camps and areas where drug-producing plants are cultivated.'[6]

Such is the extent of landmine use in Colombia that landowners hire paramilitary groups to lay anti-personnel mines around their property. Coca, poppy and marijuana growers use landmines to keep the authorities away from illegal crops. In areas such as Chocó, Santander and Antioquia, farmers manufacture 'pig mines' to protect crops and livestock. Other home-made Colombian mines include the *minas quiebrapatas* (leg-breakers), *kleimor* (copies of American claymore mines) and *cazabobos* (fool-hunters).

The rise to prominence of the guerrilla led to the landmine finding a new role. Guerrilla warfare is generally described as a series of raids by small groups of irregular fighters based in remote areas. Government and guerrilla armies fighting battles of insurgency and counter-insurgency used the weapons to control the movement of civilian populations. The landmine had become a weapon of terror. A key objective for any government force fighting a guerrilla war is to constrict the movement of the rural population. Loss of agricultural production, an additional refugee problem and potential loss of terrain to insurgent forces are to be avoided at all costs and landmines became increasingly useful in reducing civilian movement.

Ambassadors of the revolution

Following the successful overthrow of Batista, Che Guevara assumed the role of Cuban international ambassador of the revolution, leading guerrilla groups in the Congo and Bolivia. Inspired by Castro's exploits guerrilla groups sprang up in Venezuela, Guatemala, Uruguay, Brazil, Argentina and Chile. The military regimes in these countries had learned the lessons of counter-insurgency well and they quickly suppressed any uprisings. Not until twenty years after the Cuban revolution did Latin American guerrillas taste success again. When victory came it was truly spectacular.

In Nicaragua the Sandinistas removed the region's longest lasting dictatorship in 1979. Nicaragua, the largest country in Central America, had been under the control of the Somoza dynasty for nearly half of the twentieth century. Anastasio Somoza ruled the country from 1933 until his assassination in 1956 when his son Luis took over, followed by Luis's brother, General Anastasio Somoza Debayle. During the brief interludes when the Somozas were not officially in charge, they installed puppet presidents. The Somozas pillaged Nicaragua. They owned 10 per cent of the cultivable land in a country where such land was in short supply; they also owned the only airline, a television station, a newspaper, sugar refineries, breweries and distilleries. They even embezzled a large part of the aid sent to rebuild Managua, the capital, following the earthquake in 1972. Their excesses led the three principal left-wing opposition groups to form the Front Sandinista de Liberación Nacional which immediately attracted widespread support from the landless peasantry. Committed to armed insurrection, the Sandinistas fought a protracted guerrilla campaign against the National Guard that descended into a full-blown civil war in 1976. By the time the war ended in 1979 some 50,000 Nicaraguans had been killed.

The Sandinistas formed a government led by Daniel Ortega in 1979 which, initially at least, proved to be extremely popular. Somoza estates were returned to the state to be farmed by worker cooperatives. Programmes were introduced to tackle problems in education, health and housing. The regime, however, made the United States in particular very nervous. It was becoming increasingly radical and more heavily dependent on aid from the Eastern bloc. After the revolution, the Nicaraguans who opposed the Sandinistas were seeking allies. They didn't have to look far: neighbouring Honduras was prepared to give them a base and the CIA director, William Casey, ensured that they received the fullest support of the agency. The Sandinista government soon found itself embroiled in its own counter-guerrilla war. Calling themselves the 'Jackals', the early anti-Sandinista fighters had been trained at Fort Bragg in North Carolina, Fort Benning in Georgia, or at the Jungle Warfare School at Fort Gulick in Panama. Among the key lessons was landmine deployment: 'Former US Special Forces troops showed the combined guerrilla forces how to make improved mines and place them at critical points along the Nicaraguan road network. Harassment tactics to tie down Sandinista resources, such as planting old hubcaps to force Sandinista engineers to treat them as mines, were also taught.'[7]

The anti-Sandinista fighters eventually became known as the FDN Contras and they found a willing ally in the Reagan administration. The United States' principal reason for supporting the Contras (freedom fighters) at the outset was not the removal of the Sandinistas from power in Nicaragua. The US was more concerned with events in El Salvador and its government reasoned that, if the Sandinistas had their own problems within Nicaragua, they would be too preoccupied to continue supporting the anti-government guerrillas in El Salvador. When exiled former land-owners and National Guard officers formed the Fuerzas Democráticas Nicaragüensas, the United States offered financial and logistical support to recruit a fighting force. The Contras numbered some 10,000 and started to launch raids into Nicaragua from bases in Honduras and Costa Rica. Mines were used by both sides in the war. Government forces used landmines primarily to protect their own bases and installations as well as the border country to prevent cross-border movement of rebel troops. The Contras attempted to destabilise the government by using mines to disrupt the country's economy and infrastructure. The heaviest mine deployment was in the provinces of Matagalpa and Jinotega where there were hundreds of reports of civilian casualties during the war. The Jinotega and Matagalpa departments are the major food sources in Nicaragua as well as the areas which produce 60 per cent of the country's coffee crop. Coffee is Nicaragua's main export commodity. The area is also crucial in terms of infrastructure. The most important routes for internal trade cross here and it is also the site of the Planta Centroamericana de Apanás, one of the largest hydroelectric projects in the whole of Central America. The other areas of extensive Contra mine laying were the roads leading to the borders to protect their own bases and to hinder any cross-border pursuit by government troops. A *New York Times* reporter described the devastating effect of Contra mining on Nicaragua's roads:

Government soldiers interviewed at several outposts said they had lost comrades when blasts tore through troop transport trucks.

Landmines are reported to have destroyed trucks on all three of the rugged dirt roads that spread north from the provincial capital [of Jinotega]. Twisted wrecks of vehicles are visible near the roads in several places.

The roads, strewn with rocks and at times impassable, are vital to both the Sandinista army and the thousands of peasants who live in this poor agricultural zone.

For the rebels, mining the roads would allow them to strike against concentrated groups of government troops without risking firefights.[8]

Landmine deployment intensified in the build-up to the planned Contra offensive to mark the seventh anniversary of the Sandinista takeover. The offensive did not take place but there was strong evidence pointing to large shipments of mines reaching Contra hands during 1985. 'The Contras have gone into mines in a big way',[9] one diplomat was reported as saying. One of the most infamous incidents of the war in Nicaragua was the mine explosion on 2 July 1986 that killed thirty-four civilians, riding on a truck, on the main road in San Juan del Bocay near the Honduran border. The only survivor was one of the last to board the vehicle who was perched on the rear bumper. He was blown into a tree several yards from the wreck of the truck. The scene was horrifying: the mine had caused a reserve fuel tank to explode and the bodies of most of the victims were incinerated. Some of the bodies had been dismembered to the extent that it took several days for investigators to work out exactly how many casualties there were.

Conspiracy theories, endorsed by the White House, circulated that the mine had actually been laid by the Sandinistas. In its report to Congress the White House claimed that 'on 3 July, the official Nicaraguan press reported that a civilian truck had struck a mine deployed by the resistance, resulting in the deaths of thirty-four civilians. Simultaneously with the Sandinista report, resistance headquarters was informed that a grenade thrown at a resistance unit by Sandinista forces had hit a passing truck, causing an explosion that resulted in the deaths of thirty-one civilians, including an evangelical pastor. There is no evidence to confirm either version of events.'[10]

Nicaragua was at war for nearly twelve years, leading up to the presidential and parliamentary elections in 1990. The United States had been supporting the Contra effort in Nicaragua for a decade. It had cost hundreds of millions of dollars and was a source of extreme inter-national embarrassment, especially the illegal diversion of money to the Contras from the sales of arms to Iran and the CIA's involvement in mining Nicaraguan ports which was condemned by the International Court of Justice. Nicaragua, however, was only the sideshow for the United States in Latin America. Its real concern was its neighbour, El Salvador. Much of the aid given to the Contras was actually given to disrupt Sandinista support for Salvadorian guerrillas.

El Salvador

El Salvador seemed primed and ready to follow Nicaragua into communist revolution. By the late 1970s the country was completely out of control. Death squads roamed the streets, massacring civilians, guerrillas and soldiers alike and dumping their bodies on roadsides. Like most other Latin American conflicts, the root cause of the barbarity lay in the complete dominance of power and land by a handful of leading families. El Salvador is a small, densely populated country and the majority of its people try to live off the land. The dominant families kept control of such a volatile situation by giving the army money and power, which in return suppressed peasant uprisings with extraordinary brutality. Hundreds of thousands of landless peasants were forced to flee through hunger and fear, mostly to El Salvador's much larger neigh-bour, Honduras. This influx coincided with a period of internal unrest in Honduras when industrial agitation threatened to destabilise the military government. Hondurans resented the loss of employment to their immigrant neighbours. This was a time of economic dispute between the two countries as the fledgling Central American Common Market struggled to establish itself. The less developed Honduran industrial sector wasn't able to compete against aggressive Salvadorian companies and in April 1969 legal measures were taken against the immigrant workers resulting in the repatriation of several thousand Salvadorians.

At a time when the relationship between the two countries had deteriorated to a potentially dangerous level, Honduras and El Salvador were scheduled to play each other in two football matches to determine which country would qualify for the 1970 World Cup finals in Mexico. The first leg was played in the Honduran capital, Tegucigalpa, and passed with only the occasional scuffle between rival supporters. The return, in San Salvador, was a different matter. Anti-Honduran demonstrations escalated to a point where fans were attacked and their flag insulted. Outraged Hondurans took their revenge on immigrant Salvadorians, several people were killed and a mass exodus of Salvadorians began.

Within a few weeks of the football match the countries were at war with each other. El Salvador moved its troops to the border, its air force began to attack military bases and its navy attacked Honduran islands in the Gulf of Fonseca. At the outset it looked as if the Salvadorians were winning as they crossed the border into Honduras. The Hondurans responded with the aerial bombing of Salvadorian fuel depots, effectively ending the Salvadorian advance. After only four days, both sides agreed to a cease-fire. Although El Salvador appeared to win the 'soccer war', the consequences of the conflict proved to be catastrophic. For a country already over-populated the return of 60,000 to 130,000 expatriates was economically devastating.

In much the same way as a football match sparked the war with Honduras, it was a beauty contest that triggered the fighting within El Salvador itself. The government had spent $1.5 million on staging the 1975 Miss Universe pageant; students and left-wing activists were outraged and violent protests ensued. The National Guard killed tens of demonstrators and twenty-four simply 'disappeared'. The era of the death squads had begun. The Democratic Revolutionary Front, comprising opposition parties, religious groups and trade unions, was formed and immediately became the prime target for the death squads. Under the banner of the FMLN, guerrilla groups throughout the country united to fight back against the government and its trained killers. For the Reagan administration in the 1980s, the unholy alliance between the wealthy oligarchy and the military was preferable to another Sandinista-style communist guerrilla uprising. The United States trained and equipped the Salvadorian army for counter-insurgency. Once again the landmine was a crucial weapon. Between 1981 and 1990, the United States supplied Salvadorian government forces with 37,000 anti-personnel landmines.[11] The majority of the estimated 20,000 mines laid by the FMLN guerrillas were improvised 'home-made' weapons. These were buried in a totally indiscriminate manner. Among the mines manufactured by the FMLN were the *mina de chuchito* (clothes pin mine), the *mina abanico* (fan mine) and the *mina de pateo*, or *quita pata* (the kick mine or the mine that removes feet). Officers of the El Salvador army expressed admiration for the ingenuity of the guerrillas in the manufacture of landmines. The *mina de chuchito* was detonated by a tripwire usually laid across a path or attached to doors, vehicles or even bodies. Americas Watch reported numerous civilian casualties in El Salvador including the story of José Aguedo Rosa, a forty-year-old farmer from the Usulután district. José was forced to hunt for rabbits and lizards in an area he knew to be mined to feed his pregnant wife and four children. On one expedition he stood on a mine that had been hidden by leaves and garbage. He was saved from bleeding to death by a passing patrol of soldiers who subsequently found three other mines concealed in the same garbage pile.[12]

Land was a central issue in sparking the civil war and the subsequent fighting only served to intensify the problem. The war divided El Salvador into three parts: FMLN-controlled areas, government-controlled areas and the conflict zones. It was the military need to move large numbers of displaced people from one area to another that served to exacerbate El Salvador's mine problem. The population became very fluid during the fighting with refugees seeking fertile land that became increasingly scarce. Americas Watch reported: 'War, displacement, overpopulation, counter-insurgency tactics, economic pressures, and landmines combine to make life grimmer than usual for the rural poor of El Salvador.'[13]

Both sides drove out rival supporters from their territories. The government forces were keen to deny the FMLN a civilian base. In a process that became known as 'draining the sea', the military carried out a series of aerial bombardments backed up by roving patrols and crop-burning missions. During their incursions into FMLN territory, the armed forces displaced large numbers of civilians and destroyed food crops and buildings. One of the biggest casualty tolls was in Chalatenago, by the Gualsinga river, where fifty civilians were killed by government troops inside FLMN territory. These attacks led to the guerrilla forces laying even more landmines to defend their lands. During the height of the fighting the Archbishop of San Salvador, Monsignor Arturo Rivera y Damas, condemned the FMLN for the use of landmines and called upon them 'not to locate mines in places frequented by the civilian population, because in the majority of cases, innocent victims result from the explosion of these devices'.[14] In a broadcast on Radio Venceremos on 31 July 1986, the FMLN claimed always to remove mines from an area when they no longer served any strategic purpose. The spokesman said that the FMLN demined an area as soon as government troops withdrew.

Reversing the population flow was critical for a government that needed its civilian supporters to secure any newly conquered land. The National Plan of 1983 required the government's supporters to be organised into civil defence groups to retain territory. One such town is Chirilagua which passed from FMLN to government control and back again several times. Knowing that government troops used the *alcaldía*, or mayor's office, as a command post when they entered the town, the guerrillas mined the building. In November 1985 a government soldier was killed by a mine inside the *alcaldía*. The following month another soldier, aware that the building was mined, was searching the *alcaldía* for further devices and lost his arm when a mine placed in the ceiling was detonated. The FMLN and the El Salvador government army used mines and booby traps to set up ambushes. Landmines were extremely useful for the FMLN both in terms of defending the territory they held and in impeding government incursions. The El Salvador army claimed that the FMLN deliberately used mines to maim and injure, as opposed to killing, as a demoralisation tool. The government forces in turn claimed only to use mines to protect military bases, important installations such as dams and in perimeter belts around temporary camps. Americas Watch, however, claims to have interviewed a government soldier who admitted to planting mines for ambushes. According to its report, the soldier said that the army buried the mines to trap the FMLN, then, as soon as the operation was over, the mines were removed and reused in further actions. In an article in the *Dallas Morning News*, an army official explained how he ordered the repositioning of FMLN mines: 'The guerrillas use mines in southern Usulután to protect their supply routes. Sometimes these routes are several kilometres wide. They also use mines to protect their camps. If we find mines around their positions we will move them to disrupt the guerrilla patrols once they return, but we do not transplant mines if there are civilians living near by.'[15]

During its study in El Salvador, Americas Watch found several victims of army-laid landmines. Most of the incidents it reported appear to have happened immediately after the army had swept through an area, then retreated. For example, following an eight-day raid into the town of San Antonio, in the Cabañas region, some of the civilians began to return. One man, Bernabé Hernández, attempted to salvage bananas he'd hidden from the army, only to trip a wire on his journey. He died two hours after the explosion.

The defeat of the Sandinista government in the Nicaraguan elections in 1990 forced the Salvadorian rebels to rethink their strategy. Attacks against non-military targets were suspended and negotiations with the government commenced. The rebels also declared that they were no longer communists or Marxists. The Peruvian Secretary General of the United Nations, Javier Pérez de Cuéllar, brokered a deal between the FMLN and the government and a formal peace treaty was signed. The rebels emerged from the jungles and the FMLN was disbanded. In return, the Salvadorian armed forces were cut in half, the most violent officers were thrown out and the various paramilitary defence forces – the death squads – were disbanded. In May 1992, representatives of the Salvadorian armed forces and the FMLN, along with UNICEF and UNOSAL members, formed the Committee of the Programme for the Prevention of Accidents from Mines (PAM). The committee embarked on a programme to mark and clear the minefields and to educate the population about the danger presented by landmines in peacetime. Following the cessation of hostilities, both sides provided maps of known minefields and within two months 425 minefields had been fenced off. This was a difficult task. The Salvadorian Armed Services had dropped thousands of mines from the air and the records kept by the FMLN were incomplete. A commercial Belgian demining company, International Danger and Disaster Assistance, signed a $4.8 million deal with the government to clear known minefields over a two-year period, and by 1994 United States mine experts reported that El Salvador had been completely cleared of landmines. According to their findings, many of the improvised mines used by both sides had neutralised over time: the batteries that powered the electrical fuses had degraded to the point where they no longer carried enough charge to detonate the mines. In an interview with the ICBL, Colonel Sidney Rendón said: 'We have given a certificate where we declare that El Salvador is a mine-free zone. Of course, there is always a margin of error, but we haven't had an accident.'[16]

Nation against nation

Not only did Latin America host a whole series of Cold War revolutions and civil wars, but the region is also a melting pot of national states in border disputes with each other. Ecuador has a territorial claim against Peru which in turn is in dispute over land with Bolivia and Chile. Meanwhile, Chile disputes the Beagle Channel with

Argentina (which still, incidentally, claims the Falkland Islands from Britain) and disputes territory with Paraguay. Paraguay also stakes a claim to land in Brazil and Uruguay that led to the Chaco wars. Border fighting and landmines are old bedfellows and all these disputed lands have been extensively mined.

Peru's landmine problem reflects its recent turbulent past, both in terms of border conflicts with Chile and Ecuador and internal fighting within the country. Peru is home to the most brutal and violent of all Latin American terrorist organisations. The Communist Party of Peru for the Shining Path was formed in the remote mountain region of Ayacucho and quickly established cells in small towns and villages throughout the Andes. The Shining Path has a reputation for attacking religious groups, aid and welfare workers and civilians, and for fighting the Peruvian army and the police, as well as the Tupoc Amanu Revolutionary Movement. The latter was formed with the support of Fidel Castro in 1983 and is both anti-Shining Path and anti-United States. It differs from the Shining Path in terms of membership: the Tupoc Amanu Revolutionary Movement tends to draw from the educated middle classes as opposed to the peasantry which forms the rank and file of the Shining Path. The Peruvian army tried to form a peasant militia to fight the guerrillas, but they were badly organised, underequipped and offered little resistance to the Shining Path. With no communist neighbours to supply it with arms, the Shining Path relied upon drug cartels to supply it with arms, which they did in exchange for protection. The Shining Path then embarked on a campaign of bombing key infrastructure installations, especially the electricity grid, in order to cut off power supplies to Lima. At one point in 1991 the Shining Path blew up so many pylons that they knocked out 90 per cent of the country's power supply. They succeeded in splitting the country along the Sierra spine to isolate Lima from food supplies.

The other major area of landmine deployment in Peru is along its borders with both Ecuador and Chile. Ecuador and Peru have disputed territories to the north of the Amazon since both countries gained independence from Spain nearly two centuries ago. The dispute simmered on until armed conflict broke out in 1941 during which Peru occupied almost half of Ecuador. A peace treaty that was signed in Rio de Janeiro in 1942 ceded eastern Ecuador to Peru. The new border was to be guaranteed by the United States, Brazil, Argentina and Chile. A demarcation process started immediately, with both countries required to lay down markers along the borderline. This work continued until 1950 when the countries started to argue again and the process was suspended, leaving 78 kilometres unmarked along a section of the Cenapa river in the Cordillera del Cóndor region.

Ecuador was never satisfied with the Rio Protocol and sporadically launched campaigns to reclaim parts of its former eastern territories. Minor skirmishes occurred in 1981 and 1991 but in 1995 war broke out. The fighting lasted only three weeks in which time the Peruvian army had moved several thousand troops into the area and started to bomb Ecuadorian army positions. The casualty toll was relatively small but the Latin American Association for Human Rights has accused both Ecuador and Peru of burying more than 130,000 anti-personnel mines during the conflict.[17] The border country between Peru and Ecuador consists of dense jungle. Consequently mapping the minefields proved to be impossible. Patterns of heavy rainfall further confuse the picture. The native people of the area, the Shuar, Achuar, Aguaruna and Huambisa, were displaced during the war and the continuing presence of landmines is having a prohibitive effect on their ability to return.

In southern Peru, along the border with Chile, prime agricultural land is also being denied to the population because of mines laid during the conflicts of the 1970s and 1980s. In 1997 a Chilean Defence Ministry official claimed that Chile had planted nearly a million landmines on its borders with Argentina, Bolivia and Peru.[18] Argentina and Chile were on the brink of war in 1978 and there's still a great deal of uncertainty as to where exactly the mines were buried along the mountainous border; indeed there are claims and counterclaims as to who actually deployed them. The Argentinians have always denied that any landmines were laid on its side of the border, yet there have been many stories and rumours of mined mountain passes ever since. In August 1999, journalists writing about the discovery of three infant Incan mummies near the saltfields of Mina La Julia and Mina La Casualidad on the Argentinian side of the border were warned away by locals because they were 'full of landmines'.[19] The Argentinian Foreign Ministry does claim, however, that one part of the country is severely mined. In what was later to be described as a 'freak of history, almost certainly the last colonial war that Britain will ever fight',[20] Argentina invaded the Falkland Islands and so precipitated one of the most bizarre conflicts of the twentieth century.

The Falkland Islands

Since the nineteenth century, the United Kingdom and Argentina have disputed the Falklands Islands, known to the Argentinians as the Islas Malvinas. The long-running dispute turned into war in 1982 following the Argentine military invasion of the islands. The timing of the Argentine offensive was influenced by two major factors. By the early eighties Argentina was a country in crisis and the ruling military junta was falling apart. General Leopoldo Galtieri replaced General Roberto Viola as president in December 1981 after securing the support of the commander of the navy, Admiral Jorge Anaya. The admiral had for long advocated the reclamation of the Malvinas and Galtieri won his backing by promising to oblige by the end of 1982 – the 150th anniversary of British occupation. The other factor was the United States. When the Reagan administration took office in 1980 the Argentinians were invited to help in so-called anti-terrorist campaigns in El Salvador and to train the Nicaraguan Contras. The United States' permanent representative to the United Nations was one of Reagan's closest aides and was a well-known supporter of the Galtieri regime. Galtieri believed that all boded well for United States' support for his forthcoming enterprise in the Falklands. He'd soon be disappointed.

On Friday, 1 April 1982 Argentine special forces landed on the Falklands. Shots were fired and suddenly the Falklands Islands had become Las Malvinas. Within a few days, the British task force set sail for the South Atlantic. During the eight weeks before the British landed on the islands, the Argentinians laid extensive minefields on the Falkland Islands. The minefields were laid in the coastal areas where the Argentinian forces anticipated the task force would attempt to land. These minefields were carefully designed, fenced and recorded. The second phase of Argentine mine laying occurred after the British had unexpectedly landed to the west of Port Stanley. These proved to be randomly laid, badly recorded and ultimately proved to be very damaging both during the conflict and in the subsequent clean-up operation. Stanley is surrounded by a hill-line comprising Mount Harriet, Mount Longdon, Tumbledown, Two Sisters and the appropriately named Sapper Hill. By the time the British soldiers arrived each hill was a minefield heavily defended by machine guns. Such were the weather conditions, with driving snow and rain, that visibility on the top of the hills was down to around 20 metres. It was impossible to pinpoint Argentine defensive positions or minefields. A way had to be found of attacking from the flanks and so every night patrols were sent out into the mountains to find the Argentinian minefields.

Before the attack on Mount Harriet, Nick Vaux, the officer commanding 42 Royal Marine commandos had predicted that the low ground between the Argentine and British positions would be heavily mined. The first patrol proved him right: one of the marines stepped on a mine that blew off most of his foot. It took over seven hours to get the injured soldier out of the minefield under Argentine shelling. The distance between the lines was roughly 6,000 metres and the ground was bare of cover.

> Our feet were continually submerged. After about 1.5 kilometres we came across a single low strand of barbed wire. After having a look I informed the officer commanding that this was an enemy minefield . . . Corporal Fairburn and myself went into the minefield to try and find out the density and type of mines, using our bayonets as prodders . . . Total length of patrol 20 kilometres, approximate duration sixteen hours.[21]

Gathering this information proved to have grave consequences. One marine who lost a foot in the minefields was carried back fully conscious because in the extreme cold the morphine failed to anaesthetise him. The patrols played an extremely important role under very dangerous conditions. The sappers eventually cleared paths for 42 Commando to attack by hand, in pitch darkness and in freezing conditions. Even after this work had been carried out, the minefields still presented a formidable barrier. On the morning of the attack, Nick Vaux briefed his men for the battle ahead. He is reported as saying, 'If you find yourself in a minefield remember that you must go on. Men must not stop for their oppos, however great the temptation. They must go through and finish the attack, or it will cost more lives in the end.'[22]

The battle for Mount Longdon, which would prove to be the most costly land action of the war, was triggered by a landmine explosion. A corporal in 3 Commando Brigade's B company stepped on a mine that shattered his leg. The noise drew the first enemy fire and the ensuing battle cost twenty-three British lives with a further forty-seven wounded.

Twenty years after the fighting stopped on the Falklands, the British military estimates that there are around 16,000 landmines still buried on the islands. According to the Ministry of Defence:

18,000 mines of all types were laid, including 14,000 anti-personnel mines. British forces carried out some clearance immediately after the conflict, lifting about 1,400 mines, but stopped after several injuries to those involved. The remaining 101 minefields are marked and fenced, and therefore not an immediate hazard. The garrison conduct a public campaign to warn of the dangers. They make regular patrols and destroy mines which become exposed on the surface of the ground. The Argentines have given us their minefield records.[23]

In an interview with *La Nación* in 1999, the military commander in charge of laying Argentine minefields during the conflict, Colonel Manuel Dorrego, claimed to have handed over all records and maps of the minefields upon surrender to the British. 'We thought we were going to stay in the islands, and that after a while, we would have to remove the landmines ourselves. We never had doubts about keeping records.'[24] The landmine issue has become part of the political mire that surrounds the whole Falklands–Malvinas issue. Former Argentine President Carlos Menem argued that Argentina is 'impeded access to anti-personnel mines in the Malvinas in order to comply with the Mine Ban Treaty because of the illegal occupation by the United Kingdom.'[25] Private mine clearance companies from the United States and Europe have offered their services, but so far the British military have refused assistance. Argentina has offered money to help with the work – on condition that it is not carried out by the British military. Unsurprisingly this offer has also been refused. The joint statement issued after a meeting between Foreign Affairs Minister di Tella and the British Foreign Secretary Robin Cook read:

As agreed in October 1998 by the president of the Argentine Republic and the Prime Minister of the United Kingdom, the two governments will continue to work together to evaluate the feasibility and the cost of the removal of the landmines still present in the Falkland/Malvinas Islands . . . We are fully committed to the Mine Ban Treaty, which requires us to clear all anti-personnel landmines from the Falkland Islands within ten years of entry, unless we can show good reasons why an extension should be granted. Such reasons may include humanitarian, environmental and technical considerations. Mine clearance in the Falkland Islands is both difficult and dangerous and we shall be keeping these points in mind.[26]

VIGNETTE 4: The Psychological and Social Impact

The psychological and social impact of a landmine injury can be devastating especially in developing countries. The spilt-second action of stepping on a landmine changes a person's life instantly and completely. In many mine-contaminated countries victims face prejudice and isolation. Women may be abandoned by their husbands. Many women and some men lose their chance to marry. If a woman loses her arm, it is assumed she won't be able to look after a baby. A man who loses his arm won't be able to tend his crops so he will not be seen as a good marriage prospect either. In a poor country someone who can't work is an economic burden. Children may be kept away from school, or may be too ashamed to go at all. It has been reported that some amputees have formed gangs to deal with rejection from the society they were once part of.

War surgeons talk of seeing a response akin to grief from someone the day after they have undergone surgical amputation. The realisation that they may have to beg to survive, that they may lose their job, or that they may not be able to support their children, slowly dawns once they know they have survived the landmine explosion. Even if it's only temporary, victims also find the loss of independence hard to accept. One amputee says she refused to use the hospital bedpan, preferring to crawl to the bathroom. Victims talk of feelings of depression, isolation, of suicidal thoughts, loneliness and anxiety. One said that losing his leg was like losing a spouse or a child and the same grieving process applied. Many wished they had died in the minefield before being rescued. Depression may also extend to family members. Children struggle with issues relating to their peers. They face the prospect of not being able to play with their friends in the same way and are seen as different. Victims in developing countries who can't shake off their depression don't find much sympathy, because they are surrounded by people who face a daily battle to survive anyway.

Not all react negatively, however, for prostheses can offer some respite from the host of negative emotions mine victims experience after their injuries. Reactions can range from ecstatic delight at being given a new lease of life to no emotional change at all in someone who is already depressed and suicidal. The physical strain of learning how to walk on a prosthesis adds to the mental stress. During this time victims can also experience phantom pain. Finally, victims are sometimes haunted by memories and images of the actual accident.

In Muslim fundamentalist countries such as Afghanistan, there are cultural objections to amputation, because it is important that when

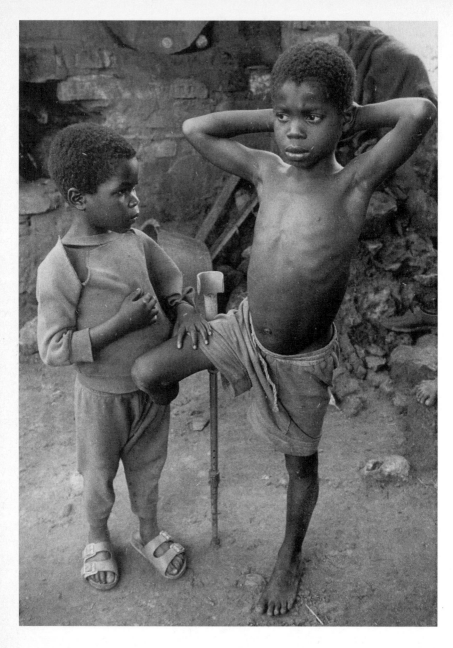

Angola, December 1997 (*photograph © Sean Sutton/MAG*).

someone dies they are buried in one piece, without any body parts missing. Surgeons sometimes face long, difficult discussions with relatives about amputating a shattered foot or leg. It's impossible to comprehend what it's like for victims trying to reintegrate into society if they do lose a part of their body yet, if those long discussions lead to the infection spreading, because surgery is delayed, the victim has to cope with an even higher amputation.

5

Africa's Longest Plague

I N the 1970s and 1980s parts of southern Africa became a bloodbath involving independence struggles as well as regional and Cold War rivalries. Landmines became key weapons in campaigns of destruction, disruption and terror. The legacy of the fighting is clear for all to see. The two former Portuguese colonies of Angola and Mozambique are now among the world's poorest and most heavily mined countries. As Angola and Mozambique broke free from Portuguese rule at the height of the Cold War, they soon descended into civil war. The old adversaries, the former Soviet Union and the United States, still fighting for domination, seized the opportunity to raise the stakes between internal warring parties. But a new player also entered the theatre of war. South Africa's agenda included white supremacy, regional domination and a swift end to black nationalism. Both sides in the Angolan and Mozambican wars, namely young Marxist governments and the insurgents fighting to topple them, were propped up by foreign weapons, training and troops. The result was prolonged, bitter and bloody conflict. Angola's war, which still rages today, has involved regional and major powers from Portugal to South Africa, the Soviet Union, Cuba and the United States. Mozambique's conflict added the former Rhodesia and China to the mix.

The landmine scourge infiltrated Angola and Mozambique from the outside, and it's a typical scenario in the developing world. The majority of the world's most heavily mined countries are not, and never have been, major landmine producers themselves. Angola and Mozambique are not known to have produced a single landmine. The

Cold War powers, who fought proxy wars on their territory, supplied thousands of landmines as part of arms packages. The landmine plague affected Africa so badly because it is the ideal weapon for guerrilla warfare and for poor armies. It is cheap, effective and easy to use. Mines are now everywhere in Mozambique and Angola: on roads, railway lines, power plants, bridges, airport runways, fields, riverbanks, wells and around towns, villages and schools. The most heavily mined countries are also the most poverty-stricken – and therefore the least able to cope with the problem. Landmines have a disproportionate impact on the poor. They help to keep Third World countries firmly locked in the Third World. Landmines compound the suffering by shackling the economy and by making people constantly fearful. Both Angola and Mozambique are rich in natural resources – especially Angola, with its diamonds, oil, gold and other mineral wealth. Both countries are blessed with excellent climates and fertile soil. However, in Mozambique the presence of landmines prevents crucial develop-ment and in Angola both warring parties are using landmines to assist them to exploit the natural resources for their own ends.

Angola and Mozambique reborn: the end of empire

The wars in Angola and Mozambique can be traced back to the collapse of the Portuguese empire and the ensuing struggle for independence. In the fifteenth and sixteenth centuries the Portuguese settled in coastal areas of Angola and Mozambique to provide themselves with points of supply en route to India and the Far East. The ports later became lucrative trading points for slaves (destined for Brazil), gold and ivory. Colonisation followed at a much later stage. In fact, Portuguese rule only began in earnest in the late nineteenth and early twentieth centuries. During this time cotton plantations and a coffee industry were established in Angola. Most African colonies had gained independence and had been decolonised in the 1960s, but Angola and Mozambique were among the few exceptions. The fascist government in Portugal claimed it would never give in to increasing demands for decolonisation. This obstinacy resulted in bitter and prolonged struggles for independence. The stirrings of discontent in both Angola and Mozambique had turned into armed struggle by the early 1960s. In 1974, Salazar's regime was overthrown in Portugal and the new government admitted it could no longer sustain the fight to keep its long-held territories. Within a year, Portugal had abandoned Angola and Mozambique. Little did the anti-colonialists know back then, however, that their long-awaited freedom was in essence the beginning of a descent into long, bloody civil war.

Angola is now home to Africa's longest running civil war. Three decades of fighting began with the war against colonial Portugal in 1961 and has continued in the current civil war that began after independence in 1975. The first report of a landmine buried in Angola was as early as 1961, but the majority were laid between 1975 and 1988. There were several different movements all struggling for control of Angola, the largest of which was the MPLA (Popular Movement for the Liberation of Angola), essentially a Marxist organisation. The other organisations were the FNLA (National Front for the Liberation of Angola) and UNITA (National Union for the Total Independence of Angola), a breakaway from the FNLA. The three movements appealed to different ethnic groups. The FNLA got its support in the north of the country from the Bakongo tribe while UNITA, led by Jonas Savimbi, was supported in central and southern regions by the largest tribe, the Ovimbundu. The MPLA tried to appeal across tribal boundaries, although it got most of its support from the Kimbundu tribe of north-central Angola.

In preparation for independence in November 1975, the three groups agreed to share power, but this pact was broken by both the FNLA and UNITA. By mid-1975 all sides were at war but the MPLA prevailed to form a one-party socialist government. The MPLA, led by José Eduardo dos Santos, was receiving assistance from Cuban troops, and more indirect support from the Soviet Union. South Africa was backing UNITA and Zaire supported the FNLA. South Africa's apartheid regime sought to stamp out the threat of black nationalist movements in its backyard. At home South Africa was fighting the African National Congress (ANC), which had training bases in both Angola and Tanzania. South Africa was also fighting SWAPO, the South West African People's Organisation, which began its struggle in 1966 at the time the United Nations legally terminated South Africa's authority over Namibia. SWAPO had some help at first from UNITA, and then from the MPLA. In the early 1980s South Africa occupied part of Angola in its campaign against SWAPO bases in the country.

The FNLA dropped out of Angola's internal battle at an early stage, leaving the MPLA and UNITA bolstered by big military powers to continue fighting. Angola had become a fully fledged player in the

Cold War. By the mid-1980s what had initially been covert American support of UNITA was now in the open. Patrick Brogan noted that UNITA secured around $15 million a year in weapons from the US, which prompted the Soviet Union to send the MPLA government $1 billion in military assistance every year. Brogan recalls: 'For the United States, it was an exceedingly cost-effective way of putting pressure on the Soviets, the reverse of what happened in Vietnam.'[1]

The prize for either side was considerable, notably Angola with its substantial oil and mineral resources. The wars in Angola, from independence to the proxy war being fought by the Cold War powers, to today's civil war, have always been as much about money as ideology and politics. Angola should be able to benefit from being one of the richest countries in Africa but its resources are being wasted and abused. Oil is keeping the government forces going and UNITA has a hold over the country's diamond mines. Although the United States didn't recognise the Angolan government in the 1980s, it remained the government's main trading partner and American oil companies contributed to Angola's trading surplus of $642 million with the US in 1986.[2]

UNITA uses Angolan diamonds to pay for its weapons. Angola is one of several countries in a guns-for-diamonds loop, where illicitly mined 'hot rocks' or 'blood diamonds', travel from African countries to Antwerp in Belgium to pay for weapons that make their way back into Africa, often from Eastern Europe. When the United States, Cold War supporters of UNITA, recognised the former Marxist government in Angola in an attempt to maintain peace and carry out successful elections in 1992, UNITA leader Jonas Savimbi used the respite from fighting to focus his attentions on doubling his diamond mining operations because he wasn't getting CIA funding. As a result his take from the diamond mines was around $750 million a year.[3] When Savimbi lost the election and resumed the war, he was able to buy new supplies of weapons from Eastern Europe. Human Rights Watch claims to have evidence that UNITA planned to purchase anti-personnel landmines in return for diamonds in preparation for the resumption of war yet again in 1998.

Throughout the conflict in Angola all sides have used landmines. However, the majority of mines have been deployed by UNITA and Angolan government forces. Landmine use increased markedly in the late 1970s and early 1980s with the involvement of Rhodesia and South Africa. Anti-personnel mines have been used in large numbers. The government forces have used mines to defend strategic locations including roads, oil installations, diamond mines and water pipelines. They have also laid large defensive minefields around towns to counter UNITA advances, in line with Soviet military doctrine. The pattern of mine-laying by UNITA across the countryside has been much more indiscriminate. UNITA has used landmines to destabilise the government through the disruption of daily life. Roads, villages, agricultural land and water sources have all been mined. Soldiers fleeing destroyed vehicles have been blown up by anti-personnel landmines buried in roadside ditches. UNITA and South African forces also used a lot of improvised mines and booby traps, including anti-lift devices, which ensured the mines would go off if anyone tried to clear them.

Like the Angolans, the Mozambicans launched their war of independence against the Portuguese in the early 1960s and they also suffered a brutal civil war after winning their freedom. Frelimo (the Mozambique Liberation Front) launched its guerrilla campaign in 1964. Frelimo was a Marxist-Leninist organisation founded by Eduardo Mondlane, the man who led the campaign for independence. The first recorded incident of a landmine being laid in Mozambique was in 1965, probably by Frelimo forces. When the Portuguese withdrew from Mozambique, Frelimo gained control of the country. It introduced a radical socialist agenda by nationalising land and industry, but it lacked the capacity successfully to implement its sweeping plans and to rebuild the country. Industrial and agricultural production plummeted. When the Portuguese left, much of the country's skilled labour and capital had disappeared, which severely damaged Mozambique's economy. In the late 1970s drought exacerbated the problem.

The seeds of discontent in Mozambique were sown when Frelimo decided to support international sanctions against its neighbour, Rhodesia, and to give refuge to Rhodesia's independence fighters. Mozambique was thus dragged into the Rhodesian war. Dissatisfaction with the economy and with the new government spread among Mozambique's people and Renamo, or the Mozambican National Resistance, emerged. Renamo, which had been fostered and supported by Rhodesia, sparked a sixteen-year civil war in which it earned a notorious reputation for banditry, terrorism, mutilation of civilians and mass murder. Its campaign centred around the destabilisation and destruction of the country's infrastructure including schools and health clinics. When Rhodesia gained independence, becoming Zimbabwe, in 1980, South Africa took over the support of Renamo, supplying the movement with arms and other forms of military aid. Both Rhodesia and South Africa trained Renamo in mine warfare and supplied it with mines.[4] Just as it got involved in Angola's affairs, South Africa was prepared to fight both communism and black freedom movements in general. Although the ANC didn't train in Mozambique, guerrillas travelled through the country to launch attacks in South Africa. The Soviet Union and China sent aid to Mozambique's Marxist government, but stopped short of supplying troops. Human Rights Watch was told by the Mozambican government's chief mine expert that soldiers received mine warfare training in the Soviet Union and from a British Military Assistance Training Team course in Zimbabwe.[5]

As in Angola, landmines were laid by all sides in Mozambique's war. Frelimo and Renamo laid most of the mines in the struggle to control the country, between 1978 and 1990. Frelimo government forces used defensive mines around military bases, towns and villages, water and electricity supply points, roads, tracks, paths, bridges and railway lines. It also laid large defensive minefields along the South African border in the early 1980s in case of a possible South African invasion. Both sides used mines randomly against civilians, to deny access to agricultural land, water and fishing points. Renamo targeted civilians with mines to discourage refugees from returning home. Mines have been found in water wells, clinics, schools, small factories, cashew nut groves and cattle-dip tanks. Both sides used improvised mines and booby traps. Renamo regularly practised ambush mining using both anti-tank and anti-personnel mines. It planted mines along roads and tracks to disrupt opposition supply routes. It also mined airstrips.

Mozambique also introduced another dimension to mine strategy. Mines were used as a psychological threat – people were told that some areas were mined when in fact they weren't. This tactic was used in World War II where troops who didn't have time to lay proper minefields would lay out the traditional markings of a minefield and found that this was still an effective way of repelling the enemy. The huge difference in Mozambique is that the mines weren't marked – and civilians were involved. Land suspected of being mined was thus simply abandoned. In some instances, people stayed away from their villages for years before mine clearers moved in to find just a few mines or no mines at all. It makes no difference whether land is rumoured to be mined, whether it has three mines or three hundred mines. From an economic point of view the effect is the same. Even the indiscriminate scattering of a few mines can render a huge area unusable.

Mines in Angola and Mozambique have a clear, strategic purpose. The use of the mine has to be seen in a geographic as well as an economic context. Mines answer the crucial dilemma of how to lay claim to vast areas of land with a small, poorly equipped army. Whoever lays mines can automatically claim that land, because no one else knows where the mines are and they usually don't want to risk injury and death finding out. Mines can be given to inexperienced guerrillas and they can use them. They don't require expensive or time-consuming training. Angola and Mozambique are vast countries: Angola is more than 1.2 million square kilometres in size (about half the size of Western Europe), while Mozambique is slightly smaller in area, but is long and narrow. Angola has a population of about twelve million people, and Mozambique has around sixteen million. Their armies are relatively small. Roads are extremely bad and getting from one place to another is difficult and time-consuming. It's not unusual for someone to walk all day just to fetch water or food. Vehicles are scarce (even the police are not issued with vehicles in Angola; they resort to waving down expatriate motorists and demanding lifts).

At the time of Angola and Mozambique's civil wars a fully fledged landmine industry was thriving. The Vietnam War had sparked a proliferation of landmines being produced and shipped around the world. The major producers of landmines over the last quarter of the twentieth century were China, Italy and the former Soviet Union, with the United States not far behind. The United States have exported more than 4.3 million anti-personnel mines since 1969.[6] The cocktail of mines found in Mozambique includes weapons produced in Russia, China, South Africa, Italy, Portugal, Belgium, Bulgaria, France, America, Britain, Zimbabwe (as Rhodesia), Germany and the former Yugoslavia. A great majority used by both Frelimo and Renamo, however, are of Soviet or Eastern European origin. A similar array has been found in Angola, including landmines from Russia, China, Germany, Egypt, Britain, America, Spain, Italy, former Czechoslovakia, Belgium and the United States.

Tracing exactly how foreign mines ended up in Africa is a complex process. Human Rights Watch tracked one French shipment of anti-personnel mines found in Mozambique's soil. The mines were first sent by the French to Algeria during colonial times. After Algeria's independence, Algerians lifted the mines and offered them as solidarity weapons to the Frelimo government, who then replanted them. Foreign manufacturers, governments and arms dealers have all supplied mines to Angola and Mozambique. The anti-personnel mines they provided have been variously described as the 'nuts on top of the sundae', 'stocking fillers' or 'freebies'. There is some debate about whether these terms are accurate. Disagreement centres around whether mines, because they are so cheap to produce in comparison with other weapons, were typically given away free to developing countries as part of military aid packages, or whether they paid for them. It's likely that in shipments running into the millions, substantial profits were made. Whatever the case, it has not been difficult in the past for armies to secure huge numbers of landmines. In 1997 the *News of the World* in Britain claimed their undercover reporters were offered 30,000 Chinese mines from just £10 each from an arms trader.[7]

In 1988 the Soviet Union abandoned Angola and the Cubans were ordered to withdraw. A peace agreement was reached in 1991 and UN-sponsored elections were held the following year, which the MPLA won narrowly. Savimbi couldn't accept the result, claimed the election was unfairly fixed and went back to waging war. The United States had by this time dropped its support for UNITA. Superpower involvement was further eroded by Namibia's independence from South Africa in 1990. Another UN-brokered cease-fire agreement, the Lusaka Protocol of 1994, ushered in a tenuous peace until fighting resumed in 1998. UNITA continues to control many of the diamond-producing regions of the country and the government has access to oil reserves (most of the oil sector is offshore anyway and hasn't been directly affected by the fighting). Both sides have the means to keep buying arms. The war, which has already left an estimated half a million dead already, drags on, and landmines continue to be laid.

By 1984 the Mozambican economy was in such bad shape that Frelimo saw no option other than to turn to its rich neighbour, South Africa, for help. South Africa agreed to withdraw its support of Renamo, while Mozambique agreed to withdraw its support for the ANC and to allow South African investment into the country. South Africa, however, reneged on the agreement and continued to support Renamo. However, South Africa couldn't resist the inevitable for long as the days of apartheid came to an end. When a tide of political and humanitarian change began sweeping through southern Africa in the 1980s, South Africa's support of Renamo diminished. The Soviet Union abandoned Mozambique in the late 1980s when it also left Angola and Ethiopia. In 1990 the Frelimo government switched from socialism to a market economy. A peace agreement was reached in

1992, elections were held and Renamo is now in peaceful political opposition. While violence has stopped in Mozambique, however, landmines continue to hinder reconstruction and development.

Most historians agree that the Cold War and regional powers at the very least prolonged the civil wars in Angola and Mozambique. Aside from the military aid, Soviet involvement also had a negative effect on the economies of both countries, which abandoned Marxism once the Soviet influence had gone. William Minter, a leading United States specialist on southern Africa, claimed that if the major powers hadn't got involved in the former Portuguese colonies there would have been no war at all in Mozambique and a more decisive, shorter war in Angola.

> Angolans and Mozambicans had their own internal reasons for disagreement, and perhaps even for some measure of violent conflict. But the wars of the 1980s attained their deadly height as a result of external forces, which raised destruction to levels far beyond the capacity of the societies to resist. It was, above all, the intertwined pacing of apartheid's death struggle and the end-game of the Cold War that determined their rhythm and intensity.[8]

Jesmond Blumenfeld, a southern Africa specialist, suggested that without big power involvement Mozambique would have stagnated until the government came to realise that its economic policies were counterproductive. However, he stressed that while Renamo was firstly a creature of the Rhodesians and then of the South Africans, it did play on, and build on, the very genuine disaffection with the Mozambican state. Whatever the case, it's doubtful whether Angola and Mozambique would ever have had the capacity or the inclination to mass-produce their own mines. A landmine industry benefited from the wars in Africa and now another industry is working tirelessly to clear the mines. Whatever the reasons for giving aid to Angola, there are also advantages for Western governments being seen to support the government. Angola offers multinational companies some of the most lucrative and exciting prospects for oil exploitation.

Extent of the problem

As is often the case in guerrilla wars, fighting has raged back and forth over different areas in Mozambique and Angola, affecting most of the country at some stage. Landmine records in both countries are few. The maps that do exist are more likely to refer to defensive minefields laid around strategic military sites than to the randomly laid mines that are a much bigger problem.

Angola is often grouped with Cambodia as having one of the world's highest number of amputees – although, as with much landmine-related data, estimates of casualties in Angola range widely. They probably number in the tens of thousands. Life is grim for children born in Angola, especially in provinces of the country where as many as three out of every four mine casualties are children.[9] According to UNICEF, Angola has now become 'the worst place in the world to be a child'.[10] Parts of one eastern province, Moxico, were so heavily contaminated with mines at one point that even rebel UNITA forces were told not to enter them. Civilians don't always have the option. Father Conor Courtney, an Irish missionary who has worked in Angola for a decade, described an 'I'll believe it when I see it' attitude, because Angolan farmers are so desperate to work the fields they are prepared to accept the risk of landmines. The 'luckier' Angolans will be the ones who own a plough; the cattle pulling it will be the first to detonate any mines. Many animals have thus ended up as landmine victims. Sometimes people will be injured chasing animals that have strayed into minefields, because cattle are such valuable assets. Father Courtney says what changes their attitude is when just one landmine goes off and they see the consequences. Then they 'abandon the land as if it has a thousand mines in it'.

The laying of landmines and the renewed fighting in Angola have forced thousands of refugees over neighbouring borders. When they do come back, it is often to a mined area. A local official in the provincial capital, Luena, mistakenly told returning refugees to resettle in a suburb that was still mined. As a result, one woman was blinded after touching a mine, before two more mines and twenty-four pieces of unexploded ordnance were found in the area. A month later in the same suburb two people were killed by an anti-personnel mine.[11] The mining of the eastern provinces of Moxico and the Lundas 'presented almost insurmountable problems' for the return of refugees, according to a Human Rights Watch report in 1994.[12]

The continual laying of landmines in the areas where fighting is at its worst prevents the supply of international food and medical aid. Angola's economy has been in ruins since the failure of MPLA's Marxist policies in the 1970s, inflation is out of control and basic social services are practically non-existent. When fighting began again after the failed peace attempt in 1992 many displaced people took refuge in towns that were surrounded by mines. Because roads were mined, some towns could only be reached by aircraft, making the international relief operation in 1994 one of the most complicated and expensive in history. Over 200,000 tons of food were distributed among two million people at an estimated cost of $100 million. When aid couldn't be airlifted in, mine injuries rose as people were forced back into mined land, looking for food. Humanitarian aid workers have also become landmine victims. In 1993, a Russian aircraft was shot down after delivering food. The crew survived but found themselves in a minefield and it wasn't long before an explosion killed one person and injured several others. All those problems arose again as a result of renewed fighting in 1999 and 2000.

Indiscriminate mining and mines laid against civilians have made Angola a terrifying place to live. Areas frequently used by people continue to be mined because it keeps the population in a constant state of fear and, therefore, under control. Mines can be used to lock people in one place, or to displace them elsewhere. The *Independent* reported: 'In the proxy conflicts of the Cold War during the seventies and eighties mines became what napalm had been for the sixties. Originally designed for use against armies, they increasingly became weapons that took their chief toll upon civilians.'[13]

. Father Conor Courtney was asked about the presence of landmines by a group of deminers who were working in southern Angola. He pointed out a particular area he knew had a big problem and about six months later was invited to visit the cleared area. The minefield had ended in a graveyard. Mines had been planted exactly where someone would kneel next to a grave to arrange flowers, remove weeds or to say a prayer. 'I find it hard to imagine the mind of someone who would put a mine in a place like that – but that's what I've seen.' Father Courtney said most people know to keep away from defensive mines around military installations, but it's impossible to avoid the mines deliberately laid to disrupt their basic needs.

I mean, if there is a closed bush or jungle with one pathway through it, you have to take that pathway, and everybody knows this, so if a landmine is put on that pathway and it explodes it was put there purposefully to maim everyone who uses that pathway . . . the people who are going to the fields every day or the market or whatever.

When you see landmines by the side of a river everybody knows that people have to go to the river to get water; cattle have to go there to drink. Water is the life source of an agricultural community, which Angola is.

Spates of mine accidents have occurred when people have returned to villages following UNITA attacks or military activities. Many injuries have happened along paths, roads and roadsides. Many victims did not know the areas were mined. Sometimes civilians stumble on stacked mines – anti-personnel mines buried on top of anti-tank mines. The practice of reinforcing anti-tank landmines was introduced during the war as a response to South African anti-landmine vehicles that were resistant to anti-tank mines. When someone stumbles on both mines they detonate together and the force of the combined explosion is so strong it vaporises the victim.

While anti-personnel mines pose the most immediate risk to civilians, there is also a large quantity of unexploded bombs and ordnance in Angola. Residents of one bairro in Cunene province unearthed a 500-pound Russian aircraft bomb, which failed to explode when it hit the ground. Smaller bombs, which can explode in a similar way to anti-personnel mines if they are tampered with, are more common. Many are Russian.

Some of Mozambique's most heavily mined areas lie along the border with Zimbabwe and in western, central and southern provinces. Human Rights Watch estimates the number of landmine victims to be between 10,000 and 15,000.[14] The number of casualties is not as great as in Angola but it still poses a big social and economic problem. More than half of the population lives beneath the poverty line and infant malnutrition and mortality rates are among the world's highest. Food production in Mozambique has gone into sharp decline because mines restrict transportation on the major roads. Landmines have helped reduce the ability of people to meet their own needs, and Mozambique has become an economic burden on the global community. Like Angola, children are being killed and maimed by landmines on a regular basis. The children who are 'lucky enough' to survive an explosion become a huge burden on society because of their disabilities so early in life.

Machua village lies deep into the bush in southern Mozambique, miles from anywhere. It consists of a hundred or so villagers living in bare little thatched huts. Skull and crossbones signs fixed to branches of trees or stuck on posts driven into the ground on several paths around the village warn of mines because no one has fenced off the minefields. The only aid this village gets is a touring company of mines' awareness actors, who stage plays showing the children what happens if they pick up strange objects in the fields. In 2000, one young boy was killed and two of his friends were injured when he began playing with a landmine in the bush near the village. He was trying to break open the mine when it exploded; it killed him instantly. In trees not far from the scene of that accident lies the body of a woman blown up three years ago. The locals are too scared to retrieve her, as she was killed stepping on a landmine. If someone does step on a mine out there, help is a long way away.

The devastating floods in February and March 2000, which made headlines around the world, have caused some further mine problems in Mozambique. Southern and central parts of the country were hit by torrential rain and cyclones, which resulted in the worst floods for half a century. Initially it was thought shifting landmines would pose a huge problem and years of demining progress would be undone. In reality, only a handful of accidents are thought to have occurred as a direct result of mines having moved in the floodwaters. The real problem has been that reference points have been washed away: houses, trees, fences – anything that villagers once used as an indicator of unmarked mines and minefields. Another problem has been that displaced people have been forced to move to areas that are closer to minefields than their old homes were. Mozambique experienced more flooding in 2001. Two people were reported killed when their truck hit a landmine as it crossed an alternative stretch of road being used after the main road had become flooded. The alternative road was in the process of being demined.

A poor standard of care

Medical treatment and rehabilitation for landmine victims in Angola and Mozambique are sadly lacking. The problem is particularly acute in Angola, where even local doctors are refusing to work in war-ravaged southern provinces. When someone is injured by a landmine, an expatriate working for any of the international aid agencies may own the only car in a 50 or 100 kilometre area. A wheelbarrow or cart might be the next best alternative. It can be days before casualties reach hospital. Amputations are sometimes carried out without anaesthetic. If adult patients are 'lucky' they might be given a mouthful of local brew before the operation. Decades of war have left Angola's health system in ruins. Everything has to be bought on the black market. Even if a good surgeon is available, the family will often have to find all the equipment needed for the operation, including rubber gloves, soap, sutures, needles, anaesthetic, bandages and even the bags for blood transfusions. Not surprisingly, some families can't afford to buy the necessary supplies and patients die as a result. Medicines provided as part of international aid packages that aren't locked away are likely to be stolen for sale on the black market. Health has become an extremely expensive luxury in Angola.

To its credit, when Frelimo first came to power in Mozambique it considered basic social services a high priority and established a rudimentary primary health care system, but much of it was destroyed during the war as part of Renamo's destabilisation campaign. International medical aid has become crucial. It is possible for people to get free prostheses at provincial clinics, but all transport, food and accommodation costs have to be paid for, so some amputees return home before having a limb fitted because they can't afford it. It is not known how many people have no way of making the journey from remote areas to a clinic in the first place. As in Angola, often the only way to get people to hospital is to carry them or wheel them in a cart or on a bicycle – and that often takes days. Sometimes the only source of local first aid is a traditional village healer and some healers refuse to treat mine injuries. The potential for infection is great, especially when patients don't get antibiotics quickly enough. Patients can thus die of fairly minor injuries. Only central hospitals, such as the one in Maputo, or military hospitals are equipped to perform surgery in Mozambique. Because the country is poor, the government has a big problem motivating people to work with mine victims.

The bare, run down orthopaedic centre of the main hospital in Maputo, the capital, makes its own prostheses and fits them. The artificial plastic limbs are painstakingly moulded by hand. With shelves full of plastic feet and legs, there is a never-ending demand for its wares.

Solving the problem

Both Angola and Mozambique have non-governmental organisations working to reduce the mine problem. Some landmine organisations in

Angola have struggled to maintain their programmes because of a lack of funding and security problems. Others have suspended operations altogether. Mechanical demining equipment lies idle in fields. The Mines Advisory Group was forced out of the heavily mined Moxico province in 1998 and re-entered with a smaller demining programme further south, in Cunene province. Areas it had demined in Moxico became new battlegrounds and some were even remined. MAG was able to re-establish its programme in Moxico in late 2000. One non-governmental organisation was asked to clear an area by the Angolan military. Once it had finished it found out the military only wanted the old mines taken out because they no longer knew where they were. Their plan was to remine the area once it was made safe – at the expense of donor money. In June 1999, Norwegian People's Aid reported that remining had occurred in several provinces. However, another demining agency, the HALO Trust, reported that none of the 100 to 150 minefields it had cleared over a period of six years had been remined.[15] Angola is flouting the Mine Ban Treaty and there have been rumours of large-scale remining. Concern has spread among donors, who are questioning the point of continuing to fund clearance programmes. Up to the end of May 2000, 2,610 minefields had been identified in Angola, of which 517 had been cleared.[16]

Mozambique has a host of international organisations attempting to clear its mines. The country is saturated with aid agencies: every second vehicle on the streets seems to be emblazoned with an aid logo. The first thorough, nationwide survey is finally underway after delays due to the flooding. There is a long way to go, however. Mozambique has received $25 million dollars in 'mine action' funding (a term used to describe funds for demining, mine awareness and victim assistance), which is about a tenth of what experts believe the country needs in order to get back on its feet properly.[17]

Demining in Africa is a long, hot, laborious task. The earth is hard and dry, so precious water has to be used to soften it up when trying to locate mines. To make things worse, deminers also have to cope with the presence of certain natural hazards, such as snakes. The ubiquitous puff adder, for example, which has a potentially fatal bite, is camouflaged in the greenish-grey tones of dry African grasses.

Angola is increasingly becoming a dangerous and frightening place for anyone to live and work in. On the road bandits usually kill their victims even if their motive for ambushing a passing vehicle is robbery. Sometimes, criminals with no other agenda than robbery and violence will falsely claim UNITA allegiance. Westerners are increasingly being targeted by rebels who know they'll achieve more personal notoriety and more publicity for their cause by kidnapping or killing an expat. Long gone are the days when a Red Cross logo or the badges of independent humanitarian aid organisations were protection enough. In 1997 two mine clearance experts were murdered in Angola. They are believed to be the first people to be killed for their efforts to make the land safe. Tom Sauber and Rayson Pongweni, both working for a German agency, were attacked as they inspected an area in the notoriously dangerous province of Benguela. In the days leading up to their deaths the two had reportedly been warned by UNITA soldiers not to clear the area. In 2000, a Catholic missionary priest was ambushed near Ondjiva and hacked to death. He was travelling in a convoy of vehicles but even that failed to protect him. It is standard for missionary priests to have armed escorts. A deterioration in security led to the departure from Angola in 1999 of demining experts from South Africa, Germany, France, the Netherlands and New Zealand, all of them vowing not to return until a cease-fire was adhered to. Western organisations still working in Angola and Mozambique impose curfews, because of the risk of banditry as well as road accidents.

The futures of Mozambique and Angola

Angola and Mozambique have a shared history, as has been shown, but their paths diverged considerably in the 1990s and they now face very different futures. Mozambique, although chronically poor, has reached the end of a difficult road to peace and, more importantly, peace has lasted. Angola is still deeply entrenched in bloody civil war. No one dares to suggest Angola has a chance of peace, let alone a landmine-free existence.

One of the reasons an end to Angola's war seems unlikely is that both UNITA and the MPLA have the cash to keep them armed. Renewed war and general security problems have wide-ranging implications for the mines issue. They affect everything from donor funding, to the ability of international organisations to continue demining, to the provision of immediate medical care, rehabilitation and prostheses. Mines Advisory Group director Lou McGrath went as far as saying there has been some advantage for the Western powers to Angola being at war and that no real effort to secure the Lusaka Protocol was made:

Many of the countries were actually taking the wealth out of Angola while this peace process was going on. That enabled organisations like UNITA to buy huge amounts of arms. What chance of peace is there if these organisations are able to build up a substantial amount of arms? They're going to see an advantage in going back to war in order to maybe make one last ditch attempt to take control of Angola.

Michael Ignatieff, however, maintains that the failure of the international community to stop the fighting in Angola is certainly not due to a lack of effort.

In Afghanistan the international community stops and sucks its thumb and doesn't know what to do and a million people die. Angola's a case where there has been real engagement. There's been UN deployment, there have been endless peace efforts, attempts to quarantine it in terms of weapons embargoes . . . You name it – the international community has tried it in Angola. I think this is a brush fire that will have to burn itself out and I know what I'm saying: that means a lot more people will have to die.

Ignatieff believes that sometimes the only way to end the type of guerrilla conflicts and civil wars that sprang up during the closing Cold War years is actually military intervention. He claimed that in order to bring to an end a world where people get maimed and brutalised by landmines, we may have to maim and kill a few more people in the process. Even if peace could be forced on Angola though, the landmine problem will be a huge barrier to reconstruction, just as it still is in Mozambique. He says: 'Mines in those places really are like one of the seven curses of Egypt. It's like the locusts, or the rain of blood . . . because it visits the consequences even a decade after peace is achieved. Angola can't start again even if it could get peace because, without an infrastructure – no economy. As someone said it's the gift that keeps on giving.'

In Mozambique, with the once-feared Renamo now in peaceful opposition, the government is trying to attract as much aid and investment as it can. However, a vast majority of the workforce still relies on subsistence farming where landmines pose a constant threat. Flood and famine are also never far away. Landmines are hampering the production and trade in the tropical fruits and nuts that could be in plentiful supply, cashew nuts, oranges, pineapples and coconuts among them. Even on the outskirts of Maputo poverty is rife. Development has a long way to go. Agricultural, hydropower and transportation resources are still under-utilised. Jesmond Blumenfeld claimed the issue of how Mozambique should get foreign aid has proved to be problematic:

> Aid of course gets linked with various kinds of conditionalities of either a political or an economic nature, in that the international financial institutions, the World Bank, the IMF, for example, and the major Western donor countries have been trying to encourage African countries to move towards a more democratic political system and towards greater economic reform . . . There's considerable resentment on the part of the aid recipients about these linkages because it's by no means clear for example . . . that the adoption of a Western-style democratic system is necessarily in the interests of all African countries.

Before the floods of 2000, Mozambique was being heralded as the 'African Tiger', and it was one of the fastest growing economies in the world. The floods have been a major setback. Within days of the rains, hundreds of thousands of people were displaced. Mozambique is poor and its people are extremely deprived. The United Nations estimates within the current rate of clearance that 'those minefields representing the biggest obstacles to sustainable development' in Mozambique will be cleared of mines within five to seven years.[18] Patrick Brogan believes Mozambique's prospects for remaining at peace, given its history and the strain it is under, do not look good.[19]

Currently, no new landmines are being laid in Mozambique. Both sides in Angola's war, however, continue to lay landmines. Rumours were circulating in 2000, at the second Ottawa Treaty meeting in Geneva, that Angola had quite recently imported a shipment of mines. For now, mine clearers are still reporting that they are finding old stock. Ottawa Treaty campaigners claim the international trade in landmines has slowed to a complete halt. Of the former powers that fuelled the wars in Angola and Mozambique, the United States is noticeable for its assistance in cleaning up the mine problem. Donald Steinberg, President Clinton's adviser on global humanitarian demining, was the United States ambassador to Angola from 1995 to 1998. He viewed the destruction in Angola first-hand, and described how millions are suffering psychological, economic and political degradation. Aware of the criticism that the United States is not doing enough to put right its contribution to Angola's landmine problem in the first place, he is quick to point out that the US has spent more than $20 million over the past decade in demining and mine awareness, but admits 'Nothing can overcome the tragedy that has faced that country for four decades, but indeed we all have a commitment, both political and moral, to address the problem there.'

Another key issue dividing Angola and Mozambique is that they have very different attitudes towards international law relating to landmines. Mozambique has signed, ratified and been a very vocal supporter of the Ottawa Treaty banning landmines. Angola, on the other hand, has made something of a mockery of the treaty. The government signed the treaty in December 1997, but stopped short of ratifying it when war started again the following year and both sides resumed the use of landmines. UNITA and the MPLA continue to use landmines. The government has recently been making noises about ratifying the treaty despite the ongoing war, to ensure continued funding for mine clearance and assistance programmes. If Angola did ratify the treaty while continuing to lay landmines, the States Parties to the Ottawa Treaty might not have the clout to bring a legal case against the Angolan government anyway. According to Adam Roberts the actions that can be taken by the States Parties are still unclear.

> One solution is that there is within the treaty some kind of mechanism for reporting infraction, for a meeting of the States Parties to the Treaty to decide on what action to take and so on, but one cannot be frankly optimistic that all that will work. What sometimes happens when there are clear infractions of a treaty of this kind is that the UN Security Council takes action . . . if, for example, it is one side that is principally using landmines there could be action authorised by the UN Security Council in favour of the other side . . . and ultimately there may also be action before the International Criminal Court . . . so there are possibilities of action but we've yet to see how it will work out in practice and one can't be optimistic. None of these treaties can be described as self-enforcing; they always require tough decisions to enforce them and those decisions aren't always forthcoming.

As noted in Chapter 1, the best vehicle for legal action could be through the Convention on Conventional Weapons – and only then if the United States is successful in its proposal that the rules and restrictions in the CCW governing the use of landmines be applied in civil wars and internal conflicts as well as in international wars.

Donors are increasing their pressure on governments to make the ultimate commitment to the Ottawa Treaty if they want aid to continue. Mine clearance agencies, meanwhile, continue to argue that because civilians maimed and killed by landmines have nothing to do with international treaties, mine-related funding should not be linked to the actions of governments. The response of Angolan officials to the fact that mines are being laid in contravention of the government's international obligations is simple: Angola is at war. When the country is at peace, they say, they will give up landmines. At the moment, mines are too useful and humanitarian issues therefore take a back seat. The stakes are much too high for both sides.

The proxy wars in Angola and Mozambique are over and the end of the Cold War has brought some benefits. Major powers stopped fuelling the supply of weapons and troops into these countries – and, in the case of Mozambique, peace followed. The end of the Cold War also made it easier for humanitarian aid organisations to enter mine-affected countries. However the end of the Cold War has had no significant impact on the stability of Angola. The main outside interest in Angola centres around oil; the government needs revenue from oil to buy arms. To the international community, the poverty-stricken and war-ravaged cities, towns and villages of Africa are not prime real estate. The First World is. Former Bomb Disposal Officer Paul Jefferson argued there were more landmines in the whole of Europe after World War II than there are today across the entire globe. He said Europe's landmines were cleared within ten years, and over half of the problem had been dealt with within two years. At the end of the Gulf War in 1991, Kuwait was very heavily mined, but those mines were also cleared within two years. If the international will were strong enough, he believes, Africa would get the same treatment.

> If downtown Washington was mined or the outskirts of London were mined, people wouldn't be crying out for a landmine ban, they'd be screaming out for mine clearance. But if it's downtown Luanda, then people campaign for a ban and go to conferences instead, and get celebrities involved . . . that's how we deal with the problem when it's not in our own backyard. It becomes an indulgence.

Mozambique and Angola have an abundance of natural resources that are being wasted and abused. In Mozambique, huge stretches of land lie unused, while poverty and mines keep a stranglehold on the country's economy. In Angola, the government plunders the country's oil reserves while UNITA does the same with the lucrative diamond mines. Both sides can buy more and more weapons with the proceeds. Meanwhile, the people of Africa are suffering desperate poverty. Most toil away under the scorching sun just to survive. Mozambique is slowly rebuilding its infrastructure, but it remains one of the world's poorest countries. Natural disasters like the floods of 2000 show how easily economic gains can be undermined. The war in Angola is so horribly ingrained that no one can predict an end to it. Landmines compound all this suffering. It has been argued that Angola presents a weaker case for aid, for it is still at war. However, the few demining agencies still in the country are adamant that civilians shouldn't be penalised. Even if Angola could reach a cease-fire agreement that works, reversing the damage caused by landmines will remain a massive task. Landmines stop people using roads; without roads, food can't get to market; without local trade the local economy suffers; no local economic activity leads to a collapse of the national economy. A solution is a long way off and, until one is found, many more people will fall prey to the landmine.

VIGNETTE 5: Demining

Although it costs as little as US $3 to lay a landmine, the cost of removing one ranges from $300 to $1,000. The methods used vary but the most common is manual clearance with the use of a metal detector. Members of teams usually work in pairs: one person uses the detector, and then a probe and a trowel when a positive signal indicates that a piece of metal is buried in the ground. The other acts as an observer, and the two swap places regularly. Demining using this method is extremely painstaking, as only 20–50 square metres a day can be cleared by one person working manually. It can also be very hot work, as deminers have to wear protective clothing, including helmets with visors, ballistic jackets, vests and long-sleeved shirts, and long trousers. Manual clearance hasn't changed much since it was first used in World War II when soldiers would use crude sensors and bayonets to poke the soil. In one instance, German prisoners of war were made to walk through cleared land to show locals that the land was safe. These days, deminers will still walk through cleared land to prove to a local community they have faith in the quality of their own work.

Mechanical clearance, which is much faster, is used in some places. Machines with flails and rollers have been adapted from the old converted tanks used during World War II, to become smaller, lighter and more agile. Some machines are remote-controlled. Mechanical clearance by itself can't meet the clearance standards of the manual technique, so often the two are used together. Dogs are also used to clear mines, being trained to recognise the smell of certain explosives. Electronic sensors, on the other hand, pick up every piece of metal, whether it contains explosive or not. Dogs are used in conjunction with manual teams. Any dog over 18 inches in size can do the job but poodles are especially effective. Apparently, however, some former military men find poodles a little embarrassing, and prefer to use more macho-looking dogs . . .

The main methods of clearance for non-commercial or humanitarian demining organisations remain manual, mechanical and the use of dogs. However, there is a large research and development industry dedicated to finding new ways of detecting landmines. How many methods will ever be used on a wide scale remains to be seen (some people argue that tens of millions of dollars are being spent on technological advances that will never be practical in the real world) but researchers are testing new advances all the time. In some cases, companies that used to manufacture mines are now researching ways of detecting them. In the United States, honeybees and bumblebees are

The stake mine POMZ 2, a directional fragmentation mine, made in the USSR (*photograph by Stephen Hart*).

being used in landmine-detection experiments. Bees, in particular, are being used to try to pick up TNT residue. Rats have also been used in trials to detect landmines. In Scotland scientists have developed a small remote-controlled pyramid-like structure on wheels, which detonates mines while taking the blast of the exploding mine through its sparse structure into the air. In New Zealand researchers have invented a self-propelled trolley carrying a microwave generator, designed to locate plastic anti-personnel mines. A British company has developed a low flying airship that uses radar technology to map minefields, and in Korea it is hoped that a microbial landmine detection system, by which landmines are found with genetically manipulated bacteria that go crazy when they come across TNT components, will be able to locate landmines along the Korean border. Yet other experimental work includes developing chemical 'sniffers' to locate explosive.

6

A Return to Europe

THE end of the Cold War and the disintegration of communist states sparked a new round of wars, as smaller nations struggled for independence and their own identity. The break-up of the former Yugoslavia unleashed nationalist extremism, ethnic civil war and genocide. Neighbours who had been friends, despite different religious and cultural roots, took sides and turned against each other. Conflicts broke out in several areas of the former Yugoslavia in the 1990s. Bosnia-Herzegovina, Croatia and Serbia fought each other as Serbia began to lose its grip over Yugoslavia, before tensions between ethnic Albanians and Serbs in the southern Serbian province of Kosovo spilled over, igniting yet another war. In both cases a Serbia ruled by Slobodan Milosevic was responsible for much of the aggression. The onset of ethnic war unleashed the massive stocks of Yugoslav landmines, once part of Tito's prized military machine, into Bosnia, Croatia and Kosovo. Tito's regime in Yugoslavia had encouraged the growth of military industries, including the production of landmines and compulsory mine-warfare training for all Yugoslav men. The former Federal Republic was one of the most prolific and sophisticated producers of mines in world and Yugoslav plastic anti-personnel mines are among the most difficult to detect and clear. A degree of evil ingenuity that defies belief has gone into the design and use of Yugoslav mines and booby traps. The cleverest and most detailed methods have been devised to lead unsuspecting enemy soldiers or civilians into the trap of detonating explosives. Almost all of the mines now littering the Balkans are domestic mines. The landmine scourge in the Balkans, unlike the ones in Africa and Latin America, came from within. However, this does not exempt the world's powers from a responsibility for the landmine problem. They may not have been providing the Yugoslav army with shipments of landmines, but it can be argued that they have at times prolonged or exacerbated the Balkan conflicts. Through its air campaign in 1999 NATO also created a cluster bomb problem in Kosovo.

The Balkan wars are among the most reported in history. A media frenzy was sparked by the realisation that genocide had returned to Europe. Many people were shocked that such hatred and violence could exist on the very doorstep of Western Europe in the late twentieth century. The historic city of Sarajevo was besieged for three years while in the countryside mass atrocities were committed. The term 'ethnic cleansing' became common currency resulting in the eventual establishment of a war crimes tribunal in The Hague. Some of the killers booby-trapped dead bodies to prevent the collection of war crimes evidence. A few years later in Kosovo, Serbs began the cleansing of the seemingly never-ending stream of ethnic Albanian refugees who poured out of Kosovo into makeshift camps in Macedonia and Albania.

An endless cycle of conflict

The Balkans are no stranger to conflict and conquest. Tensions and divisions can be traced back to the Roman Empire and Byzantium, when the region was split along Catholic and Orthodox lines. More recently Slovenia and Croatia were absorbed into the Austro-Hungarian Empire, while the Ottoman Turks conquered Bosnia-Herzegovina and Serbia. After winning its independence from the Turkish Empire, Serbia went about seizing Montenegro, Kosovo and northern Macedonia before the outbreak of World War I. By this time, Austria had also annexed Bosnia. After World War I and the defeat of Austria-Hungary, a new kingdom of Serbs, Croats and Slovenes (called Jugoslavia) was formed out of Slovenia, Croatia, Serbia and Bosnia-Herzegovina, although it was dominated by Serbia and ethnic tensions remained. World War II brought a new round of atrocities on all sides. Hitler took over Yugoslavia and divided his spoils between various collaborators. During the war Croatia's fascist leadership killed an estimated 700,000 Serbs and Jews[1] and many more were forcibly deported or thrown into concentration camps. The Serbs never forgot their treatment at the hands of the Croats.

From 1945 to 1991 Serbs, Croats and Muslims lived together relatively peacefully in the state of Yugoslavia, under the communist rule of Josip Broz Tito. The former Yugoslav Federation was made up of six republics: Bosnia-Herzegovina, Croatia, Slovenia, Macedonia, Serbia and Montenegro. Tito suppressed ethnic tensions, stressed the importance of unity and equal status and encouraged travel and interaction with the West. Like many communist leaders Tito also placed a high priority on building up a strong military. The former Yugoslavia became one of the biggest producers of anti-personnel mines in the world, for domestic use and for export, especially to developing countries. Bosnia was home to many of the weapons factories.

In May 1980 Tito died; his death destroyed the stability of Yugoslavia. The economy went rapidly downhill. By 1989, communism had collapsed and political change was sweeping over Eastern Europe. Slobodan Milosevic came to power in Serbia in 1987, and under his leadership the most powerful republic attempted to dominate its neighbours once again. In 1989 Milosevic stripped the Serbian province of Kosovo (the poorest region in Yugoslavia) of the autonomy that Tito had awarded it in 1974, sowing the seeds of wider conflict. The Serbs, outnumbered by one to every nine ethnic Albanians in Kosovo, began severely repressing the Albanian majority and taking away their rights. (It was at the famous battle of Kosovo Polje that the Turks defeated the Serbs in 1389.) Milosevic rekindled old resentments by siding with the Serbs resisting Albanian demands for independence. Claiming Albanian terrorists were persecuting Serbs, Milosevic whipped up a Serb nationalist frenzy – essentially for his own political ends. His campaign evoked images of a Kosovo that held great historical and religious significance; that, in essence, it represented the heart of Serbian national life and should never be surrendered. The rebellion that broke out in Kosovo stopped short of full-blown war, albeit only temporarily. As the other Balkan states suddenly descended into brutal conflict Milosevic had other concerns on his mind. Open conflict was put on the backburner and the Kosovar Albanians began a campaign of peaceful resistance against their Serb oppressors.

How mines infiltrated Bosnia-Herzegovina and Croatia

The inevitable disintegration of the former Yugoslav Federation began in 1991. It was a bloody process, especially as Serbia was resolutely against the break-up of the Federation. Hundreds of thousands were killed and injured and millions were displaced in a decade of warfare. Slovenia and Croatia were the first to launch their battles of independence, and broke away in 1991. Large numbers of Serbs in parts of Croatia became extremely unhappy at the prospect of living in an independent Croatia and began to demand autonomy themselves. Violence in Croatia spread, while a brief war in Slovenia largely spared one Balkan republic from the ensuing carnage. Memories of Serbian persecution at the hands of the Croatian fascists during World War II, repressed under Tito, resurfaced. The Yugoslav army supported Serbian irregulars in Croatia, and Serbs embarked on their notorious campaign of ethnic cleansing. During six months of bloodshed in Croatia an estimated 10,000 people died and hundreds of thousands were displaced. Peacekeepers entered Croatia in 1992, but fighting continued as attention turned to Bosnia-Herzegovina, which proclaimed its independence from the Socialist Federal Republic of Yugoslavia in the same year.

Until war broke out in Bosnia, the country had enjoyed a very cosmopolitan outlook, including mixing and intermarriage between ethnic groups. However, shortly after Bosnia's declaration of independence war broke out between the Muslim majority and Serb and Croat minorities. All three groups began persecuting minorities in their midst, but the main thrust of the war was the desire of both Croatia and Serbia to annihilate Bosnia's Muslims. The bulk of the fighting was carried out between the Bosnian government army (ARBiH), the Bosnian Croat army (HVO) and the Bosnian Serb army (VRS), which was backed up by the Yugoslav army.

All sides committed atrocities, but the Serbs were the worst perpetrators. Muslim buildings were destroyed. In April 1992 the infamous siege of Sarajevo began. Sarajevo is hemmed in by mountains, so its half a million citizens had no way of escaping the onslaught. A tunnel under the airport was the only link to the outside world. Sarajevo was left without telephone lines, water, gas and electricity and the siege that lasted for three years was probably one of the longest in modern history. Snipers killed indiscriminately. Around 10,000 people were killed in Sarajevo alone, and more than 50,000 were injured. The football pitch in the shadow of the Zetra stadium had to be turned into a cemetery to cope with the dead. By late 1992 thousands of UN troops were in the country, but in several well-publicised incidents they proved to be notoriously ineffective. After a Serb mortar attack on the main outdoor market in Sarajevo left sixty-eight people dead and 200 injured, NATO issued the Serbs with an ultimatum to remove their guns from around the city or suffer the consequences. They relented.

By 1994, despite their own hostility towards each other, the Bosnian Muslims and Croats had united against the Bosnian Serbs. The fighting continued and in 1995 the Serbs attacked the 'safe haven' of Srebrenica, slaughtering 6,000 Muslim men as they fled. In the same year Croatia forced out thousands of Serbs and retook territory. NATO finally bombed Serb military positions throughout Bosnia. The air strikes and increasing diplomatic pressure finally resulted in a cease-fire and the signing of the Dayton Agreement in November 1995. A quarter of a million people had died and another 200,000 had been injured. Millions had been displaced and the country was in ruins. The Dayton Agreement, signed by the presidents of Serbia, Croatia and Bosnia-Herzegovina, recognised two entities within Bosnia: the Federation of Bosnia-Herzegovina (Muslim/Croat) and Republika Srpska (Serb). The two entities have their own armies, governments and parliaments, so the ethnic divide remains.

All sides in the Bosnian and Croatian wars laid landmines. The Yugoslav army had quick, easy access to mines, as Serbia had been left with substantial stockpiles of landmines dating back to the Tito era. Before the break-up of Yugoslavia, all men were required to complete one year of compulsory military training in the Yugoslav army. They were ready to use mines as soon as war broke out.

> JNA [the Yugoslav National Army] military doctrine relied heavily on the widespread use of mines as a deterrent against invasion and, while its engineering units had primary responsibility for mine-laying, all its soldiers were taught mine warfare techniques. Field engineering handbooks contained detailed instructions on how to lay various types of anti-personnel, anti-tank and mixed minefields. They also explained how to mark and record minefields.[2]

About half the weapons produced in the former Yugoslavia came from Bosnia and landmines continued to be produced in Bosnia and Croatia during the conflicts. Unlike many of the civil wars in the late twentieth century the front lines were fairly static and to begin with, at least, the three armies laid many of their minefields in a disciplined manner. This was in line with Yugoslav military doctrine. Some efforts were made to map minefields on paper during the war. More minefield records were kept in Croatia than Bosnia, but generally these records have been inaccurate and not very helpful. Some commanders have been reluctant to hand over records, despite cease-fire agreements requiring them to cooperate. Some minefield records were burnt during the war. Markings were in short supply and rarely used. Those that were used were often part of a subtle code that only soldiers would understand, such as carvings on trees or crossed branches in the middle of a path. Such markings were seldom permanent. Sometimes soldiers marked minefields when they were laying them but then removed the markings when they had finished. Along many of the front line positions civilians had already fled, so the soldiers may not have thought that markings were needed to protect residents. Some minefields were laid over existing minefields in an attempt to exert an even tighter grip on an area. Mines have also moved due to flooding or shifting soil.

Throughout Bosnia and Croatia the Serbs made extensive use of indiscriminate mine-laying and booby-trapping in order to terrorise and control civilians. Mines became one of many tools the Serbs used to 'ethnically cleanse' Bosnian Muslims. Assisted by the Yugoslav Federal army, Bosnian Serb forces brutally expelled the Muslim population from northern and eastern Bosnia to create a 3,000 kilometre corridor joining Serb ethnic areas in the west of Bosnia and in Serbia. Concentration camps and mass atrocities became a main feature of the campaign. Just as mines were used in Cambodia and Angola to control the movement of populations, so they were used by the Serbs to facilitate their plans to create ethnically homogenous populations. The Serbs used mines offensively and defensively during the campaign, forcing tens of thousands of Muslims and Croats from their homes. Mines were used to close off some areas and to channel populations into other areas. Anti-tank mines were used to destroy homes, and anti-personnel mines were placed in rubble to prevent rebuilding of houses.

Bosnia was the booby-trap capital of the world's minefields. Serb and Yugoslav forces would rig bombs and mines to everyday objects in and around houses or farms, such as doors, televisions, cars or even household ornaments. Many booby traps were designed to threaten the basic needs of returning residents in the aftermath of war, such as food, heating and water. The warning signs that a house was booby-trapped were subtle and civilians could easily miss them. They might have included a closed or partly closed door or cupboard, an item that had been moved out of place or something valuable that had been placed to attract attention, tempting someone to pick it up. Booby traps can be simple, such as a grenade attached to a door, or more complex. In one reported case in Bosnia, a stack of anti-tank mines in a loft was wired to detonate as soon as the doors to the house were opened. In another example, a pile of hidden anti-tank mines was linked through a wiring system to the kitchen tap. If someone had unwittingly turned the tap on, the house would have exploded, to devastating effect.

Anti-personnel mines have often been booby-trapped. Mines attached to tripwires are reportedly the most common and the most lethal. Fikret Zahirovic, the father of three young children, was walking in central Bosnia one summer's day with a friend in a field where they used to collect strawberries. He trod on a stick, which was connected by a rope to a mine. The mine exploded, severing Fikret's leg. He has faced a long battle back from illness and depression since the accident and his bitterness towards the person who laid the mine is still acute: 'When I think about the man who put the mine in the ground I imagine a man without family, without anybody. I would say a man without a soul.'

Former soldier Nihad Dzigic encountered a booby trap during the war when he and his friend went looking for water. Just as he realised they had walked into a minefield his friend pulled a rope connected to a mine, which exploded next to him, throwing him 10 metres across the field. He was left with arm, leg and chest injuries.

Yugoslav mine warfare techniques also included all sorts of switches that can transform everyday objects into lethal killers. One such device is designed to be fitted to any object that can be rotated, from a tap to a cap on a fuel tank. It is fitted to the object and then attached to a mine or bomb. The action of rotating the object then causes the explosion. One Yugoslav landmine has a timer mechanism. Soldiers abandoning a building can wind up the timer in the mine for a delayed reaction of anything up to twenty-four hours. They remove the pin and leave the mine ready to explode when civilians or enemy soldiers enter the building.

Some improvised mines, which are not as stable as those produced in factories, were also used in Bosnia. One example was the 'Gorazde mine', a tripwire-operated fragmentation stake mine produced in small workshops in Gorazde during the war.[3] The mostly Muslim defenders of Sarajevo responded in the same way as the Cambodians when faced with death and torture at the hands of the Khmer Rouge. They laid home-made mines to keep out the Serbs. The lines between soldiers and civilians had been well and truly lost in Bosnia and Croatia. The ethnic hatred which engulfed Bosnia and Croatia led to former neighbours and friends waging war against each other − and that happened in the case of laying mines as well. According to Michael Ignatieff it made a lot of sense for the Muslims to lay mines, even if it doesn't seem morally acceptable: 'I think it easy to condemn what people do when their very survival, their existence, is threatened . . . and I think there's a huge difference between amateur landmine laying by threatened populations and the deliberate seeding of mines by countries engaging in conquest and invasion.'

The mine problem has penetrated the very heart of Bosnia-Herzegovina and Croatia. Unlike many landmine-affected countries, which only have a rural problem, the front lines of Croatia and Bosnia ran not only through open farmland and rugged mountains, but also through the middle of cities, villages and even playgrounds. Many key cities are mined including Vukovar, Dubrovnik, Split and Zadar in Croatia and the Bosnian capital, Sarajevo, Banja Luka, Gorazde, Mostar and Tuzla. Mines have affected both countries' agricultural sectors, as well as Croatia's once-booming tourist industry. There are few areas untouched by mines and the list of places the weapons can be found is endless: they include military sites, telecommunications networks, industrial sites, waterways, railways, bridges, power sources, tourist areas, agricultural land, along mountain trails, in forests and around villages, houses and roads. When one Bosnian soldier who survived the war stepped on not one but two anti-personnel landmines buried at a roadside within days of demobilisation, his comment was 'Now I understand war'.[4] The border between Bosnia and Croatia is also mined. Mines have been found in fourteen of the twenty-one counties of Croatia.[5] Many minefields were laid defensively to keep out the Yugoslav forces. All cantons within Bosnia-Herzegovina are contaminated with mines and some of the most heavily populated are the most heavily contaminated. More than 18,000 mined areas have been reported but it's estimated that up to 30,000 exist. By March 2000 just over a quarter of a million anti-personnel mines had been found, along with some 50,000 anti-tank mines.[6] There are fewer mined areas in Republika Srpska than there are in the Federation. According to the ICRC Bosnia is home to more than 4,300 mine victims.[7] However, the number of mine victims in both Bosnia and Croatia has been dropping.

A new round of mine warfare in Kosovo

Peace in the Balkans didn't last long. After years of Serbian repression following Milosevic's revocation of Kosovo's autonomous status, ethnic tensions finally came to a head again in the winter of 1997–98. War broke out in Kosovo between the Yugoslav army and the Kosovo Liberation Army (KLA), which was supported by ethnic Albanians seeking independence from Yugoslavia. The international community supported the Albanians' demands for autonomy, but not for fully fledged independence. However, Milosevic finally provoked NATO into action. After another long campaign of ethnic cleansing by the Serbs, failed peace negotiations and Milosevic's blatant disregard for international demands to stop the continuous expulsion of Albanians from the province, NATO launched air strikes against Serbia between March and June 1999. Despite criticism that NATO's action served to worsen the Serbian campaign of terror against the ethnic Albanians, the air strikes did finally force a cease-fire and once again international peacekeepers poured into the Balkans. Both the Serbs and the KLA used mines in Kosovo, although the KLA used far fewer. The Yugoslav army laid barrier minefields along the borders with Macedonia and Albania. It has been reported that Serb forces laid both anti-personnel and anti-tank mines along the entire Kosovo–Albania border, which is 80 kilometres long.[8] Minefields were also laid inside Kosovo protecting army sites such as airports, strategic bases and military installations as well as power stations. Mines have been laid across rich farm land. The Serbs also laid mines along the routes where NATO would have invaded with a ground force, had it decided to send in troops. The Yugoslav army recorded and mapped most of its major battlefield minefields and the United Nations gained access to those records. They show that the Yugoslavs laid 620 minefields.[9] KLA forces have denied using anti-personnel mines, but evidence suggests they did carry out some indiscriminate mining against the Yugoslav army, and they did lay some defensive minefields.[10] It's not clear where the rebel army would have obtained its mines, although some unsubstantiated allegations implicate Albania.

The scale of mine contamination in Kosovo is not as severe as the problem in Bosnia and Croatia. Not only are there far fewer mines, but a lot of the mine-laying by the Yugoslav army was ordered. There was a lot less booby-trapping than there was in Bosnia and Croatia. However, based largely on the experience of Serb mine-laying and booby-trapping in Bosnia, the mine problem in Kosovo was at first feared to be huge. The number of mines was predicted to be as high as several million. It turned out to be much less of a crisis and estimates of tens of thousands are more realistic. To the end of March 2001 more than 6,000 cluster bombs, 12,000 anti-personnel mines and almost 5,500 anti-tank mines had been found.[11] Because of the publicity concerning landmines generated by the Ottawa Treaty, awareness about the expected landmine problem was high. The HALO Trust entered Kosovo speedily after the war to produce a survey of the whole area. However, the landmines have had their intended effect. They have rendered land unsafe and have created fear among civilians. Up to June 2000, 472 people had been killed or injured by mines or unexploded ordnance.[12] People in the Balkans are also so conditioned to the threat of mines that vast tracts of land have been abandoned due to the perceived threat of mines.

The Yugoslav army behaved in a much more disciplined way than the irregular forces that specialise in indiscriminate mining. However, there was some indiscriminate mining in Kosovo, in gardens and around agricultural land, especially by Serbian Interior Ministry Special Police and Serbian paramilitary forces, in their bid to prevent refugees returning and to injure civilians. There was some booby-trapping of schools and houses, but the Yugoslav army didn't have time to booby-trap extensive areas before the UN peacekeeping forces moved in. Inhabitants of Tenoches, on the Kosovo–Macedonia border, described the kinds of booby traps awaiting them when they returned to their village in June 1999. A chicken stuffed with explosives was found in a cupboard with a detonator wired to the door. A water heater switch was wired to a bomb. Even a video cassette found near a path had been ruined: it exploded when it was thrown away.[13]

Just as significant as the landmine problem in Kosovo is that caused by cluster bombs, many of which were dropped by NATO. The properties of cluster bombs have been explained in Chapter 3; they were just as problematic in Kosovo, where they often failed to explode when they landed in many of the wooded areas in Kosovo. One type of bomblet used by NATO is intended to have three processes in the way it operates. The first is an explosion on impact designed to penetrate tank armour; the body of the bomblet then fragments, spraying hundreds of shards of metal which rip through soft targets; a flammable coating then increases the destructive impact. By 1 July 2000, several hundred more cluster bomblets than anti-personnel mines had been found – a total of almost 4,600.[14] By August, that number had increased to more than 11,000.[15] Donald Steinberg outlined the dangers of NATO's own cluster bombs in June 1999: 'The cluster bombs that are on the ground are a particularly dangerous element. They are, in some cases, small balls that are silver; in other cases, they look almost like soda cans, painted orange, in many cases, or yellow. They unfortunately are very attractive to young children . . . These are dangerous things.'[16]

NATO has provided records to the United Nations Mine Action Coordination Centre (MACC) regarding 333 cluster bomb strike areas upon which almost 1,400 bombs (each containing hundreds of smaller bomblets) were dropped. The MACC estimates that as many as 30,000 bomblets may have failed to explode.[17] Some have been found buried up to 50 centimetres below the surface. A US demining agency has been charged specifically with clearing cluster bombs. Rae McGrath said it didn't seem as if any lessons had been learned – or at least no changes to strategy had been made – since the Southeast Asian conflict and Operation Desert Storm in the Middle East. He believes none of the military achievements of the cluster bomb campaign can be justified in light of the civilian toll: '. . . it seems clear that the use of cluster bombs proved disproportionate to the military advantage gained. As time passes the bomblets become harder to locate and, often, increasingly unstable. Further civilian deaths and injuries will continue to illustrate the uncontrollable and disproportionate nature of cluster bombs.'

The risks of both known and unknown dangers

In April 2000 three children were killed by a landmine in Bosnia when they strayed into a minefield outside Sarajevo. One of them, an eleven-year-old girl, screamed for help for hours as would-be rescuers watched, unable to go to her aid because of the risk of further explosions. Police, NATO peacekeeping troops and a demining team arrived shortly after the blast. By the time a path had been cleared, two hours later, all the children were dead. Residents said they knew the area was mined and it was marked, but it wasn't fenced off. Awareness of mines and cluster bombs is generally very acute in the Balkans, especially among people who lived through the wars and didn't flee. Aid workers have identified certain attitudes within local communities which work against their efforts to ensure people's safety. Sometimes, people know about mines but they don't understand the dangers facing them. Two incidents were recorded where people injured by landmines had gone into forested areas that had been mined, believing that, because there had been mine accidents there already, the area had been cleared. One man, who was inside his house on the outskirts of Sarajevo with his son, heard an explosion outside. Despite the fact that he knew his wife was in the garden he didn't panic – he told his son the explosion couldn't possibly have been in their garden because he had walked through it the previous day and there had been no evidence of mines. He was wrong.

In Croatia the United Nations has become aware of a gun culture, where one in five sets of parents are actually keeping weapons at home.[18] If people have a desire to hoard weapons they may try to collect landmines and unexploded bombs as well. Schoolchildren are therefore taught to encourage their parents to hand over any bombs or landmines they are hoarding to peacekeeping forces. A macho attitude has also been identified among Croatian teenagers living in heavily mine-contaminated areas.[19] In some countries such teenagers show their machismo on the road; in Croatia they display it around landmines. Landmine victims in the Balkans are typically male, in their late teens to early twenties. Many are farmers. Curiosity was the downfall of one teenager on the outskirts of Peja in Kosovo. He went with his cousin to inspect the damage from the war. They were running alongside the main road in an area that used to be a Yugoslav army and Special Police Force's camp when he stepped on a mine. He lost a leg and his cousin sustained injuries to his chest, eyes and a leg. In Kosovo, the three high-risk activities that have been linked to mine and unexploded ordnance are individual movement, farming and unsanctioned mine clearance.[20] The ICRC has observed: 'It is especially important to address the reasons why people continue to take risks. A lack of personal concern is often the result of economic necessity, peer group pressure, bravado, trauma suffered during the war or plain overconfidence around mines.'[21]

The ICRC has further identified a wider problem involving the way people perceive the landmine threat. Johan Sohlberg, who has worked in different areas of the Balkans for the ICRC, believes the sheer horrors of the Balkan wars have actually made people more blasé about landmines: 'Some people tend to have a feeling that they survived the conflict – the actual hostilities – and now it's calm again that problem no longer exists . . . it's peace and it's safe. It's not, of course, but it's very easy to forget.'

Education programmes are seen as crucially important, even if it is just to remind people about the danger of mines. After all, many mines are completely invisible. It's harder for children to understand that an area that looks exactly the same as it did before the war has suddenly become dangerous. Children, for example, return to play in the grounds of their schools unaware that such a familiar place might be mined. In Bosnia it has been found that some children who lived through the war have detailed knowledge about mines and booby traps, including how each weapon works. Others, especially refugees and displaced children returning home, know very little. They form the highest risk group with the highest incidence of mine accidents.

One of the characteristics of all the Balkan wars has been the massive displacement of people. Ethnic cleansing has led to millions of people leaving their homes. Since the signing of peace agreements many of these refugees and displaced people have been returning to their old homes after cease-fires were declared. If their area isn't prioritised for clearance, people often have no idea where the mines are. Several post-war incidents were reported in Bosnia of new mines being laid to prevent the return of refugees. This was in clear contravention of the Dayton Agreement, which required all parties to allow ethnic minorities to return to their homes. Sometimes, as in the case of Cambodia, refugees are so desperate to return home that they place themselves in danger. By late June 1999, just days after NATO forces entered Kosovo, about a quarter of a million refugees returned home, despite warnings about mines. Political efforts since 1999 to speed up the repatriation of thousands of Serb families have been tempered by the reality that many of these people face rebuilding their lives in abandoned, heavily mined rural areas. Others who have returned have been unable to farm the land because of mines and are existing on state benefits. In rural Bosnia many places are still waiting for clearance to begin. The few hundred locals, who have returned to rebuild their houses in the village of Donja Bistrica, are still surrounded by landmines. Their only hope of earning an income is to start farming, but they are afraid to work the land. Their power lines and water supply were destroyed during the war. None of it can be repaired until demining begins. The village of Cekrcici, on the road between Zenica and Sarajevo, is still waiting for deminers. Two returning refugees have already died after stepping on buried landmines while walking around their houses. One resident working in the fields says he found five or six unexploded mines and threw them in the river.

The central Bosnian canton of Zenica was one of the worst affected areas for mine contamination during the war and many returning refugees now live with the daily threat of injury or death. One in ten households in Zenica reported that it had experienced a landmine incident.[22] On one scenic hillside, a former front line, twenty-five children were injured by landmines over a three-year period. One young man – a double amputee – had to cope with the additional tragedy of his father being killed by a landmine during the war. Another young man lost a leg when he stumbled on a mine when he was walking on a well-trodden path. He said he didn't know there were mines there and claimed to know many other people in the area who'd lost legs to landmines. One teenager lost his hand when he went fishing in a river close to his village with two friends. He picked up a mine in the water. Another teenager also lost a leg when he went fishing. A group of children had found a landmine while he was at the river. They took the mine to a man nearby, who threw it back in the river. It exploded on impact. One young boy was playing near his house when he picked up a strange object. It exploded before he could throw it away and he lost an eye.

Clearing the mines: yet more disputes

In the central Sarajevo suburb of Dobrinja, a former front line runs along the hill behind Serdarevic Rifet's house. Serdarevic had put his life savings into the house by the time he finished building it in 1991. Not long afterwards war broke out and he was forced out of his home by the Yugoslav army. While the Bosnian and Serbian armies slogged it out behind his house, he camped in an abandoned apartment building 500 metres down the road. After the war he returned to find his house destroyed and mines littering his garden and the rest of his land, which ran up the hill. With the help of his brother and a friend he cleaned up the area around his house, but he wanted to wait for trained mine clearers to make the hill safe. Despite the fact that he lives a short drive from the headquarters of the Sarajevo Mine Action Centre, it took deminers four years finally to reach his house. In mid-2000, deminers were still working their way around his and neighbouring properties. Mine contamination prevented Serdarevic from working his land and from grazing animals. It also meant he couldn't have his young daughter living in the house, in case she wandered out of his sight.

The mine clearance operation in Bosnia has been widely criticised by both the country's residents and international aid agencies for being extraordinarily slow. Questions have been raised about the efficiency and quality of work being done in both Bosnia and Croatia – but Bosnia is the more complex and controversial case. Demining has been a difficult process from the outset. When the Dayton Agreement was signed, initial responsibility for clearance of other areas was given to the warring parties. They were also given a ridiculously short deadline to complete the clearance – a mere thirty days. Some commanders were reluctant to hand over maps, and there was a lack of training and a general lack of motivation. Nationwide clearance organisations (Mine Action Centres) have since been handed over by the United Nations to national authorities. Most demining in both countries is now being carried out by private or semi-private companies. High priority areas for resettlement and rebuilding are still mined.

Allegations of inefficiency, *ad hoc* initiatives, mismanagement and the rigging of contracts have plagued the mine clearance programme in Bosnia. Commercial organisations have been accused of cutting corners under the pressure of competition to secure contracts. Private companies, on the other hand, have alleged that non-governmental organisations are wasting money by being overly cautious and inefficient. There is a huge range of agencies working in Bosnia, from national and commercial interests, to non-governmental organisations and the military. In the military, demining teams are divided along ethnic lines. There are few non-governmental demining agencies working in Bosnia compared with the number operating in other heavily mined countries. However, there are more than twenty commercial demining companies working there.[23] This has resulted in a strange situation whereby huge machines are being used to clear unpopulated areas while residential suburbs languish in mine-contaminated land.

Mines Advisory Group (MAG) director Lou McGrath claimed a huge amount of money has been wasted buying equipment and training people and very little effort has been made to organise proper, safe clearance. MAG attempted to set up a programme in Bosnia in 1998 focusing on an area in Zenica that was both populated and mined, but it never got off the ground. The HALO Trust undertook initial assessments in 1994 and 1995 but stopped short of establishing a fully fledged clearance programme, believing the situation was about to turn into a 'complete circus', according to its director, Guy Willoughby. Willoughby said that by mid-1996 there was an 'agonisingly complex quasi-commercial contract system' in place.[24] Other NGOs, such as Norwegian People's Aid and HELP, did set up programmes and are still working in Bosnia. Pivic Enes of the ICRC in Zenica agreed that a lot of money had gone into demining and that many people in Bosnia believe the process has been too slow. The World Bank is a major funder of the demining effort in Bosnia, along with American, Canadian and European donors.

General Jusuf Jasarevic, who heads the Sarajevo regional office of the Federal Mine Action Centre (FMAC), admits clearance has been too slow. He believes about a fifth of the estimated total number of mines has been cleared. He claimed this to be a big success, but admits it is disproportionate to the amount of time that has elapsed. He blamed the lack of progress on a shortage of funds, and said 500 deminers were unemployed because there wasn't the money to pay them. He also said the armies didn't give FMAC any maps or records. The FMAC admits only 61 per cent of their planned operations for 1999 were actually carried out. That, too, was blamed on a lack of money. Continuing funding shortfalls have led to reports that the Mine Action Centre in Bosnia may have to close down altogether.

Despite a few criticisms the Croatian Centre for Demining (CROMAC) has a happier record than Bosnia in terms of progress made. It successfully implements its annual plans. However, large areas still require surveys and mine clearance and the problem isn't likely to be solved in the short term. The Croatian government contributes more to demining than its Bosnian counterparts, but it has the revenue to support it from tourism and commercial activities. Many industries in Bosnia before the war were defence-related and are therefore no longer allowed to operate. Industrial production in Bosnia has fallen by as much as 90 per cent since 1990.[25]

The progress of mine clearance in Bosnia and Croatia is being hampered by a host of other difficulties. There are booby traps, built-up areas, hills and mountains for the deminers to negotiate. Over time grass has grown over mines, making them more dangerous and difficult to find. Heavy brush is also a problem. Over the past four to five years, areas that used to be farm land have almost become forests. Small trees have to be removed before demining can begin. Severe winters, during which much of the ground is covered in snow, have also hampered mine clearance. The Yugoslav plastic mines are difficult to detect with an electronic sensor, the most important tool for manual clearance. Thanks to Yugoslav mining strategies, deminers have to watch out for various hidden traps. Anti-tank mines have been rigged in such a way as to make them explode as easily as anti-personnel mines. So-called anti-handling devices can cause the anti-tank mine to explode with changes in heat, light, sound and movement. Some mines with low metal content have been buried in a stack of three, the top two without fuses, to prevent detection. Sometimes extra mines have been planted in ordered enemy minefields so that, when the enemy tried to lift its minefield in order to relay it somewhere else, a nasty surprise would await them.

Kosovo's mine clearance programme is based around a completely different philosophy to that of the other Balkan programmes. Most importantly, a time limit has been set for international clearance to finish, making the Kosovo programme the first United Nations demining programme to be completed. Once the UN has left, local deminers will take over to undertake what little clearance remains. In the absence of an elected government, the United Nations is in charge of the whole demining operation in Kosovo and it controls where international demining agencies (comprising commercial and non-governmental) should work. Kosovo is not a huge area and the United Nations Mine Action Coordination Centre has estimated that by the end of 2001 (a year earlier than scheduled) landmines will be cleared to the point where they don't pose any great danger. MACC programme manager Lieutenant-Colonel John Flanagan said that the UN wants to achieve the same standard of clearance that was reached in Western Europe after World War II.

> We accept that we are not going to clear 100 per cent of the mines and UXO [unexploded ordnance] in Kosovo . . . Therefore we believe in acceptable risks and that is what we practise. We can spend tens of millions of dollars looking for the last mine or CBU [cluster bomb unit] in Kosovo, and we'll never find it . . . This is not to say we cut corners at all, but we approach things from a totally different perspective than other programmes. We believe that we focus more on the solution, rather than the problem, as occurs in other areas.[26]

Lieutenant-Colonel Flanagan's philosophy is only to use manual deminers if there is a 100 per cent probability that they will find a mine in a short period of time; otherwise he believes it is best to use mechanical clearers or dogs in conjunction with manual clearance. Mechanical clearance is being used to help cover areas more quickly, sometimes simply to ensure that a suspected mined area is clear. Flanagan maintains that any organisation using only manual clearance without considering other options is helping to perpetuate 'the myth that the world mine problem cannot be solved in the next 100 or 200 years'.[27] Various European countries and Canada, Australia and the United States are contributing funds or resources to help solve Kosovo's mine problem. Lieutenant-Colonel Flanagan believes that if donors know a clearance operation has a time limit they're more willing to give money. The uncertainty of an indefinite commitment can put donors off.

> The battle against mines is as much psychological as it is physical, as this has a major impact on post-conflict recovery and development. Investors are not going to spend money on infrastructure if they are convinced that every road, bridge and field is mined. Therefore, it is essential that the 'mine affected' label be removed from every country as soon as possible. And that does not mean clearing every single mine.[28]

It became apparent early on that most of the demining in Kosovo would take place in large, ordered minefields. Deminers have said that in the bigger Yugoslav-army minefields, once they find a few mines a pattern emerges and it is relatively easy to locate the remaining ones. When it started its demining programme the United Nations asked agencies to hire former KLA soldiers to carry out clearance. 'When the UN and KFOR [Kosovo Force] first came in, they didn't want the KLA running around armed or idle, so the UN specifically asked demining NGOs to hire ex-KLA soldiers . . . basically to keep them off the streets and to give them something to do,' explained Neil Elliot, MAG's Kosovo Programme Manager.

Some of the former KLA soldiers had valuable knowledge about where the mines were, but unlike deminers in other countries who signed up voluntarily, some said they didn't enjoy the job at all. Others, however, said they felt happy to do something for the children. One former KLA soldier said he was fighting for his people during the war, and by clearing enemy mines he was fighting for his people again, by making their lives safer.

Lieutenant-Colonel Flanagan believes that if other Balkan countries, especially Bosnia, had the same philosophies adopted in Kosovo, they 'would be close to completing the clearance of all high priority areas, and probably a large number of medium priority areas.'[29] He went on to say, 'The fact is, they do not even know what constitutes a high, medium or low priority area yet.'[30] Flanagan further argued that the fact that Kosovo's mine problem is relatively small in comparison to the other Balkan countries has little to do with the potential results he believes could be achieved with a different approach.

Future prospects for the Balkans

Ethnic divisions still characterise the Balkans, tensions still simmer, issues remain unresolved and the spectre of conflict is never far away. Thousands of NATO peacekeepers are still enforcing a tenuous peace. Milosevic has been ousted from power, but although he did much to precipitate past wars, the future stability of the Balkans depends on many things. Kosovo is controlled by UN administration and a return to a multi-ethnic, harmonious society is still a long way off. The border between Kosovo and Serbia remains volatile. In 2001 it was the scene of clashes between ethnic Albanian guerrillas of the Liberation Army for Presevo, Medvedja and Bujanovac (LAPMB) who were demanding the area be joined to Kosovo. Kosovo's neighbour, Macedonia, came close to civil war more than once in 2001. Ethnic Albanian guerrillas based in Kosovo calling themselves the National Liberation Army (NLA), were fighting Serb and Macedonian forces. The rebels, linked to the former KLA, were demanding that the Macedonian constitution should be rewritten to guarantee equal status with majority Slavs. The government argued that the move would lead to a *de facto* division of Macedonia. Macedonia had Western backing for its fight against the rebels, but it was also under international pressure to make concessions to ethnic Albanians. A peace agreement was signed by the country's main Albanian and Macedonian parties in August 2001, allowing for key changes to the Macedonian constitution. NATO sent in British-led troops to oversee the disarmament of the ethnic Albanian rebels amid doubts about whether a cease-fire was sustainable. Violence had intensified in the week before the signing of the peace agreement and it included 18 Macedonian soldiers being ambushed or blown up by landmines.

The long-term future of Bosnia-Herzegovina is, at best, unclear. Tensions still simmer in Bosnia and the administration of the country is divided along ethnic lines. In April 2001 NATO peacekeepers were injured when hard-line Croatian separatists rioted as part of a campaign for a Bosnian–Croat mini state. Commentators agree that when, or if, the international community leaves Bosnia to its own devices, war between all three ethnic groups will resume at once.

> The Dayton Agreement is so fragile that the war will start again should the international troops ever leave . . . The way the maps defining Serb, Croat and Muslim-controlled territory are drawn undermines the economic development of all three communities, while the political arrangement discourages cooperation between them. The settlement is, in short, full of anomalies and frictions.[31]

Montenegro has expressed a desire for independence from the Yugoslav Federation. Doing so would sound the final death knell for Yugoslavia as a federation. If Montenegro divorces itself from Yugoslavia, it could have repercussions in Kosovo. There is a large Albanian minority in Montenegro and Kosovar Albanians may well wonder why they should stay in Serbia if Yugoslavia effectively ceases to exist.

Several incidents of mine use have been reported in Bosnia-Herzegovina and Croatia since the signing of the Dayton Agreement. There have been reports of mines being laid to prevent people going back to their homes, and further reports of civilians using mines to protect property. These are familiar sounding incidents for any country where mines have been readily available in the past. Mine incidents have continued after the end of the Kosovo war. In February 2001 it was reported that Albanian militants blew up a coach full of Serbian women and children in northern Kosovo with a remote-controlled landmine. Seven people were killed and twenty-one injured. A couple of months later a Serbian policeman was killed when his vehicle hit a landmine in southern Serbia near the Kosovo border. In some landmine incidents that have occurred as a result of renewed conflict around Kosovo border regions it is not clear whether the mines dated back to the 1998–99 war or whether they were new mines.

Mine clearance still has a long way to go in parts of the Balkans, especially in Bosnia-Herzegovina. Mined areas hamper development and reconstruction. Sarajevo is a beautiful and fascinating city and tourists are gradually returning. Its colourful Turkish quarter lies next to modern commercial developments, and street sellers are now capitalising from the war by offering tourists polished and engraved shells. However, beyond the city centre there are streets where every second building is pockmarked with bullet holes. The burnt-out tower blocks on the road into the city once dubbed 'Sniper's Alley' are testament to the damage inflicted during the siege. Inner city suburbs are still mined and people are unable to rebuild their lives.

The former Balkan war zones are still reliant on international peacekeepers and aid not only for demining but for development. The war destroyed parts of Bosnia and Croatia's health system, once heralded as one of Tito's major achievements. The number of doctors in Bosnia had almost halved by the end of the war.[32] Bosnia, the poorer republic of the two, fared worse than Croatia. However, access to medical care and physical rehabilitation is generally better in the Balkans than it is in other countries with mine problems. In Kosovo, which has always been poor, public health facilities have deteriorated over a long period of time, and support for mine victims is generally inadequate. On the positive side, Milosevic's downfall means there is a greater chance of stability within Yugoslavia. The international community drew up a Stability Pact for South Eastern Europe in June 1999, largely in response to the Kosovo conflict. Its objective is to promote 'lasting peace, prosperity and stability' within the region.[33] Encouragingly, the number of mine-related deaths and injuries has either been dropping or stabilising in Bosnia, Croatia and Kosovo.

Bosnia-Herzegovina, Croatia and Macedonia are parties to the Ottawa Treaty. However, a return to war is likely to result in the laying of more landmines, possibly even before the current problem has been solved. Perhaps most importantly, Yugoslavia has not made any commitment to ban landmines. There have been unsubstantiated claims that Yugoslavia has stopped producing and exporting anti-personnel mines, but it is clear that the Yugoslav military still sees the weapon as useful. Signing the Ottawa Treaty is not an absolute guarantee that governments will not resort to the use of landmines during war anyway: Angola is an example of a signatory which went back to war after signing and began using landmines again. It remains to be seen how Croatia or Bosnia would respond if they became caught up in a war where landmines were laid against them and they couldn't retaliate in the same way. It could depend on what legal clout the treaty had in respect of violations. The booby-trapping of explosives that was so prolific in the wars in Bosnia and Croatia is virtually impossible to police. Improvised mines can be made with or without government approval. The pattern of NATO involvement in the Balkans could continue, so another cluster bomb campaign can't be ruled out. The use of cluster bombs is not included in the Ottawa Treaty. The United

States has not joined the Ottawa Treaty so it reserves the right to use both landmines and cluster bombs.

The wars in the Balkans weren't the long, drawn-out affairs that some guerrilla wars around the world have been. However, even a few years of war have left parts of the Balkans littered with mines. The stockpiles of landmines built up in the former Yugoslavia offered an immediate and steady stream of weapons, especially to the Yugoslav army and Serb paramilitary forces. Soldiers in all armies were already familiar with the landmine and with the countless ways the most harmless looking objects can be converted into death traps. Little did Tito know that so many of the weapons he encouraged manufacturers to produce would one day contaminate his country.

Valmara 69, a bounding fragmentation mine, made in Italy (*photograph by Stephen Hart*).

VIGNETTE 6: Anti-Personnel Mines – Production and Trade

In the *Landmine Monitor Report 2000* the International Campaign to Ban Landmines claims that the number of known producers of anti-personnel landmines dropped from fifty-four to sixteen during the closing years of the twentieth century. The countries that are still producing anti-personnel landmines (which include several that have stopped producing but reserve the right to restart production if they believe it is necessary) are Burma, China, India, North Korea, South Korea, Pakistan, Singapore, Vietnam, Russia, Turkey, the Federal Republic of Yugoslavia, Egypt, Iran, Iraq, Cuba and the United States. There has been one unconfirmed report that Sudan is also producing landmines – a country that hadn't been a known producer before. Russia has announced it has stopped producing blast mines, the most common anti-personnel mine found around the world. Eight of the twelve biggest producers and exporters over the past thirty years have now signed the Ottawa Treaty stopping production and export. They are Belgium, Bosnia, Bulgaria, the Czech Republic, France, Hungary, Italy and the United Kingdom. Monitoring the production of anti-personnel mines hasn't been as simple as uncovering landmine factories, though. Electronics makers and defence contractors were capable of producing components that are used in landmines as well as other common products such as alarm clocks. In 1991 Human Rights Watch released a report identifying forty-seven US companies making landmine components.

The *Landmine Monitor Report 2000* noted an almost complete halt in the trade of anti-personnel mines. The International Campaign to Ban Landmines hasn't been able to identify a single shipment in the past five years. The ICBL said that, while this does not prove there have been no covert or black market shipments, military specialists agree with their assessment. Thirty-four nations are known to have exported mines in the past. The ICBL said all of these countries except Iraq have at least formally stated they are no longer exporting. Some say many of the past landmine producers were never exporting to the Third World anyway. Others say the Ottawa Treaty has just altered the face of landmine production and that it will go underground or more mines will be manufactured at home. Yet others say the arms trade has never truly been above ground anyway. However, if nations continue to trade landmines when they say they have stopped the evidence may eventually turn up in the ground through demining. Likewise, it is impossible to know with certainty whether production has ceased in any country. The best evidence is of export shipments or of mines being found through eventual clearance by national or international demining organisations.

7

End of Empire

IT was in Afghanistan that the world suddenly began to understand just what landmines could do to ordinary people. Stories had circulated for years about this weapon that kept on killing and maiming long after the soldiers had gone, but this was different. The international media started to pick up on reports from medical aid agencies about a battleground epidemic the like of which even the most experienced war surgeons had not seen before. Afghan civilians, in their thousands, were being carried in to makeshift hospitals, and a large percentage of them were landmine victims in need of limb amputations. In Afghanistan a largely unheralded weapon of war precipitated a humanitarian crisis.

The ICRC moved into Afghanistan within a year of the Soviet invasion of 1979. Its longest serving delegate in Kabul is now one of the most renowned figures in the city. Alberto Cairo, an Italian physiotherapist, has been supplying new limbs to Afghanistan's wounded for over a decade. Since he arrived, the city has been under firstly Soviet, then Mujaheddin and now Taliban control. The front line of the fighting has moved constantly, often from street to street within the city walls. Yet Alberto remains – and the casualties keep on coming: 'Many people ask me if I'm sad and tired to see so many people coming in. And I say "yes", I am in a way. But I learn not to think too much. When I see an amputee come in with both legs missing, I don't think "poor guy – I don't think your condition is very good". I think "one month and he will walk again". If you don't think positively in Afghanistan it is very difficult.'

The prosthetics centre was established in 1988 and it grew bigger and bigger so as to be able to meet Afghanistan's need for new limbs. The centre employs local people and uses anything that's at hand to relieve the suffering of mine victims, including the treads of old Soviet tanks to make prosthetic limb joints. The ICRC now runs similar projects throughout the country, as the landmine toll shows no sign of abating. 'According to the number of patients we receive, we don't see any difference. It was bad before – it is bad now,' claimed Alberto. 'The main frustration is that whatever you do, whatever you start, you never finish. You treat a patient, you discharge a patient, but new patients, new mine victims, just keep on coming. Sometimes I feel that what I'm doing is a bit useless.'

Far from being useless, Alberto's project is one of the few beacons of hope for Afghanistan's ever increasing amputee community as Najmuddin, the manager of the orthopaedic centre in Kabul, can testify. He was driving a car one day in 1992 when he hit a mine, and lost both his legs. 'I was in the hospital for a year. After that I tried to get a prosthesis to walk again but at that time in Afghanistan it was very difficult to get artificial limbs. So for five years I was stuck at home just doing nothing. Then I heard that the ICRC had set up an orthopaedic centre in Kabul,' said Najmuddin. 'The ICRC then asked me to work with them at the orthopaedic centre – of course, for me having been at home for five years I said "yes". If the ICRC wasn't here what could people do? – nothing.'

Aid workers who arrived in Afghanistan as the war raged on soon realised that the country had a landmine 'epidemic'. The casualty rates were startling, and included Soviets, Mujaheddin and, of course, civilians. To cope with the sheer numbers, both sides in the conflict were treated in the same ward. ICRC staff often travelled through the front line to take Mujaheddin landmine victims to a Red Cross hospital in Kabul to treat them in a ward with the Soviet patients who were their enemies, before taking them back to Mujaheddin territory when they got better. 'We thought there'd be gun battles in the middle of the ward,' explained Dr Frank Ryding, 'but often you had enemies in the next bed and in fact they'd be helping each other out and feeding each other.' He also recalled one occasion when an injured Soviet military commander was shown a nearby ward full of Afghan children with mine injuries.

I took him around the children's ward when they were doing the dressings; so he saw children with no arms and no legs, and he saw the dressings being changed, and he saw the stumps of amputations, he saw newly operated amputees, and he saw them before they'd been operated on. And he turned white and started shaking because it was the first time he'd actually seen what his mines did. He'd maybe seen someone step on a mine but he hadn't seen what the problems were long term especially for people that really don't deserve that at all. And a lot of his victims were children, they were elderly, they were women, people who had nothing to do with the military side at all. It really did deeply affect him and before he left he sheepishly left us $200 to buy toys for the children.

Suffering is endemic to the people of Afghanistan. They have been pawns in a 'Great Game'[1] for more than a century. The contest began with tsarist Russia and imperial Britain fighting each other on Afghan soil. Then, as the twentieth century unfolded, Afghanistan took its turn in hosting the Cold War as the Soviet Union battled the American sponsored Mujaheddin, and as the millennium drew to a close Russia and Iran lined up behind the non-Pashtun north which squared up to the Taliban, backed by Pakistan and Saudi Arabia along the Hindu Kush. Afghanistan's woes at the hands of outside powers began in the nineteenth century when it inadvertently found itself in the buffer zone between the expanding empires of Britain and Russia. India was vital to the British empire and Britain was concerned about Russian expansion south through Central Asia. Three times the British tried to conquer Afghanistan (1838–42, 1878–80, 1919); three times they failed. It became apparent that it was easier to cut a deal with the Afghans than fight them, so cash subsidies were offered to tribal chiefs to make Afghanistan a British client state. In truth, Afghanistan served a purpose for both Britain and Russia. The superpowers had no real desire to fight each other and Afghanistan was at a very convenient safe distance between two of the world's great nineteenth-century empires.

Barely half a century after the British and Russians had last used Afghanistan as a playground, history was repeating itself. At the height of the Cold War, Afghanistan received billions of dollars of aid from the USSR and the USA. From 1956 to 1978 the Soviet Union contributed the equivalent of US $1.25 billion in military aid and US $1.26 billion in economic aid; during the same period the United States gave Afghanistan US $533 million.[2] The Afghan people had grown increasingly dissatisfied with the ruling Zahir regime throughout the Cold War years. The breaking point came after the drought of 1971–72, which reduced food production by 20 per cent and livestock numbers by 40 per cent. The resulting famine killed half a million Afghans.[3] King Zahir Shah was deposed by his cousin and brother-in-law, Sardar Mohammed Daud. The king went into exile in Rome, Afghanistan was declared a republic and Daud was installed as president. The Soviet Union was initially supportive of his regime. Communist officers within Daud's army and the urban-based Parcham party crushed a nascent Islamic fundamentalist movement in 1975. The leaders of the uprising, Gulbuddin Hikmetyar, Burhanuddin Rabbani and Ahmad Masud, would eventually wreak vengeance on their communist conquerors – they were later to lead the Mujaheddin.

Throughout his brief reign, Daud had become increasingly concerned about an overdependence on the Soviet Union and pursued a policy of purging Marxist sympathisers from his government and army. The very same officers who had fought with Daud to oppress the Islamic uprising turned against him in April 1978. Daud and his family were massacred. The new communist government immediately declared its intention totally to reform Afghan society, issuing *Basic Lines of Revolutionary Duties of Government of Democratic Afghanistan*. The programme planned to redistribute land, abolish traditional debts related to land and bride prices and most controversially, to launch a literacy campaign for women. Their highly ideological social reforms took no account of ancient creeds and cultures and they sparked widespread rural revolts. The khans and mullahs declared a jihad on the infidel government and Islamic fundamentalists took up arms under the banner of the Mujaheddin. The conflict escalated as the government was unable to control the warring factions within its own ranks, let alone fight the jihad.

The Afghan communists were already bitterly divided at the time of Daud's assassination. There were two distinct groups, the Khalq (the masses) and the Parcham (the flag). The first Khalqi president, Nur Mohammed Taraki, was murdered by supporters of the deputy prime minister, Hafijullah Amin, who then embarked on a policy of courting support from the United States. The Soviet Union was growing increasingly uneasy about the volatility within a neighbouring state and on Christmas Eve 1979 its troops invaded Afghanistan. Hafijullah Amin in turn was killed and the Soviets installed Barbrak Karmal, the Parcham leader who had fought with Daud in 1975 as president to establish a socialist regime. The Kremlin had intended a quick *coup* and the installation of a puppet leader in Karmal, but Soviet strategists had totally underestimated their neighbours. It was to be the beginning of a war that would span a decade and precipitate the eventual demise of the Soviet Union. The Afghan Mujaheddin became 'US-backed, anti-Soviet shock troops'.[4] The Soviet Union fought the war with all its military might – jet aircraft, helicopter gunships, tanks, troops and millions of landmines. The Mujaheddin fought back with increasingly high-tech arms acquired from the United States, China and other Arab nations. Eric Hobsbawn has recorded that: 'Afghanistan became – as some people in Washington undoubtedly intended it to be – the Soviet Union's Vietnam.'[5]

Soviet troops fighting alongside the communist Afghan army controlled the cities and the towns as well as the major lines of communication. The Mujaheddin held mountain strongholds and became the hidden enemy. Fortified by American weapons they launched devastating hit-and-run attacks on besieged Soviet positions. To keep out the Mujaheddin fighters, increasingly dispirited Soviet conscripts turned huge tracts of Afghanistan into giant minefields. The Soviet military's defensive philosophy was still influenced by the German invasion of the Soviet Union in 1941. They considered mines to be very effective in slowing down the advancing German army and from that point onwards, landmines were integral to the defence of the Soviet Union's extensive borders. The Soviets developed over fifty types of mine, most of them cheap, simple devices. Soviet forces used mines to build massive barrier minefields in front of an enemy, and used much smaller 'belt' minefields to protect strategically important sites such as airfields, garrisons and supply routes. According to the HALO Trust, 'the greatest long-term effect on the civilian population was the defence of the supply routes, which involved the creation of interlinked *cordon sanitaires* along the ribbon development of villages and intensive agriculture in the narrow fertile valleys'.[6] The Vietnam Veterans of America Foundation, which questioned nearly 5,000 village households throughout Afghanistan, found that 80 per cent had found landmines in their fields.[7] Prior to the Soviet invasion, Afghanistan was self-sufficient in food production. Landmines have forced the rural population into the cities, exacerbating existing problems of overcrowding and unemployment. The largest dam in the country, Kajakali, did not produce any electricity for more than a decade because the power pylons linking it to Kandahar had been mined. Rae McGrath observed, 'There was no pretence that the wide-scale use of mines was directed purely at the military opposition – the policy was area-denial and any area which could not be controlled by the Soviets was to be denied to the Mujaheddin.'[8]

The war in Afghanistan developed as an insurgency and counter-insurgency campaign. According to Rae McGrath, this kind of war 'has resulted in the most inhuman and persistent use of mines'.[9] McGrath argues that in such conflicts, landmines are used in a random and widespread manner over agricultural and communal land. The mines are used as anti-morale weapons against civilians with extensive deployment in villages, wells, religious shrines and graveyards. The Soviet military justified this use of landmines on the grounds that the enemy was 'hiding in the community',[10] so the community became a legitimate target. In addition to strategic military use, mines were extensively used in Afghanistan to harass civilians. Residential areas were frequently mined, as were livestocks grazing areas. According to one study, 'mines were used to depopulate towns, restrict the movement of people and disrupt agriculture in order to weaken support for the Mujaheddin. The Mujaheddin used far fewer mines against the Soviet and regime forces – mainly to block roads and tracks.'[11]

In addition to protective minefields around garrisons, the Soviets used scatterable 'butterfly' mines that were dropped on mountain passes, villages and Mujaheddin bases. The entire food-producing infrastructure was paralysed by extensive mining of fields and irrigation channels as well as the helicopter drops which remotely mined nearly all the available grazing land. Twisted carcasses of animals are still a common sight on hillsides throughout Afghanistan. The Soviet forces used mines to protect the major cities that lay close to the Iranian and Pakistani borders such as Kandahar, Herat, Jalalabad and Khost. Kandahar was renowned as an oasis town in the middle of a desert. Huge orchards and green fields were maintained with an extremely complex and sophisticated irrigation system. Grapes, melons, mulberries, figs, peaches and pomegranates from Kandahar often graced the tables of British Governor Generals in India during the nineteenth century. Following the Soviet invasion, both sides heavily mined the green fields of Kandahar. The Mujaheddin used the irrigation channels and orchards as cover in an otherwise flat landscape. The Soviets, isolated within the city retaliated by cutting down the trees and destroying the water channels. Such was the extent of the mine laying around Kandahar that the rural population fled to neighbouring Pakistan. When they returned in 1990, the destroyed orchards were used to cultivate opium poppies to generate income for the Taliban.

The rise of the Taliban

Mikhail Gorbachev came to power in the Soviet Union in 1986 and pledged his commitment to ending the conflict in Afghanistan. His stance received widespread support from an increasingly disillusioned Soviet population. A cease-fire was announced in 1987 and Soviet-backed President Mohammed Najibullah initiated a policy of reconciliation, which included an amnesty for opponents of the regime, safe return for refugees and the establishment of links with tribal leaders. The cease-fire did not hold, yet it would prove to be the beginning of the end of the war. The United Nations-sponsored negotiations led to the Soviet Union agreeing to withdraw from Afghanistan by 15 February 1989. The Accords were signed, which committed Afghan political parties now based in Pakistan and Iran to form a new government. They also demanded that the Russians hand over all their minefield records to the authorities in Kabul.

The Soviets eventually withdrew from Afghanistan in 1989 after a conflict that had claimed 1.5 million Afghan lives. The Soviets may have gone but the suffering of the Afghan people would continue. The Afghan interim government, based in Peshwar, was racked with internal tension and the addition of Shi'ite parties from Iran to form the Alliance of Eight did nothing to quell the rivalries. The fighting continued. The Najibullah government was finally overthrown in 1992 when the Mujaheddin captured Kabul and established the Islamic State of Afghanistan. The manner of Kabul's capture, however, would condemn Afghanistan to another bloody civil war. The warlords had united against a foreign enemy but now the only people left to fight with were each other.

For 300 years Kabul had been controlled by the Pashtuns, the ethnic group that makes up 40 per cent of the population of Afghanistan. In the weeks leading up to the overthrow of Najibullah, the feuding Pashtun parties were beaten to Kabul by the better organised Tajik and Uzbek forces. For the first time in three centuries the Pashtuns no longer ruled Kabul. It was a devastating blow and another civil war ensued immediately. Afghanistan was ruled by warlords who fought each other, made alliances with each other, and then changed allegiances again. The changing nature of the war after the Soviet withdrawal resulted in a new wave of mine laying in very different areas. When the Soviets controlled the big cities the minefields were largely confined to the perimeters of urban areas to keep the

Mujaheddin out. Now that different factions of the Mujaheddin were fighting each other in house-to-house battles, inner city areas were extensively mined.

The new regime, under the leadership of the Tajik Burhanuddin Rabbani, was doomed to fail. He controlled Kabul and its environs and was also in an uneasy alliance with the Uzbek warlord, General Rashid Dostum, who controlled northern Afghanistan. The west of the country was ruled by Ismael Khan, a former Mujaheddin war hero, while the area east of Kabul was held by the Pashtun General Gulbuddin Hikmetyar. Rabbani was surrounded as Hikmetyar laid siege to Kabul with relentless shelling. He was soon joined by General Rashid Dostum in the north who abandoned his alliance with President Rabbani and joined in the shelling.

With Kabul besieged, Afghanistan's second city, Kandahar, staged its own civil war. Tribal warlords seized houses and farms, raped women and children and slaughtered civilians in the streets as the ancient city descended into a violent abyss. For former members of the victorious Mujaheddin, who'd fought the Soviets and then the Najibullah regime, to return to lands controlled by bandits was too much to bear. From the ranks of former Mujaheddin emerged a second generation of fighters intent on restoring order to Afghanistan. War-ravaged Kandahar became the birthplace of a new wave of extreme Islamic warriors – the Taliban. The Taliban's declared aims were to 'restore peace, disarm the population, enforce Sharia law and defend the integrity and Islamic character of Afghanistan'.[12] In an effort to distance themselves from the warring factions of the Mujaheddin they called themselves the Taliban, meaning Islamic students. The idea was to portray an image of religious cleansers as opposed to power seekers. From the very outset, the Taliban's unquestioned leader was Mullah Mohammed Omar, a battle-scarred Mujaheddin warrior opposed to the criminal activities of the leaders for whom he had once fought. Many of his followers had been born in refugee camps in Pakistan and knew very little about Afghanistan or its recent history. The Taliban leaders, however, carry with them permanent reminders of Afghanistan's bloody recent history. Omar's second-in-command, Mullah Mohammed Hassan, walks with the aid of a wooden stump, refusing one of the modern prostheses that are now available to the millions of landmine amputees in Afghanistan.

The Taliban seized control of Kandahar in October 1994 before marching north and west to capture Herat and lay siege to Kabul. The Taliban victories revived hopes among the Pashtuns that they would once again dominate Afghanistan. After assuming control of Kabul, the Taliban were in no mood to forgive or forget. Former President Najibullah, who'd taken refuge in a UN guesthouse since his overthrow by the Mujaheddin four years earlier, was dragged out into the streets, castrated, beaten to death and his body left hanging from a traffic observation tower. It set the tone for one of the most brutal regimes of modern times. Under the Taliban Afghanistan became an international outcast. Former United Nations Secretary General Boutros Boutros Ghali argued in 1995 that Afghanistan had become 'one of the world's orphaned conflicts – the ones that the West, selective and promiscuous in its attention, happens to ignore in favour of Yugoslavia'.[13] The vicious faction fighting raged on and landmines continued to be buried in huge numbers.

The birth of humanitarian demining

In accordance with the Geneva Accords, the Soviet Union handed over minefield records to the authorities in Kabul and clearance began. A short-term national reconstruction plan called Operation Salam was established in 1987 and sponsored by the United Nations. It was an attempt to train 13,000 Afghan volunteers in clearing minefields at training camps in Pakistan. Military deminers from Australia, Canada, France, Italy, New Zealand, Norway, Turkey, the USA and the UK were flown in to train the nationals. This was the first attempt, anywhere in the world, to use military demining techniques with civilians. Ultimately the project failed due to lack of equipment and a failure to create any sort of infrastructure within Afghanistan to organise the clearance. The results were both disappointing in terms of the quality of the clearance work and tragic in terms of the accident rate with deminers.[14] The United Nation responded by establishing four Afghan non-governmental organisations, led by a small number of foreign experts, to start clearing the landmines. The pilot project was based in Kunar province and within a year demining teams were working throughout Afghanistan.

The real departure, however, came in 1988 when HALO set up a mine clearance programme which, in essence, was the world's first humanitarian demining programme. Up to that point the most common form of mine removal had been military breaching which, in a conflict situation, required speed in order to clear small, clearly defined paths and thus to create 'safe' routes through minefields. The standard techniques developed by the world's armies were to detonate the mines with rollers, flails and fuel-air explosives or by using armoured ploughs to push the mines aside. Humanitarian demining, however, required thoroughness not speed and the clearing of large expanses of land not narrow channels. The needs may have been different but the expertise required remained the same, as the founder directors of HALO soon realised. The late Colin Mitchell decided to use military people with technical expertise in laying mines for humanitarian demining. The first programme was in Baghlan province, in an area on the main road into the former Soviet Union. Soviet soldiers used it to bring ammunition, armoured personnel carriers and tanks into Afghanistan. Consequently the road and its surrounding areas were extensively mined by both the Soviets and the Mujaheddin. 'HALO can claim that we invented the idea of humanitarian demining in the world,' explained HALO's director in Afghanistan, Dr Farid Homayoun. The organisation now employs over 1,300 Afghan deminers in various operations across the country, from Kabul and the surrounding districts, north through the Shomali valley to the provinces of Baghlan, Kunduz, Samangan and Balkh. Despite the political instability, the rise to power of the Taliban and the continuing internal conflict, the HALO programme has continued in Afghanistan.

The war rages on. The Taliban captured Kabul in September 1996, yet Tajik and Uzbek forces still fight government forces along fronts in the northeast and northwest of the country. The Taliban deny using mines against the insurgents but the evidence suggests otherwise. The Taliban's enemies, meanwhile, are known to have received Iranian copies of American anti-tank mines. The ongoing war has prevented the United Nations from handing over its operation to the government as originally anticipated. Despite the problems and the continuing high rate of accidents, there is no doubt that the demining programme in Afghanistan is among the most effective in the world. According to Dr Farid Homayoun,

. . . there are many provinces where the problem of mines no longer exists. To give you an example of Kabul city, we finished our last demining task there at the end of 1999 and there are no mines left now in the residential areas of Kabul. Another example is Baghlan province. In Baghlan city and many of the surrounding districts there is no longer a problem with mines now because after so many years of clearance the problem has been tackled. So it's very encouraging when you're clearing land and then you hand it over to the local people. People come back, life returns to normal. People move in, resettle and you see the short- and long-term impact of the clearance with your own eyes.

Despite the undoubted success of mine clearance programmes in Afghanistan mine accidents continue to occur at an alarming rate. What's even more disturbing is that many mine casualties in Afghanistan don't reach hospital at all. They die in minefields, they are buried and no one knows about them. It's impossible to know what the accident rate really is. In 1995 the Vietnam Veterans of America Foundation reported that 59 per cent of mine victims in Afghanistan die from their injuries. This is a startling fatality rate for a weapon most commonly deployed to maim rather than kill. There are areas where up to three people a day are killed by landmines in northern Afghanistan. 'Sometimes you get tired,' said Alberto Cairo, 'you see that whatever you do there are new patients coming in. It seems that it will never end. You find problems in any job but to work in Afghanistan is not the easiest thing.'

Long before the Taliban assumed control, the ICRC surgeons working in Afghanistan faced a host of non-medical problems. 'We treated a lot of anti-personnel mine injuries in Afghanistan,' said Robin Coupland, 'but in Muslim countries there's a very specific set of cultural objections to amputation. Often we would be faced with very long and difficult discussions with the family and the patient about whether or not to amputate a severely injured limb. Sometimes this could take many days and occasionally it would result in the patient leaving the hospital against our advice and refusing the treatment we had to offer.'

Another problem encountered by a surgeon working for the ICRC was an unqualified medic who insisted on treating landmine casualties with a tourniquet. 'He thought he was doing good and whenever he got involved in a mine injury he would put a tourniquet on very tightly,' explained Dr Frank Ryding:

It did stop the bleeding, but by the time they got to the other side of Afghanistan and a Red Cross hospital, the tourniquet had been on for three days. Even after an hour you start to worry about a tourniquet, so what would have been a below the knee amputation of the leg turned into an above knee amputation simply because of the bad treatment. We sent a team into Afghanistan to try to find this person and tell them to stop it. Eventually we did but it's a prime motto of medicine: first do no harm.

Demining and remining

Afghanistan is not a party to the Ottawa Treaty. Even though the Taliban control 90 per cent of Afghanistan, the country's seat at the United Nations is still occupied by Burhanuddin Rabbani on behalf of the Islamic State of Afghanistan, or the Northern Alliance. Both sides in the ongoing conflict accuse each other of continuing to use landmines. The Northern Alliance openly admit to their deployment, the Taliban strenuously deny the accusation. Mullah Mohammed Omar issued a statement proclaiming the Taliban's unequivocal support for a ban on anti-personnel landmines. Several high-ranking officials of the Taliban appeared with UN officials in Kabul in an event staged to commemorate the 1997 Mine Ban Treaty. During the ceremony Mohammed Yousef, the head of the Taliban's Office of Disaster Response which incorporates the Department of Mine Clearance, announced that 'if someone uses a mine in a Taliban-controlled area they will be punished according to Islamic Shariat [Sharia law]'.[15] Rabbani initially declared his support for an anti-personnel mine ban in a statement to the United Nations in March 1996. However, the Rabbani government failed to turn up for a UN General Assembly vote in support of the Ottawa Treaty in December 1999 and has subsequently admitted to the Northern Alliance's continued use of landmines. The Taliban's Foreign Minister wrote to UN Secretary General Kofi Annan to ask him to help stop the flow of landmines from 'hostile' countries to the Northern Alliance.[16] In 2000, the United Nations announced that it was cutting its budget for mine-clearing operations in Afghanistan by 50 per cent. Nothing has as big an effect on those who finance demining programmes as reports of remining in a country. Afghanistan's mine clearance has been very successful to date but there is a real concern within the demining community in the country that the renewed fighting and its financial consequences will undo much of the good work.

'In the areas we've demined, thanks be to God, there have been very few reports of remining,' said Dr Farid Homayoun. 'We are now fighting donor fatigue syndrome. And if we are forced, through lack of money, to leave areas only partially cleared, it is a very dangerous situation because you only encourage more victims. If you leave Afghanistan as it is now the mine casualty figures will rise automatically. The international community has a responsibility to carry on running the demining programme in Afghanistan.' Some commentators, while applauding the efforts made to demine Afghanistan believe that it is simply a case of too little, too late. 'It's clear there is the international will to get mines out of Afghanistan but there isn't an international will to stop the civil war in Afghanistan,' said Michael Ignatieff.

Mines are part of a larger way in which we fuel civil wars and then do nothing to stop them. The Afghan war could be stopped by great power diplomacy, banging on the table, arms embargoes, shutting off the forces that put the mines there in the first place. So the mine problem is part of a much bigger problem which is that we send arms and allow civil wars to rage unchecked and then we come in with bandaids and the bandaids are mine clearance, but the bandaids aren't enough because the initial diplomatic effort wasn't enough to do anything to stop this stuff in the first place.

The onset of mine clearance on a large scale prompted a series of estimates as to how many mines had been buried in Afghanistan. As indicated in Chapter 1, the revised figures in relation to the number of mines laid in that country were used as a benchmark when assessing the numbers of mines laid in other countries. Whatever the true figure for the number of mines laid, there's no doubt that Afghanistan is one of the world's most heavily mined countries. It also has the world's largest number of displaced people. It is a lethal combination. According to some estimates, 400,000 Afghans have been killed and another 400,000 injured by landmines since the Russians invaded in 1979. One of the groups most affected by mines in Afghanistan is the Kuchi: these nomadic people became a key source of information on the whereabouts of landmines.[17] Rae McGrath argues that repatriated refugees are at particular risk from landmines. Experiences in Afghanistan have showed that the first two weeks for returnees is an especially hazardous period, one in which basic procedures regarding mine-affected terrain are completely ignored. 'Some Afghan returnees climbed mountains to view their home valley, or even to picnic, within days of being repatriated. All too often the resulting explosion led to a return to Pakistan by ambulance. Children have climbed from vehicles and run directly into fields within minutes of returning to their homeland – with inevitable and tragic results.'[18]

The ailing empire

The Soviet Union was the most prolific user of landmines in history. Some estimates claim that the Red Army laid over 200 million mines to fight the Germans in World War II. This is almost certainly a gross exaggeration but there's no doubt that the landmine was crucial in the Soviet effort during the war and the weapon has continued to be an integral part of Russian military thinking ever since. Soviet military doctrine is largely based on a siege mentality, and mines have always been regarded as the best form of protection. Countries that used to lie adjacent to the Soviet Union also used landmines to keep the Red Army out. The Finns, for example, suspended landmines below the ice on frozen lakes and rivers so that when they were detonated they shattered the ice to slow down advancing troops and vehicles.

When the Cold War ended and the Soviet Union broke up, the Russian army continued to rely on landmines to keep troublesome regions in order. Nowhere was this more in evidence than in Chechnya, the scene of one the bloodiest wars of recent times. Even experienced surgeons, such as Dr Frank Ryding, who'd witnessed the humanitarian disaster wreaked by landmines in Afghanistan were shocked by the brutality of Chechnya.

It was very different there. You had a First World power fighting a Third World community and that was very difficult to come to terms with. It was very difficult for us to appear to be neutral. Each side wanted us to be purely on their side and it was very tough to say, 'no, I'm sorry, we have to be neutral and if you can't accept that we've got a big problem'. It was a very vicious war, which had things that hadn't occurred in my experience before.

In terms of landmines, the war in Chechnya mirrored that in Vietnam with a huge force being staved off by determined guerrillas armed with ingenuity and local knowledge. The recent troubles in Chechnya started when the Chechen Republic Ichkeria proclaimed independence from Russia in September 1991. Increasing tension resulted in Russia sending troops into Chechnya on 11 December 1994 and since then both sides in the conflict have used an enormous number of mines. The Khasav–Yurt peace agreements were signed in August 1996 but relations remained strained until the Russians sent troops back into Chechnya in September 1999. During the cease-fire between December 1994 and September 1999 there were allegations that the Russians were continuing to lay new minefields. The HALO Trust reported the continued mining of Chechnya's borders with Ingushetia and Dagestan.[19]

The pattern of mine laying in Chechnya is similar to that deployed by the Russians in Afghanistan. The first phase of mine laying was to protect strategically important installations such as checkpoints, outposts and temporary positions. This was followed by air-dropped scatter mines in the Chechen mountains. The Russians used scatter mines in an attempt to cut off withdrawal routes from Dagestan and supply lines along the Russian–Georgian border. Chechens returning to their homes often found them booby-trapped by retreating Russian troops.

For sheer horror, the use of landmines in the battle for Grozny is unparalleled in recent times. Chechen resistance in the capital was weakening throughout January 2000 and a column of nearly 3,000 rebel fighters was forced to withdraw. Russian military officers claim to have lured the fleeing Chechens into a minefield by pretending to accept a bribe in exchange for safe passage from Grozny. 'Frankly, we did not expect bandits, especially the key figures, to swallow the bait,' boasted one Russian general.[20] Such was the scale of the minefield massacre that one doctor claimed to have amputated the limbs of sixty-seven casualties in two days, including the right foot of the rebel commander, Shamil Basayev. The mayor of Grozny, Lecha Dudayev was killed by a mine during the retreat. One Chechen fighter said, 'I saw dreadful things during fighting in Grozny, but that massacre was beyond comparison. We had to walk on our dead comrades to avoid stepping on unexploded mines.'[21] It did not take the Chechens long to avenge the deaths of some of its highest ranking officers. In May 2000, two senior Russian government officials were killed when their vehicle ran over a Chechen-laid mine on the outskirts of Grozny.

In a letter to the International Campaign to Ban Landmines, Alexander V. Zmeevski, Permanent Mission of the Russian Federation to the United Nations wrote:

The use of anti-personnel landmines there (Dagestan) was nothing less but a 'dire necessity'. In Dagestan we had to do everything possible not only to safeguard the territorial integrity of the Russian Federation, but first and foremost to protect the civilian population from the international terrorists.

The Russian Federation uses anti-personnel landmines only for the purposes of defence and in the first place to deter terrorists, drug smugglers and other potential illegal trespassers who wish to penetrate into our territory.[22]

The HALO Trust recently reported a triple accident in Chechnya. The chain of events was triggered when a cow was blown up by a mine. The farmer went to retrieve the animal on a tractor, which in turn was blown up by an anti-tank mine. His wife then went to rescue the farmer on another tractor only to drive over another mine. Only the wife survived but she was severely maimed. Economic desperation forced the family to continue herding over mined land. It is a common story throughout the world's most heavily mined countries, which tend also to be poorest. A Chechen military officer told the ICBL that the mines used by his fighters are all from old Soviet stockpiles and those left behind by Russian troops after the first war. He claimed that the only way the Chechens could secure a continuing supply of landmines was through 'contacts with representatives of the Armed Forces of the Russian Federation'.[23] Since the second advance into Chechnya there has been increasing evidence that the Russians have been selling mines to the Chechens to be used against their own troops. An article in *Chechenskaya Pravda* claimed that Georgian intelligence officers had stopped a vehicle leaving a Russian military base in Vazini, Georgia, with a consignment of arms destined for Chechnya.[24] In response, a television news report broadcast on Russian television claimed that the Chechens used 'serial landmines of Western manufacturing.'[25]

The continued fighting in Chechnya has led to further mine deployment along Russian borders. The *Moscow Kommersant* reported on 12 April 2000 that Russian military commanders had decided to mine the border between Russia and Georgia to stop the flow of personnel and supplies into Chechnya. The report claimed that twenty mountain passes would be mined along with dozens of pathways near the Argun Gorge. The report speculated that the deployment would be similar to that in Afghanistan with the use of helicopters to scatter the mines over the mountainous areas.[26]

Prior to the Russian advance into Chechnya in 1999, the Chechen Minister of Foreign Affairs Ilias Akhmadov, declared that he would sign the Ottawa Treaty as soon as his country was an internationally recognised sovereign state. The resumption of hostilities has changed the Chechen position. According to one Chechen government official, 'any questions pertaining to the anti-personnel mine ban, which may be put by a sovereign state during peacetime to the Chechen Republic Ichkeria, are unacceptable at the present time'.[27]

According to this same Chechen official the end of landmine deployment in his country is a very long way off:

> The question of banning the use of anti-personnel mines, which we put to some field commanders . . . caused unconcealed indignation. We considered it senseless to make further inquiries pertaining to this theme. The main conclusion made by our representatives is that mines will not be discarded from general military strategy by either the Russian army or the Chechen detachments.[28]

VIGNETTE 7: Who's Who

ICRC (International Committee of the Red Cross)

The ICRC was founded in 1863, after a Swiss citizen, Jean-Henri Dunant, became involved in tending thousands of wounded soldiers during the War of Italian Unification in 1859. Based on that experience, he suggested relief societies could be formed out of qualified volunteers willing to care for war wounded. He also suggested international conventions might be able to set out principles for the treatment of war wounded, and his writings became the basis for the Geneva Conventions. The ICRC currently operates in more than fifty countries. It has been actively involved in both the political and legal campaign to ban landmines as well as providing medical aid and mine awareness education in mine-affected countries. Based in Geneva, the ICRC is funded by governments, supranational organisations such as the European Union, public sources, National Red Cross and Red Crescent societies, as well as private donors. Its mission statement is as follows:

> The International Committee of the Red Cross (ICRC) is an impartial, neutral and independent organisation whose exclusively humanitarian mission is to protect the lives and dignity of victims of war and internal violence and to provide them with assistance. It directs and coordinates the international relief activities conducted by the Movement in situations of conflict. It also endeavours to prevent suffering by promoting and strengthening humanitarian law and universal humanitarian principles.

UN (United Nations)

The United Nations plays a significant part in 'mine action' (demining, mine awareness activities and victims assistance) around the world. The UN has set up many Mine Action Centres (MACs) that have subsequently been handed over to the countries' national authorities. However, the UN is still running programmes in such countries as Afghanistan and Kosovo. The UN also develops, reviews and updates international technical and safety standards for humanitarian demining operations. At the end of 1998, around thirty countries were receiving various levels of UN technical assistance, ranging from mine awareness programmes to assessment missions. The United Nations Mine Action Service (UNMAS) was created as the coordinating body for

Afghanistan, July 1994 (*photograph © Sean Sutton*).

the mine-related activities of eleven UN departments and agencies. UNMAS also describes itself as taking 'a lead role in developing materials which stigmatise the use of landmines and support a global ban'.

MAG (Mines Advisory Group)

The Mines Advisory Group began its first demining operation in northern Iraq in 1992. The organisation was founded by Rae McGrath, who was instrumental in setting up the first wide-scale United Nations mine clearance operation in Afghanistan. Under the directorship of Lou McGrath, MAG is now registered as a charitable company in the UK. It currently operates in Angola, Vietnam, Azerbaijan, Cambodia, Laos, Kosovo, northern Iraq and southern Sudan. It is also surveying new regions. MAG is funded by private donors, companies and charities as well as European governments, the European Union, various UN departments and the Diana, Princess of Wales, Memorial Fund. MAG was one of the six founding groups of the International Campaign to Ban Landmines.

The HALO Trust (Hazardous Areas Life-Support Organisation)

The HALO Trust was established in 1988. It is registered in Britain as a charity and in the United States as a not-for-profit organisation. HALO describes itself as a 'non-political, non-religious, non-governmental organisation' that 'specialises in the removal of the debris of war'. HALO operates in Afghanistan, Cambodia, Angola, Mozambique, southern Sudan, Somaliland, Eritrea, Ethiopia, Abkhazia and the Transcaucasus enclave of Nagorno Karabakh and Chechnya. It is also surveying new regions. HALO has divorced itself from other non-governmental organisations and demining agencies by refusing to become politically involved in the campaign to ban landmines and by declaring it 'is not distracted by involvement in campaigns and conferences'. HALO is funded by private donors and the governments of Ireland, Germany, the Netherlands, UK, Canada, Japan, USA and the Swiss Foundation Pro Victimis.

Handicap International

Handicap International was established in France in 1982. It provides rehabilitative care and socioeconomic development for people living in war-torn or chronically poor countries. Handicap staff include prosthetists, physical and psychological therapists, health-care professionals, agronomists, architects and engineers. Handicap has more than 160 projects underway around the world. It was one of the six founding groups of the International Campaign to Ban Landmines. Handicap claims that the rights of landmine victims are largely ignored and that the Ottawa Treaty has done little to improve the plight of victims and their families.

8

Desert Storms

THE Middle East is a theatre of war. Arab nation fights Arab nation. Fundamentalist Muslim states are pitched against moderate Muslim states. Traditional monarchies clash with secular republics. Petrodollars divide the rich from the poor. And in the middle lies Israel. The collapse of the Ottoman Empire in the aftermath of the Great War saw the region carved up into new states: Transjordan, Syria, Lebanon and Iraq emerged, along with the promise of a new Jewish homeland. The map had been redrawn, new boundaries appeared, new enmities created. In the vast desert expanses, where no natural boundary existed, man-made borders were delineated. Tensions within the region have also been exacerbated by its geographic position, standing as it does at the crossroads between Europe, Asia and Africa, and by the discovery of oil, which made the Middle East critical to the world's major economies. A roll call of the region's conflicts includes civil wars, religious wars, insurgencies and invasions. Vast expanses of land had to be defended along with small towns and villages. It was the ideal environment for the landmine – a zone of conflict with artificially created boundaries offering little natural terrain for defensive positions. In the fifty years from Rommel's Devil's Garden of El Alamein to the carnage of Iraqi Kurdistan, the Middle East became a patchwork of minefields.

The birth of Israel

Ever since the United Nations Palestine Commission recommended the creation of Jewish and Arab successor states in 1947, the Middle East has witnessed continuous cycles of invasion, occupation and withdrawal. As soon as the state of Israel was declared in May 1948, troops from Egypt, Transjordan and Syria entered Palestine with a further Trans Jordanian presence on the Arab West Bank. Israel promptly retaliated by occupying lands allocated to the Arabs. In 1955 Israeli troops entered the Egyptian Gaza Strip, whereupon Egypt responded by blockading Israel's new port of Elat in the Gulf of Aqaba, setting up a combined military command in the area with Jordan and Syria. Meanwhile, Egypt had nationalised the Suez Canal, provoking strong reaction from the French and the British. After secret talks with both countries Israel launched an attack on the whole of the Sinai Peninsula on 29 October 1956. Knowing that the Israelis' key weapon was the tank, the Arab forces defended their positions with barrier minefields. Though not effective enough to defend their territory against a well-marshalled Israeli tank assault, the Arab minefields did inflict severe losses on the invading forces. An entire company of Israeli armoured vehicles was destroyed in the battle for Alm Agelia when the Israelis were caught in an Egyptian minefield at Um Katef. The vehicles that did manage to avoid the mines were slowed down sufficiently to be picked off by anti-tank fire. During the same campaign a Palestinian brigade inflicted grievous damage to a combat group of Israeli tanks by protecting its position at Khan Yunis with plastic mines. Without the time to detect non-metallic mines the Israeli tanks had to drive straight through the minefield and accept the losses.

In 1967 Israel launched what it called a 'preventative war' in response to the build-up of Egyptian forces in Sinai and a renewed blockade in the Gulf of Aqaba. Within six days Israel's troops had taken the West Bank, Old Jerusalem, the Golan Heights, the Gaza Strip and Sinai. To this day, the Golan is still contaminated by the defensive minefields laid by Jordanian, Egyptian and Syrian troops prior to the onset of the Six-Day War and subsequent Israeli mining of key installations such as military bases, water stations and pipelines and electricity plants. The International Campaign to Ban Landmines has reported that a 'major danger in the Golan is the fact that many minefields are not marked or fenced and are thus easily entered by mistake'.[1]

The Golan saw further fighting during the Yom Kippur, or the October War, of 1973. In an ultimately unsuccessful attempt by Arab troops to reclaim lost territory, an attacking Syrian force breached an Israeli minefield on the Golan with a line of four or five tanks with flails exploding before them. However, as the war turned in the Israelis' favour, an Egyptian armoured brigade was destroyed when the Israelis forced it into a minefield. The Egyptian 25th Armoured Brigade of nearly 100 tanks was attempting a surprise attack along the flank of the Israeli position. The Egyptians were spotted, the Israelis counter-attacked and drove the enemy on to a defensive minefield. The Egyptians had been caught between a barrage of anti-tank guns and a minefield. They lost eighty-six tanks and every single armoured-personnel carrier.

Enter Saddam

Since Saddam Hussein took the reins of office on 16 July 1979, Iraq has been at war with Iran and Kuwait, and has experienced a Kurdish uprising in the north and a Shiite uprising in the south. This amounts to two decades of conflict, which have left over a million dead, the country's economy in ruins and its soil contaminated with landmines. Relations between Iraq and Iran have been strained ever since the British and the French redrew the map of the Middle East after 1918. The very process of partitioning created a problem. The Shatt al-Arab river, which is the confluence of the Tigris and the Euphrates, marks the southern border between Iraq and Iran. For most of the twentieth century the exact point of the boundary was disputed, with Iran claiming that the frontier point was the middle of the river, while Iraq argued that the border was the east bank, which put the waterway entirely within Iraqi territory.

Relations between the two countries deteriorated in 1961 when Iran began assisting Kurdish rebels in northern Iraq. Finally, in 1975, a deal was struck with Iraq accepting Iran's claim on half of the Shatt al-Arab in exchange for Iran dropping their support for the Kurds. The deal also contained one additional, and ultimately crucial, clause to prohibit the harbouring of any opposition movement against the prevailing regime in either country. The Iranians demanded that Iraq expel the Ayatollah Khomeini who'd lived in exile there since 1965. His expulsion served only to provide Khomeni with the means eventually to overthrow the shah while also increasing his enmity towards the Iraqis. It took Khomeini only six months to orchestrate the Iranian revolution. The shah fled the country on 16 January 1979 and on 11 February Khomeini proclaimed the Islamic republic. He wasted no time in inciting Iraqi Shiites to revolt.

The ensuing crisis in Iraq paved the way for the most ruthless, hard-line member of the government to take centre stage. Saddam Hussein, then vice-president, persuaded the president, Hasan al-Bakr, to resign, and immediately took office. Saddam killed several high-profile Shiites in a series of public executions and quickly established a brutal new regime in Iraq. He emerged as the only Arab leader with the power to defend the region from revolutionary Shiite fundamentalism and, with the support of the emir of Kuwait and the king of Saudi Arabia, he proceeded on a campaign to overthrow Khomeini, recover the entire Shatt al-Arab river and also to annex Khuzestan, the Arabic-speaking province that contains much of Iran's oil reserves.

In September 1980 Saddam Hussein's army stormed into Iran. It was the beginning of an eight-year conflict that would cost millions of lives. The early Iraqi successes were quickly reversed by the Iranians and for many years Saddam's generals fought a defensive war behind massive barrier minefields based upon Soviet warfare doctrines. The Iraqis continued to defend against increasingly exhausted Iranian offensives. Hundreds of thousands of Iranian Shiites volunteered for the Revolutionary Guard, which acted as little more than human waves pouring into the Iraqi minefields in much the same way as the soldiers of the Great War went over the top on the Western Front. The war with Iran convinced Iraqi military strategists that dense fortifications comprising massive minefields backed up by heavy artillery barrages were the key to defending desert terrain. This had been an extremely effective strategy against the Iranian infantry and the Iraqis would try to replicate these defences again a decade later, this time in an attempt to keep armies from around the world at bay.

The Gulf War

The war with Iran had left Iraq with a foreign debt of around $80 billion, which the neighbouring Gulf States, despite declarations of support at the outset of the war, were not prepared to write off. Relationships between Iraq and Kuwait soon disintegrated. Iraq wanted to renegotiate a loan it had received from Kuwait during the war with Iran in the 1980s – Kuwait refused. Iraq asked Kuwait to cut back on its oil production, which was keeping prices down – Kuwait refused. Iraq demanded that Kuwait stop drilling in a disputed oilfield on the border – Kuwait refused. And so, within weeks of the formal ending of the Cold War in July 1990, the new world order was put to the test when the Iraqi army invaded Kuwait. It took only a few hours for Saddam to proclaim that a new Provisional Revolutionary Government had taken power. In a show of post-Cold War solidarity US Secretary of State James Baker and Soviet Foreign Minister Eduard Shevardnadze issued a joint statement condemning Iraq.

Within days of the Iraqi invasion, troops from the United States, Egypt, Syria, Morocco, Pakistan, Bahrain, Oman, Qatar and the United Arab Emirates had arrived on Saudi Arabian soil. American and British combat aircraft defended Saudi airspace. Saudi Arabia was persuaded to allow non-Islamic troops on its soil when presented with spy satellite pictures of Iraqi troops massed on the border with Kuwait. The British and Americans already had warships stationed in the Gulf and as in Korea forty years earlier, the United Nations appointed an American, General Norman Schwarzkopf, to lead the coalition forces. Saddam attempted to turn the conflict into an Arab crusade and to link any withdrawal from Kuwait to an Israeli retreat from the Occupied Territories. He even settled his differences with Iran. Meanwhile, United Nations Resolution 678 established a deadline of 15 January 1991 for Iraq to withdraw from Kuwait. In a last-ditch attempt to avoid war, the UN Security Council imposed economic sanctions on Iraq that were policed by a naval blockade consisting of US, British, Australian and Western European Union ships. Iraq faced a stark choice – leave Kuwait or fight. Saddam dug in and prepared to fight the 'mother of battles'.

There are no natural barriers along the Iraq–Kuwait border. During the six months between the initial invasion and the commencement of Operation Desert Storm (the name given to the combined coalition offensive against Saddam), the Iraqis laid extensive desert minefields similar to those laid by the Germans in the North African campaign in World War II. Most of the mines were buried in regular patterns and were clearly fenced. An Iraqi military intelligence officer attached to a Divisional Engineer Unit spoke of the defensive minefield laid to defend northern Iraq:

For four months before the coalition invasion, from September 1990 I think, we were involved in building a defensive barrier in the triangle formed by the Syrian and Turkish borders. It was an extremely large-scale operation – eight divisions were moved into the front and each began preparing minefields to protect its positions

. . . for four months we laid mines throughout the front, every day, there simply weren't enough military trucks to bring them from the stores in Mosul so civilian vehicles were used as well.[2]

The minefields were built along classic Soviet defensive warfare lines. Millions of mines were buried as the nucleus of the barrier that was augmented at the front by fire trenches and anti-tank ditches. Behind the mines were the direct and indirect fire weapons. A second layer of this formation was established behind the first and the defensive line was christened 'the Saddam Line' by the Allies. Iraq's defence depended upon bringing its huge firepower to bear on coalition forces while they were slowed down in the minefields. They structured this defence in layers. The first line consisted of conscripted units with better quality units positioned further northwards and the elite Republican Guard bringing up the rear. The idea behind this formation was that any breach of the forward defensive positions by the coalition forces would be met by more experienced Iraqi armoured units. Along the coastline, the Iraqis defended the beaches with a series of electric underwater cables connected to mines in the shallow waters with wire and further landmines buried along the narrow strip between the beach and the coast road. From the outset, Iraqi landmines and sea mines were a crucial factor in influencing the Allied strategy. Coalition planners had identified three options for entering Kuwait: a direct attack across the Saudi Arabia–Kuwait border, an amphibious landing on the Kuwait coast, or an advance into southern Iraq, before heading eastwards into Kuwait. The Iraqi landmines and fortifications on the southern Kuwaiti border and the off-shore mines persuaded the coalition to choose the third option, which involved going around the Iraqi defences as opposed to going through them. General Schwarzkopf called it the 'Hail Mary play'.

Desert shield

Operation Desert Storm began at 3 a.m. on 17 January 1991. Allied planes started by attacking anti-aircraft defences, the Iraqi air force on the ground and command and communication centres. The air offensive was designed to weaken Iraqi defences to the point where coalition casualties in the eventual ground invasion would be minimal. This included British raids to drop a runway-denial system on Iraqi airfields. The system uses a mixture of bombs to crater the runways with mines that have timers and anti-disturbance fuses to hinder repair. American B52s were also used to drop a number of bombs in an attempt to detonate mines but these had 'little impact on minefields'.[3] During this time the Royal Navy attempted to clear the Gulf waters of mines. The Iraqis had mined the northern waters to an extent that the only two coalition warship casualties of the war were due to sea mines.

The ground offensive began on 24 February 1991. Five years before the onset of the Gulf War, Lieutenant-Colonel C.E.E. Sloan RE wrote that positional defence 'is extremely expensive in personnel and equipment, such that reserves are at a minimum, unable to reinforce those areas under greatest threat or to react to an unexpected enemy action. If sufficient resources are available in strength to dominate the area being defended, positional defence can be extremely effective. But few countries have the forces to fully protect all likely enemy approaches and objectives.'[4] He added that 'this form of positional defence produced "Maginot Line Mentality" which causes the defender to believe he simply has to construct a strong perimeter position, well protected, with the maximum of troops in prepared trenches and bunkers. Any attempt to breach this forward line will, of course, be repelled by firepower brought to bear on the selected killing ground. Sadly, history is full of impregnable fortifications being overrun or bypassed.'[5] Five years later, the coalition forces overran and bypassed the Saddam Line.

The key operation in the ground campaign was VII Corps' attack on the Republican Guard, which consisted of two tank and one mechanised division equipped with the most sophisticated weaponry at Iraq's disposal. The Republican Guard was reinforced by three regular army tank divisions and together this was to be the force that was to hunt and destroy coalition forces attempting to breach the defensive barrier. The Iraqi heavy divisions were positioned on the western edge of the mine-field and so precluded a simple outflanking by the Allies. Accordingly, the coalition plan was to launch an attack through the last sector of the minefield with a simultaneous manoeuvre around the flanks. The success of VII Corps' mission depended on the speed with which the minefield could be breached. This was to be the biggest breaching operation the US Army had conducted since the Korean War. The Allied strategists had been working on a formula that a massive two-hour artillery barrage was required before proceeding to breach the minefield. In the event, in thirty minutes more ordnance was dropped on the Iraqis than the Eighth Army had fired on Rommel at El Alamein.[6]

The onslaught all but destroyed the defensive units. What little defensive fire was encountered was poorly directed and breaching the minefield at the designated entry point into Iraq proved to be relatively straightforward. United States' reconnaissance teams were airlifted over Iraqi positions to ambush counterattacks while bulldozers ploughed through the minefields. The bulldozers were followed by tanks to defend the first breaches that in turn were followed by the combat engineers who fired 200-yard-long, high-explosive cord, known as 'snakes', which detonated mines and cut through barbed wire. A further wave of engineers then moved in on foot to mark the cleared lanes. Within eighty minutes, the armoured bulldozers of the 1st Mechanised Infantry Division, known as 'the Big Red One', had opened up sixteen lanes for the US cavalry units to push through. The lanes were indicated by tape and massive red and blue boards often marked with the words, 'WELCOME TO IRAQ, COURTESY OF THE BIG RED ONE'.

The static nature of the minefield-based defence strategy employed by the Iraqis meant that the coalition forces had the advantage of knowing exactly where the enemy's installations were positioned. Coalition artillery batteries used the 'shoot and scoot' tactic where they would move up quickly towards the barrier minefield so as to have their target in range, fire, and then quickly retreat out of range. Despite the fact that the Iraqi army offered little resistance and no protection to the minefields, the mines did cause coalition casualties. USMC 6 Division lost eleven vehicles, seven of which were tanks, and fourteen troops were injured.[7] The only relative success of the barrier minefield was in delaying the Arab Joint Forces Command long enough for Iraqi artillery to start raining fire down on them. Again, the weeks of aerial bombardment had greatly reduced Iraqi firepower and despite the delay there wasn't a single direct hit on an Egyptian tank. In one afternoon, the Egyptians breached the most difficult part of the Iraqi minefield and destroyed virtually an entire Iraqi division.

The way that the military dominance of the coalition was able to negate the impact of Iraqi minefields once again brought into question the contribution of the landmine in modern-day warfare. Those who argue in favour of the military usefulness of anti-personnel mines say that the mining of the beaches by the Iraqis prevented an amphibious landing by the Allies and that remotely delivered mines on the flanks of advancing coalition forces helped deter any Iraqi counterattacks. Essentially, a minefield is only as good as the defensive cover it is given, and in the Gulf War such cover was virtually non-existent: 'They [fixed defences] have often been of value, but as has often been demonstrated in history, their weakness is that a determined enemy, given sufficient time and study, can always overcome them.'[8]

Flails, rollers, ploughs, explosives–filled hoses and fuel–air explosives have all been used to clear channels through barrier minefields. In the Gulf War the coalition forces took less than two hours to breach a minefield of some nine million mines. As for Allied mine deployment in the Gulf War, one senior US Army general asked, 'What the hell is the use of sowing all this if you're going to move through it . . . We have many examples of our own young warriors trapped by their own minefields.'[9] The coalition forces used remotely delivered mines to close the gaps they had breached in the Iraqi minefield to slow down the withdrawal of Iraqi troops. In fact, the retreating Iraqi Republican Guard breached the minefields as quickly as the advancing coalition forces had done. Detractors argue that that these minefield systems actually reduced the manoeuvrability of their own troops. Once again Desert Storm called into question the strategic value of the remotely delivered mine systems that had such a negative effect on the Americans in Vietnam and the Russians in Afghanistan. The commander-in-chief of the coalition forces, General Norman Schwarzkopf, was one of the senior US officers who later signed an open letter to President Clinton claiming that a landmine ban would not undermine the military effectiveness or safety of US or other countries' armed forces.

After the storm

In the first meeting between military commanders of both sides after the cease-fire, in a small airstrip at Safwan inside Iraq, Schwarzkopf demanded that the Iraqis hand over all minefield maps. However, while it transpired that the Iraqi maps were quite accurate, in the weeks following the Iraqi surrender the number of casualties from landmine incidents actually started to rise. During the first six months following the liberation of Kuwait, seventy coalition soldiers were killed by landmines. Only 150 coalition soldiers had been killed in the actual conflict. The commander of the British forces in Desert Storm, General Sir Peter de la Billière, wrote of his concerns about the minefields: 'I banned all mine-clearance operations unless specifically approved by me. I also put out detailed instructions across the whole theatre telling commanders to ensure that no deaths were incurred through negligence or stupidity and to make everyone aware, right down to the lowest level, that death might be lurking beneath every grain of sand.'[10]

Estimates as to how many mines were laid in Kuwait during the Gulf War range from five to seven million. The vast majority were buried by the Iraqis in the massive protective minefields while the Allies dropped several hundred thousand from the air. The government of Kuwait paid commercial contractors in conjunction with foreign troops to clear the country of unexploded ordnance and landmines. The private companies came from the USA, the UK and France. The troops were from Egypt, Pakistan, Turkey and Bangladesh. The whole operation cost the Kuwaiti government an estimated US $700 million – the most expensive mine-clearance operation ever undertaken. It was also very dangerous. During the clear-up, eighty-four deminers were killed, including the five mine experts employed by the Kuwaiti military. It was this operation that's generally seen as having given birth to the commercial demining industry. The money-making potential of demining soon became apparent – as did the dangers:

> If 5–7 million mines in Kuwait were worth $700 million, how much more could be made from the reported 80–110 million mines in sixty-four other countries? ... In addition to corporations, operations in the Gulf also resulted in a large number of expatriates looking for highly paid employment in other mine-affected countries. Some of these individuals were explosive ordnance disposal specialists, but others had little specialised training. And if their approach to demining was of questionable effectiveness in Kuwait, there was no doubt that it was even less well suited to the circumstances faced by a majority of mine-affected countries.[11]

The quality of much of the work was questionable. Many areas had to be recleared after inspections and despite the extensive post-war demining programme, landmines are still being found in coastal and desert areas in Kuwait. However problematic the clearance programme may have been, many still feel that the lessons learned in Kuwait have proved to be invaluable to humanitarian demining operations around the world. One of the former military officers working on the programme in Kuwait was Steve Wilson, now director of the Mines Advisory Group in Southeast Asia.

> I think it will go down in history as one of the biggest demining operations conducted by a civilian entity. All ex-military guys [former army bomb disposal experts] were brought together to face a big task in that there was a great deal of land in Kuwait which was basically mined in the tradition of NATO patterns. At one stage there were about 250 expats there and we learned the lessons there . . . The mistakes were made, and there were some pretty horrific mistakes. Basically the standards were defined there and built upon since, but that was the turning point. Initially what we tried to do was transpose military demining rules and regulations, drills and procedures – but that was just the starting point. There was a lot of work to be done in improving the techniques because we were clearing whole minefields. It wasn't a military approach to the problem – it was humanitarian because we had to clear all the mines. That was the difference. But it was a steep learning curve and quite painful at times.

Baghdad strikes back

Kuwait may have been liberated but Saddam Hussein was still firmly in place as the leader of Iraq. In the heady days following the Allied victory, George Bush responded to criticism that the war had not succeeded in removing Saddam from office by remarking that he believed that the Iraqis themselves would do that particular job. The Kurds in the north and the Shiites in the south, assuming that Saddam's military power had been destroyed, took up the challenge. It proved to be a big mistake. The Kurds in particular would suffer at the hands of Saddam's military machine not only in battle but also in the reprisals that followed.

The Kurds have lived in the same mountain region for 2,000 years yet have never lived as one nation. Their origins are unknown but the ferocity with which they have fought each other, as well as the governments of the region they occupy, is the stuff of legend. The Kurds once found themselves living in the territory that was divided by the frontier between Persia and the Ottoman Empire and as the twentieth century drew to a close they were caught in the middle of another battle to control the Middle East. The Kurds of today live in various different countries, including Iraq, Iran, Syria, Turkey, Lebanon, Azerbaijan and Armenia. A dispute between any of these countries puts the Kurds in the front line. In the twentieth century living in the front line meant living on a minefield and the Kurds of northern Iraq in particular are among the world's most mine-affected people. As their struggle for independence enters its third millennium many Kurds believe the landmine now represents one of the biggest obstacles faced by their people. The Kurdish author, Hussain Arif, wrote in 1991: 'We have always had our dream: freedom, self-determination, a voice in our future – this is the Kurdish dream. We have come so close but so many things conspire against us, and now these mines, this blight in our fields – they will surely kill our dream, even if we are successful in all our other efforts.'[12]

Northern Iraq has suffered three phases of extensive mine laying: the war with Iran, the Gulf War, and two decades of internal conflict. As the war with Iran was coming to an end the Iraqi army returned to Kurdistan for an operation that became known as 'Anfal'. The term, taken from the Koran, means 'the spoils' taken from infidels in war. The campaign resulted in the disappearance and slaughter of tens of thousands of Kurds as well as the looting and destruction of scores of towns and villages. During Anfal, Iraqi soldiers buried mines along roads, around power lines, in agricultural land, former army barracks and extensively in villages vacated by Kurds. They embarked on a scorched earth campaign, used chemical weapons and jailed thousands of women, children and the elderly. Those not captured or killed fled in their tens of thousands to Iran or Turkey.

It's hardly surprising therefore that when President George Bush encouraged the Iraqi people to rebel against Saddam's regime, the Kurds responded. In March 1991 the Kurdish uprising began with immediate success. It looked for a while as if the uprising would succeed as towns and cities fell to the rebels but then the Republican Guard arrived. With no sign of international help Kurdish civilians fled for their lives from Saddam's most feared fighting force. An estimated one million Kurds reached Iran while a further 450,000 reached Turkey. Ultimately it was television pictures of starving Kurdish refugees on the snow-covered mountains of Turkey that forced the Allies to intervene. Thirty thousand US, French and British troops established a safe haven in northern Iraq so that the Kurds could return from exile without fear of reprisal. Further protection was offered by the no-fly zone above the 36th parallel.

The Allied intervention persuaded thousands of Kurds to return to their villages and towns, only to induce another wave of carnage, this time caused by landmines buried by the retreating Iraqi army or as part of the main fronts in the Iran–Iraq conflict. One area of particular strategic importance during the Iran–Iraq war was the Derband Gorge. This former front line is now home to returnees and mine accidents are commonplace. The Derband minefield is particularly dangerous because of the presence of booby traps, consisting of tripwires connected to 20-litre steel drums containing napalm. Reports also tell of tripwires attached to bounding mines. An unsuspecting victim would thus be exposed to a combination of burning napalm and shrapnel.

Civilian landmine accidents began to occur as soon as the Iraqi army withdrew from northern Iraq in 1991. So desperate were the Kurds to return to their home towns and villages that many took on the role of amateur mine clearers – usually with disastrous consequences.

> One disturbing practice, which is increasingly common within Kurdistan, is the burning of minefields in the belief that this will destroy the mines. The strategy is usually employed on mined grazing land, particularly mountain pasture, and, to a lesser extent, on arable land ... While some devices were detonated by heat or rendered inoperable by burning, many were either made unstable or sustained no damage at all. The obvious danger of this practice is that people may be encouraged to believe that the ground is safe for use after burning. In fact, in some instances it may actually prove more dangerous following this treatment. Burning certainly promotes increased vegetation growth, making sighting of mines more difficult.[13]

Other mine clearance techniques reported in northern Iraq included driving herds of animals over suspected areas and using shotgun and rifle fire to blow up mines. Some estimates claim that one in five of all landmine casualties in Kurdistan have occurred as a direct consequence of firing at landmines. In some cases the marksman is the victim – usually because he underestimates the effective range of the mine – but third parties are often maimed because of the lack of any warning system. The only agency currently conducting humanitarian mine clearance in the area is the United Kingdom-based Mines Advisory Group which began demining in northern Iraq in 1992. These operations continue despite the Iraqi government's view that they are subversive activities and fail 'to respect Iraq's territorial integrity and sovereignty'.[14] MAG, however, has no intention of leaving. Lou McGrath says: 'When Saddam chased them [the Kurds] into the mountains his troops went around and mined all the villages so the problem in the country is absolutely massive. We've been there since 1992 and we've made some great inroads but the problem is going to take several years to solve.'

MAG's task is not made any easier by the fact that there's continued conflict in the area. Following the end of the Gulf War in 1991, northern Iraq has been under the nominative control of the Kurdish Regional Government. This body has no formal diplomatic recognition and faction fighting in the region continues to flare up sporadically. The Kurdistan Workers Party (PKK) has launched a series of hit-and-run attacks into Turkey resulting in Turkish military retaliation. There have been numerous stories that the PKK is still using anti-personnel landmines to this day. Voice of Iraqi Kurdistan Radio carried a report on 17 July 1999 that the PKK had buried anti-personnel mines along roadsides in the Chaman border area, which resulted in serious injury to a local civilian. Such reports are supported by Turkish military claims that it has seized over 15,000 landmines from PKK bases between 1994 and 1999. Another serious and tragic setback for the demining effort in northern Iraq was the murder of a member of the United Nations' mine programme. New Zealander Nicholas Speight was killed when gunmen opened fire from a taxi near Irbil airport. All this occurs against the backdrop of Saddam Hussein's speeches claiming that deminers' lives are under threat.[15] Despite the obvious dangers and the recurrence of internal conflict, the director of the Mines Advisory Group, Lou McGrath, believes that his organisation has provided at least one stable structure in an otherwise highly volatile region:

I think the objective of our group is to help civilian populations. There are many different Kurdish groups within northern Iraq who obviously have opposing views and fight amongst themselves. I think what we've always tried to do is make them recognise that we work with all sides regardless. We obviously are aware of Saddam's threats. All our staff are aware of that and we feel that if we don't carry out this work then what future or hope have the Kurdish children. Some of the areas in which we work can be dangerous and we are threatened but our concern is for the civilian population.

According to the International Campaign to Ban Landmines, Iraq remains both a producer and exporter of anti-personnel landmines. The United States Defence Intelligence Agency found that Iraqi stocks contained not only domestically produced weapons but imported mines from Belgium, Canada, Chile, China, Egypt, France, Italy, Romania, Singapore, the former Soviet Union and the United States.[16] In October 1992, Human Rights Watch published a report entitled *Hidden Death: Land Mines and Civilian Casualties in Iraqi Kurdistan*. The report's author, the Nobel Peace Prize co-laureate, Rae McGrath, wrote that among the most common mines found in the area were the Italian-made Valmara 69 and the VS-50, both manufactured by Valsella Meccanotecnica SpA. Seven executives of the Brescia-based company were tried and convicted of illegally exporting nine million landmines to Iraq between 1982 and 1985. Valsella was unable to secure a licence to export the landmines directly to Iraq, so it formed a new company in Singapore, which was not subject to any export ban, to take delivery of the weapons before re-exporting them to the Middle East. The company's defence at the trial claimed that the Italian government was fully aware that the mines were eventually destined for Iraq. According to a United States State Department report 'it is possible to find almost every variety of landmine manufactured around the world in Iraq'.[17] Rae McGrath argues that the ready supply of landmines on the international market has allowed Saddam's regime to continue its campaign of terror against the Kurds indefinitely:

> Part of the problem lies in the fact that, since vast quantities of landmines were readily available, vast quantities were sown, far in excess of the needs of military strategy . . . It is a reasonable conclusion that the Iraqi army laid and abandoned these millions of mines to make large areas of Kurdistan unusable for all time. Though several mined areas were fenced, warning markings were only deployed in isolated cases. The omission of warnings is unconscionable as they would not have vitiated any legitimate military purpose of the mine fields in the slightest.[18]

The statistics alone appear to prove McGrath to be right. Although Iraq relinquished maps and records of minefields laid in Kuwait as one of the conditions of surrender following the Gulf War, they have not supplied any information about mine laying in the north. In the meantime in northern Iraq nearly 3,000 people have been killed, and a further 5,000 have been maimed by mines and unexploded ordnance.

After the sixth day

Minefields provide a useful guide to the geography of the wars staged in the deserts of the Middle East. Landmines are the war historians' fossils. Anyone brave enough to wander into these areas could tell who fought whom and when just by the live explosive left in the ground. But unlike cenotaphs and statues, these memorials leave visitors with permanent reminders of bygone battles. Jerry White, a co-founder and director of the Landmines Survivors Network is a casualty of a battle fought when he was a baby living on the other side of the world. Nearly seventeen years after the end of the Six-Day War Jerry travelled to Israel on a break from his studies. During the trip he went hiking in the Golan with two friends.

It was a sunny day in April 1984 and we had packed up our camp and were heading down the side of a picturesque hillside in northern Israel. And suddenly boom, everything exploded around me with all the dirt and smoke and we thought we were under some sort of terrorist attack. But as it turned out we were in a minefield and I had detonated a landmine that had ripped off my right foot immediately and blew open my left leg. So my friends had a choice of watching me bleed and die or summoning up the courage to carry me out of that minefield.

As Americans, we don't have mines in our country, it was a shock. I had no expectation or education about the issue or that I had been in an area that was heavily mined. As it turned out this was a horrible area that had been a stronghold in the 1967 Arab–Israeli war and was littered with every type of mine that was conceivable. So my two friends picked me up and proceeded to walk down the hill and took a path that was probably the most difficult way down the hillside in the hope that there would be less mines in this craggy, rocky area.

I think the moment of the injury is surreal and traumatic. There's something seared into my mind about what happened to me. So much so that even when I walk across a beautiful park in the United States . . . I will always remember the smell, the taste, the feeling, the pain of what happened when I suddenly stepped on the earth and it exploded. And to this day when I walk in a park or go hiking I always remember back and think that it was on a beautiful day like today on a nice grassy area that I was walking on that the earth exploded. So I never cross a park again without thinking about it at some level even in countries without minefields.

Epilogue

Wars are inevitable. All humanity can hope to achieve is to exert some form of control over the conflict, to curb man's capacity for carnage. Upon these principles, a complex web of treaties, proclamations, commissions, conventions and protocols has been spun into what is commonly known as international humanitarian law, and forms what is essentially a rulebook by which wars are to be fought. This somewhat bizarre notion of sanitising the slaughter is not new. Codes of chivalry operated across the battlefields of medieval Europe in a similar way to the samurai codes of Japan. A breach of the rules resulted in a loss of honour – a fate worse than defeat in battle.

Attempts to minimise the suffering to both soldier and civilian during times of war also go back many centuries. The use of poisons in battle, for example, has been considered unacceptable for hundreds of years, but the first real attempt to draw up a code of conduct for warfare can be traced back to a Swiss traveller in northern Italy in 1859. Jean-Henri Dunant watched from the hills around Castiglione as the French and Austrian armies slaughtered each other on the battlefield of Solferino. In his account of the scene, Dunant wrote of the 'new and frightful weapons at the disposal of the nations'. His response was to establish the Red Cross movement and the organisation has been at the forefront of efforts to 'civilise' warfare ever since. Following Dunant's lead the Swiss government hosted a meeting of sixteen of the world's most powerful nations eventually to sign what became known as the Geneva Convention. There was no policing mechanism to ensure that opposing armies complied with the regulations, nor was there punishment for non-compliance, but the Geneva Convention did put certain behaviour beyond the pale. Essentially the victims of war were to be treated humanely.

Geneva and later The Hague became the two cities that hosted a series of international conferences and conventions that would shape the future of global humanitarian law. Meetings at The Hague tended to concentrate on issues that governed the general conduct of war, such as the prohibition of certain weapons. Geneva Conventions, on the other hand, were primarily concerned with the legacies of wars staged immediately prior to the conference.

The Martens Clause in the introduction to the 1899 Hague Convention states that its aim is to control war with the 'laws of humanity and the dictates of the public conscience'. It was at the 1899 Hague International Peace Conference that a prohibition was placed on the use of the newly developed exploding, or 'dumdum', bullets that expanded on entering the body causing horrific wounds. Like the Ottawa Treaty nearly a century later, the two major military powers of the time (in the case of the Hague Declaration it was the United States and the United Kingdom) objected to the ban. In what could be a hopeful sign for the ICBL, this initial high-powered opposition soon gave way in the face of widespread opposition. Dumdum bullets were subsequently banned as part of customary international law. The extensive use of poison gas in the Great War led to the Geneva Protocol on Poisonous and Asphyxiating Gases in 1925. Regulations against chemical and bacteriological warfare were further strengthened in 1972 by the Biological Weapons Convention and in 1993 by the Chemical Weapons Convention.

International humanitarian law has been developed to minimise the suffering of civilians and combatants in warfare. It requires states to honour three principles during times of war: humanity, proportionality and discrimination. The principle of humanity is that no party, in any conflict, has an unlimited right to use weaponry against an opponent. In practical terms this prohibits the use of weapons that cause unnecessary suffering. Proportionality demands that the decision to go to war is a balanced response to another aggression and that the methods and weaponry deployed are proportionate to the primary objective of the conflict. In other words, military actions have to be balanced against the humanitarian consequences of those actions. Discrimination obliges combatants to distinguish between soldier and civilian. This is essentially a requirement to protect non-combatants in times of war.

The first principle, that of not causing unnecessary suffering, is the one that proves to be of the greatest difficulty for advocates of a landmine ban. Few soldiers would discriminate between landmines and high-velocity bullets or air-burst artillery shells, for example, in terms of weapons that cause unnecessary suffering or superfluous injury. The majority of landmine survivors would rather be amputees than be dead. The truth is that the landmine causes no more or less unnecessary suffering than other weapons.

Proportionality is also a problematic principle when considering anti-personnel landmines. Pro-ban campaigners point to the existence of unmarked minefields after the end of a conflict as a direct violation of the requirement only to use weapons as a means to an end. When the fighting ceases, guns are put away while landmines continue to kill and maim. The continued threat is deemed to be out of proportion to the original goal. A possible objection to this theory arises when the deployment of landmines has served a very real strategic purpose that no other weapon could have served. If an unmarked minefield protected a Cambodian village from the Khmer Rouge, or a community of Muslims from Serb paramilitaries, can the use of those landmines ever be deemed to be out of proportion to the threat otherwise presented? Also, international laws cannot stop threatened civilians from laying home-made mines. However, on the total scale of landmine use worldwide, the number used by the Cambodians and the Bosnian Muslims is relatively small. Even from a military point of view only, the principle of proportionality is useful for landmine ban campaigners. A Pentagon report finally admitted in 1992 that the use of landmines during the Vietnam War was more of a hindrance than of military benefit to US troops.[1] A number of UN soldiers were also killed by their own mines in Korea.

It is the principle of discrimination that truly sets the anti-personnel landmine apart from other conventional weapons in terms of inter-national humanitarian law. Victim-operated traps cannot distinguish between combatants and non-combatants for the simple reason that they are triggered by the victim not the opponent. The use of landmines is therefore a flagrant breach of the requirement to protect civilians in times of war. However, current international treaties regarding landmines are falling considerably short of banning landmines.

Is it actually possible to ban a weapon that's cheap and easy to make and that has formed a staple part of an army's arsenal for the best part of a century? That anti-personnel landmines represent a humanitarian catastrophe across large tracts of the world's poorest countries is beyond dispute, but the plausibility of a global prohibition on what is essentially a simple victim-operated trap is highly questionable. An additional problem for the pro-ban community is that many of those working to clear the world's minefields not only doubt the viability of a ban but consider the international campaign to be counterproductive in alleviating the suffering of communities whose lives are currently blighted by landmines. Wars will be fought, weapons will be used, and people will be killed and maimed. The only way to deal with the problem is to clear up the theatre of war when the fighting is over. So say the ban sceptics.

As discussed in Chapter 1, the deployment of anti-personnel landmines is addressed in international treaty law under the catchy title of the 1980 United Nations Convention on Prohibitions or Restrictions of the Use of Certain Conventional Weapons Which May Be Deemed to Be Excessively Injurious or to Have Indiscriminate Effects (CCW). The protocol in this convention that deals with the use of mines and booby traps is largely held to be useless by the anti-landmine lobby for its failure to regulate the use of mines in civil wars or internal disputes. Future wars are likely to continue to be sparked internally – along ethnic, nationalist and religious lines. World wars are no longer the main threat to global population. Civil wars, cross-border conflicts and 'low intensity' campaigns are now commonplace.

One of the reasons the landmine is still considered useful is because of the simplicity of the concept of the victim-operated trap. It is easy and quick to use, and one landmine can take the place of several soldiers at very little cost. Landmines have been used in many different ways for a variety of purposes. They were deployed in massive barrier minefields in World War II, in the Iran–Iraq war, the Gulf War and they are still buried in their thousands along the 38th parallel that separates North Korea from South Korea. They have been laid in small numbers by guerrilla forces intent on frightening and controlling civilian populations, and by the civilians themselves, desperate to save their families from would-be aggressors. In the Balkans individual mines have also been booby-trapped by Serb irregulars by attaching them to a myriad tripwires, switches and other complex wiring systems.

Developments in landmine technology are likely to keep the arms manufacturers one step ahead of ban campaigners, international legislators and treaties. Two areas of landmine design in particular offer great potential for manufacturers to beat the ban. Switching mechanisms, which incorporate the latest developments in sensor technology, undermine the fundamental argument that anti-personnel landmines do not discriminate between soldier and civilian. The argument, however, that switching mechanisms and sensors protect civilians doesn't take into account human or mechanical error. The use of lasers and the latest advances in telecommunications allow armies greater control over a landmine's target. In the past the greatest limitation of landmines with electronic sensors was the need for a power supply on the mine. Ironically, the high-profile campaign for a ban was used by the manufactures to their advantage. The batteries fitted to power electronic sensors eventually degrade, theoretically rendering the weapon 'safe' after a certain time. The United States is currently at the cutting edge of 'smart' mine technology and sceptics claim that it will sign the treaty once it has developed a weapon that is not banned under the terms of the convention. There is inevitably a failure rate with all new technology and campaigners argue that however small this rate, any percentage is totally unacceptable. Self-neutralising mines are inherently more problematic than self-destructing mines as deminers or civilians wouldn't be able to tell for certain that the weapons were safe just by looking at them.

Stigmatisation may prove to be more useful than any treaty. There have been serious questions as to whether Canada, the home of the mine ban treaty, is adhering to the spirit of its own initiative. Canada's arsenal still includes claymore mines that are buried in the ground and detonated by a soldier using an electronic trigger. They are generally used to protect military bases and are not banned under the Ottawa Treaty because they are not victim-operated. Remotely detonated mines are argued to be no different to a shotgun aimed and fired at someone when they are in range. However, the truth is that military boffins design their way around arms-control treaties. Customary international law is useful in ensuring parties comply with the spirit and not just the letter of treaties.

With its 'no exceptions, no reservations, no loopholes' mantra, the ICBL was aware of this pitfall from the outset. Where a particular mine lies in the 'dumb-smart' spectrum is a debate that could undermine a ban agreement. The debate over landmine technology also engenders suspicion of developed countries by developing countries. The Third World argues that international laws are biased towards those with the most technically sophisticated production capabilities.

Customary international law, a branch of international humanitarian law, is likely to be extremely important to the ICBL. Customary international law is essentially a body of uncodified principles that represents man's attempt to retain a semblance of civility in the theatre of war. It is potent because of its widespread acceptance as opposed to any formal structure. Because the law is generally applicable to all, it makes the use of anti-personnel landmines unacceptable whether a state is a party to a ban treaty or not. It is the stigmatisation of biological and chemical weapons as much as the body of international laws covering these types of warfare that helps to keep them off the battlefield. Landmine campaigners often voice their hopes that the landmine can be stigmatised in the same way that chemical and biological weapons have been. When a device is just too simple to ban, maybe the best chance of reducing the numbers of landmines in the ground is to revert to the days of chivalry. The ICBL has unashamedly blitzed a previously unsuspecting public with a barrage of images graphically illustrating what a landmine does to the human body. There has been a noticeable reduction in the number of countries producing, stockpiling and transferring conventional anti-personnel mines. Princess Diana's crusade, the Ottawa Treaty and the Nobel Peace Prize have all raised the general level of awareness about landmines. Governments, politicians and the general public now know something about the horrors of landmines. The real success of the international campaign has been to make the use of landmines unchivalrous. This is especially important in conflicts where public perception and international sympathy for the cause are key factors in dictating strategy. Even if it escapes the confines of a formal ban, the landmine has already been dishonoured.

Notes

Introduction

1 According to the International Campaign to Ban Landmines' *Landmine Monitor Report 2000* (p. 23), there were new landmine and unexploded ordnance victims in seventy-one countries in the period March 1999 to May 2000.

1: 'No Exceptions, No Reservations, No Loopholes'

1 US Defense Intelligence Agency, *Landmine Warfare: Trends and Projections* (1992).
2 *New Internationalist*, September 1997, p. 24
3 Asia Watch & Physicians for Human Rights, *Landmines in Cambodia: The Coward's War*, September, 1991, pp. 102–3.
4 Jody Williams and Steve Goose, 'The International Campaign to Ban Landmines', in *To Walk Without Fear: The Global Movement to Ban Landmines* (Ontario, Oxford University Press, Canada, 1998), p. 22.
5 E-mail to the authors, 25 April 2001.
6 *Sunday Telegraph*, 2 February 1997.
7 *New York Times*, 3 April 1996.
8 Robert Muller, 'Pentagon Proposal to Continue Landmine Use Denounced', 10 May 1996.
9 *Time*, 13 May 1996.
10 Cameron A. Maxwell, Robert J. Lawson and Brian W. Tomlin (eds), *To Walk Without Fear*, p. 165.
11 *Financial Times*, 22 May 1997.
12 *The Times*, 15 January 1997.

13 *Daily Mirror*, 16 January 1997.
14 Bruce Anderson, Spectator 15 February 1997.
15 *The Times*, 19 August 1997.
16 Williams and Goose, p. 41.
17 Declaration of the Brussels Conference on Anti-Personnel Landmines.
18 *The Times*, 19 August 1997.
19 *ibid*.
20 *Time*, 29 September 1997.
21 *International Herald Tribune*, 4 December 1997.
22 *ibid*.
23 *Daily Telegraph*, 18 September 1997.
24 *Guardian*, 25 October 1997.
25 *ibid*.
26 *International Herald Tribune*, 25 November 1997.
27 International Campaign to Ban Landmines, *Landmine Monitor Report 2000*, p. 3.
28 E-mail to the authors, 25 April 2001.
29 Edward Cummings, Geneva, Switzerland, 3 April 2001.

2: The Demon from the Trenches

1 For further reading, see William C. Schneck, *The Origins of Military Mines: Part 1*, Engineer (US Army Engineer School, Fort Leonard Wood, Missouri, July 1998), and Mike Croll, *The History of Landmines*, (London, Leo Cooper, 1998).
2 Croll, *The History of Landmines*, p. 9.
3 Eric Hobsbawm, *Age of Extremes: The Short Twentieth Century, 1914–1991* (London, Michael Joseph, 1994), p. 22.
4 J. A. S. Grenville, *The Collins History of the World in the Twentieth Century* (London, HarperCollins, 1994), p. 95.
5 Alfred William Lewis, *Wanderers in a Strange Land: The Story of Alfred William Lewis in the 1914–1918 War*, Local History Group of the Clevedon Civic Society, p. 35.
6 Rae McGrath, *Landmines and Unexploded Ordnance: A Resource Book* (London, Pluto Press, 2000), p. 3.
7 *Ibid.*, p. 1.
8 Bert Chaney, 'The First Tanks in Action, 15 September 1916', *The Faber Book of Reportage* (London, Faber and Faber, 1987), p. 465.
9 John Keegan, *The First World War* (London, Hutchinson, 1998), p. 442.
10 Major Charles Heyman, *Trends in Land Mine Warfare* (Coulsdon, Surrey, Jane's Information Group, 1995), p. 17.
11 International Campaign to Ban Landmines news report, 13 April 2001.
12 Lewis, *Wanderers in a Strange Land*, p. 33.

13 *Diary of G. A. Handford*, Imperial War Museum, London.

14 Croll, *The History of Landmines*, p. 37.

15 Anti-handling devices are still a matter of much debate as they can act like anti-personnel mines, but they are not covered by the Ottawa Treaty banning landmines.

16 Hobsbawm, *Age of Extremes*, p. 35.

17 Dr Chris Smith (ed.), *The Military Utility of Landmines*, Centre for Defence Studies, King's College, University of London, June 1996, p. 13.

18 Croll, *The History of Landmines*, p. 37.

19 Russel Stolfi in Ballistic Research Laboratories Report 1582, *Mine and Countermine in Recent History, 1914–1930* (Maryland, April 1972), p. 21.

20 McGrath, *Landmines and Unexploded Ordnance*, p. 5.

21 Stephen E. Ambrose, *Citizen Soldier* (Simon & Schuster, New York, 1997), pp. 143–4.

22 S. Brooks (ed.), *Montgomery and the Eighth Army* (London, The Bodley Head, 1991), p. 149.

23 Croll, in *The History of Landmines*, pp. 27–8, cites a type of pipe mine used by the Germans in World War I as probably the first operational device designed to wound rather than kill.

24 E-mail from Major William C. Schneck, 4 May 2001.

25 Alan Clark, *Barbarossa: The Russian–German Conflict 1941–45* (London, Phoenix Press, 2000), p. 30.

26 Paul Corell, *Hitler's War on Russia: The Story of the German Defeat in the East* (London, Harrap, 1964), pp. 235–6.

27 Clark, *Barbarossa*, p. 322.

28 J. N. Westwood, *Eastern Front: The Soviet–German War 1941–45* (London: Hamlyn, 1984), p. 152.

29 Clark, *Barbarossa*, p. 330.

30 Peter Teed, *Dictionary of 20th-Century History 1914–1990* (London, BCA, 1992), p. 257.

31 Janusz Piekalkiewicz, *Tank War: 1939–1945* (Blandford, Blandford Press, 1986), p. 134.

32 Teed, *Dictionary of 20th-Century History*, p. 257.

33 International Campaign to Ban Landmines, *Landmine Monitor Report 2000*, Human Rights Watch, 2000, p. 667.

34 Lieutenant-Colonel C. E. E. Sloan RE, *Mine Warfare on Land* (London, Brassey's 1986), p. 43.

35 Erwin Rommel, 'Blitzkrieg: German Breakthrough on the Meuse, 15 May 1940', in *The Faber Book of Reportage*, p. 528.

36 R. J. Hutchings, *The Private Diary of a Young Campaigner*, Imperial War Museum, London, pp. 12–13.

37 Robin Williams, *A Time in My Life*, Imperial War Museum, London, pp. 23–4.
38 McGrath, *Landmines and Unexploded Ordnance*, p. 5.
39 Clark, *Barbarossa*, p. 336.
40 McGrath, *Landmines and Unexploded Ordnance*, p. 5.
41 E-mail from Major William C. Schneck, 4 May 2001.
42 *Guardian*, 9 December 1997.
43 International Campaign to Ban Landmines, *Landmine Monitor Report 2000*. Human Rights Watch, 2000, p. 926.
44 Landmines Struggle Centre promotional material.
45 *Guardian*, 9 December 1997.

3: A New Front Line

1 J. A. S. Grenville, *The Collins History of the World in the Twentieth Century* (London, HarperCollins, 1994), p. 434.
2 Charles Messenger, *The Century of Warfare; Worldwide Conflict from 1900 to the Present Day* (London, BCA, 1993), p. 321.
3 International Campaign to Ban Landmines, *Landmine Monitor Report 2000*, p. 501.
4 Robert G. Gard, Jr, 'The Military Utility of Anti-Personnel Mines', in *To Walk Without Fear: The Global Movement to Band Landmines* (Ontario, Oxford University Press, Canada, 1998), p. 141.
5 MAG Vietnam briefing document, July 2000.
6 Rae McGrath, *Landmines: Legacy of Conflict*, Oxfam, 1994, p. 3.
7 Messenger, *The Century of Warfare*, p. 353.
8 The Arms Project & Physicians for Human Rights, *Landmines: A Deadly Legacy*, Human Rights Watch, New York, 1993, pp. 21–2.
9 *Victim Assistance: Thematic Report 2000*, Handicap International, September 2000, p. 68.
10 *The Cowards' War: Landmines in Vietnam*, Handicap International Belgique, 1991, p. 12.
11 *The Cowards' War*, p. 15.
12 International Campaign to Ban Landmines, *Landmine Monitor Report 2000*, p. 547.
13 Asia Watch & Physicians for Human Rights, *Landmines in Cambodia: The Coward's War*, Human Rights Watch, September 1991, p. 2.
14 International Campaign to Ban Landmines, *Landmine Monitor Report 2000*, p. 383.
15 Shawn Roberts and Jody Williams, *After the Guns Fall Silent: The Enduring Legacy of Landmines*, Vietnam Veterans of America Foundation, Washington, 1995, p. 120.

16 John Pilger, *Distant Voices* (London, Vintage, 1992), p. 176.

17 *Ibid.*, p. 178.

18 Roberts and Williams, *After the Guns Fall Silent*, pp. 121–2.

19 Pilger, *Distant Voices*, p. 231.

20 ICRC news report, 28 February 1996.

21 Asia Watch, *Landmines in Cambodia*, p. 40.

22 Pilger, *Distant Voices*, p. 191.

23 International Campaign to Ban Landmines, *Landmine Monitor Report 2000*, p. 383.

24 Archie Law, interview for *The Devil's Gardens* TV series, 2000.

25 International Campaign to Ban Landmines, *Landmine Monitor Report 2000*, p. 388.

26 *Ibid.*, p. 396.

27 *Ibid.*, p. 387.

28 Rae McGrath, *Landmines and Unexploded Ordnance: A Resource Book* (London, Pluto Press, 2000), p. 44.

29 *Lao*, Mines Advisory Group, May 1999.

30 United Nations, *Portfolio of Mine-related Projects*, October 2000.

31 International Campaign to Ban Landmines, *Landmine Monitor Report 2000*, p. 505.

32 Rae McGrath, *Landmines and Unexploded Ordnance*, p. 23.

33 *Ibid.*

34 *Lao*, Mines Advisory Group, May 1999.

4: The Age of the Guerrilla

1 Eric Hobsbawm, *The Age of Extremes: The Short Twentieth Century, 1914–1991* (London, Michael Joseph, 1994), p. 434.

2 *Miami Herald*, International Edition, 27 April 2001.

3 Americas Watch, *Landmines in El Salvador and Nicaragua: The Civilian Victims*, December 1986, p. 12.

4 Stephen Kinzer, *New York Times* , 10 November, 1986.

5 *Armamento Popular*, quoted in Americas Watch, *Landmines in El Salvador and Nicaragua*, December 1986, p. 25.

6 United Nations, *Portfolio of Mine-related Projects*, October 2000, p. 61.

7 Leroy Thomson, *Ragged War: The Story of Unconventional and Counter-Revolutionary Warfare* (London, Arms and Armour Press, 1994), p. 76.

8 Stephen Kinzer, *New York Times*, 19 July 1986.

9 *Ibid.*

10 White House Report, in Americas Watch, *Landmines in El Salvador and Nicaragua*, December 1986, pp. 60–1.

11 Human Rights Watch & Physicians for Human Rights, *Landmines: A*

Deadly Legacy, New York, October 1993, p. 185.

12 Americas Watch, *Landmines in El Salvador and Nicaragua*, December 1986, p. 31.

13 *Ibid.*, p. 17.

14 Monsignor Arturo Rivera y Damas, quoted in Americas Watch, *Landmines in El Salvador and Nicaragua*, December 1986, p. 13.

15 Chris Hedges, *Dallas Morning News*, 10 August 1986.

16 International Campaign to Ban Landmines, *Landmine Monitor Report 2000*, p. 270.

17 UMAS, *Mine Action Assessment Mission Report: Peru*, 3 December 1999.

18 *La Tercera*, 8 September 1997.

19 Antonio Oieni, *El Tribuno*, 16 August 1999, quoted in International Campaign to Ban Landmines, *Landmine Monitor Report 2000*, p. 222.

20 Max Hastings and Simon Jenkins, *The Battle for the Falklands* (London, Michael Joseph, 1983), p. 7.

21 *Ibid.*, p. 328.

22 *Ibid.*, p. 332.

23 *Hansard*, 30 Nobember 1999.

24 *La Nación*, 21 July 1999.

25 International Campaign to Ban Landmines, *Landmine Monitor Report 2000*, pp. 219–20.

26 *Hansard*, 30 Nobember 1999.

5: Africa's Longest Plague

1 Patrick Brogan, *World Conflicts* (London, Bloomsbury, 1998), pp. 18–19.

2 *Ibid.*, p. 19.

3 *Newsweek*, 10 July 2000.

4 Human Rights Watch Arms Project & Human Rights Watch Africa, *Landmines in Mozambique*, Human Rights Watch, New York, 1994, pp. 15, 36.

5 *Ibid.*, p. 37.

6 Alex Vines, 'The Crisis of Anti-Personnel Mines', *To Walk Without Fear: The Global Movement to Ban Landmines* (Ontario, Oxford University Press, Canada, 1998), p. 121. (US Department of Defense Document obtained by Human Rights Watch.)

7 *News of the World*, 14 September 1997.

8 William Minter, *Apartheid's Contras: An Inquiry into the Roots of War in Angola and Mozambique* (London, Zed Books, 1994), p. 285.

9 International Campaign to Ban Landmines, *Landmine Monitor Report 2000*, p. 150.

10 *Newsweek*, 10 July 2000.
11 International Campaign to Ban Landmines, *Landmine Monitor Report 2000*, p. 150.
12 Human Rights Watch Arms Project & Human Rights Watch Africa, *Landmines in Mozambique*, Human Rights Watch, New York, 1994, p. 42.
13 *Independent*, 15 January 1997.
14 Human Rights Watch Arms Project & Human Rights Watch Africa, *Landmines in Mozambique*, Human Rights Watch, New York, 1994, p. 42.
15 International Campaign to Ban Landmines, *Landmine Monitor Report 2000*, p. 133.
16 *Ibid.*, p. 134.
17 According to Mike Wilson, Programme Director of the Canadian International Demining Centre.
18 United Nations, *Portfolio of Mine-related Projects*, October 2000.
19 Brogan, *World Conflicts*, p. 95.

6: A Return to Europe

1 Patrick Brogan, *World Conflicts* (London, Bloomsbury, 1998), p. 441.
2 International Committee of the Red Cross, *The Silent Menace: Landmines in Bosnia and Herzegovina*, 1 February 1998, p. 3.
3 International Committee of the Red Cross, *The Silent Menace*, p. 4.
4 *Newsweek*, 8 April 1996.
5 International Campaign to Ban Landmines, *Landmine Monitor Report 2000*, p. 614.
6 Information provided by the Bosnia-Herzegovina Mine Action Centre, 2000.
7 International Campaign to Ban Landmines, *Landmine Monitor Report 2000*, p. 599.
8 *Ibid.*, p. 562.
9 *Ibid.*, p. 879.
10 *Ibid.*, p. 877.
11 Statistics from the UNMIK Mine Action Coordination Centre, 2001.
12 Data from ICRC, Kosovo.
13 Mines Advisory Group report on Kosovo.
14 International Campaign to Ban Landmines, *Landmine Monitor Report 2000*, p. 875.
15 *Guardian*, 8 August 2000.
16 Transcript of US State Dept. Briefing on Kosovo Landmine Problem, 28 June 1999.
17 Lieutenant-Colonel John Flanagan, *Mine Action Program in Kosovo/*

Background.

18 United Nations, *Portfolio of Mine-related Projects*, October 2000, p. 64.

19 *Ibid.*

20 *Ibid.*, p. 100.

21 International Committee of the Red Cross, *The Silent Menace*, p. 16.

22 Shawn Roberts and Jody Williams, *After the Guns Fall Silent: The Enduring Legacy of Landmines*, Vietnam Veterans of America Foundation, Washington, 1995, p. 203.

23 International Campaign to Ban Landmines, *Landmine Monitor Report 2000*, p. 596.

24 E-mail from HALO director Guy Willoughby, 10 April 2001.

25 *Hidden Killers: The Global Landmine Crisis*, report released by the US Department of State, Bureau of Political-Military Affairs, Office of Humanitarian Demining Programs, Washington, DC, September 1998.

26 E-mail from Lieutenant-Colonel John Flanagan, 3 May 2001.

27 *Ibid.*, 4 May 2001.

28 *Ibid.*, 3 May 2001.

29 *Ibid.*, 4 May 2001.

30 *Ibid.*

31 Misha Glenny, *The Balkans 1804–1999: Nationalism, War and the Great Powers* (London, Granta Books, 1999), p. 652.

32 *Victim Assistance Thematic Report 2000*, Handicap International, September 2000, p. 71.

33 *Stability Pact for South Eastern Europe*, Cologne, 10 June 1999.

7: End of Empire

1 Ahmed Rashid, *Taliban: Islam, Oil and the New Great Game in Central Asia* (London, I. B. Tauris, 2000), p. x.

2 *Ibid.*, p. 13.

3 United Nations Children's Fund, *Situation Analysis of Afghan Children and Women*, January 1992, p. 4.

4 Rashid, *Taliban*, p. 13.

5 Eric Hobsbawm, *The Age of Extremes: The Short Twentieth Century, 1914–1991* (London, Michael Joseph, 1994), p. 479.

6 *The HALO Trust: 1988–1998 The First Ten Years*, The HALO Trust, p. 2.

7 Christine Aziz, *New Internationalist*, September 1997, p. 26.

8 Rae McGrath, *Landmines and Unexploded Ordnance: A Resource Book* (London, Pluto Press, 2000), p. 14.

9 Rae McGrath, *Landmines: Legacy of Conflict*, Oxfam, 1994, p. 22.

10 *Ibid.*, p. 23.

11 Shawn Roberts and Jody Williams, *After the Guns Fall Silent: The Enduring Legacy of Landmines*, Vietnam Veterans of America Foundation, Washington, 1995, p. 43.

12 Rashid, *Taliban*, p. 22

13 *Ibid.*, p. 207.

14 *Afghanistan: The Development of Indigenous Mine Action Capacities*, Department of Humanitarian Affairs, New York: United Nations, 1998, pp. 12–13.

15 International Campaign to Ban Landmines, *Landmine Monitor Report 2000*, p. 455.

16 *Agence France-Presse*, Kabul, 5 July 2000.

17 Rashid, *Taliban*, p. 126.

18 McGrath, *Landmines*, Oxfam, 1994, p. 35.

19 Carlotta Gall, 'Land Mines, Chechnya's Hidden Killers', *Moscow Times*, 21 May 1997.

20 'Minefield Massacre Bleeds Rebels; Russia Says It Was a Trap', *Associated Press Newswires*, 4 February 2000.

21 *Ibid.*

22 Letter to the International Campaign to Ban Landmines, Alexander V. Zmeevski, Permanent Mission of the Russian Federation to the United Nations, New York, 22 October 1999.

23 International Campaign to Ban Landmines, *Landmine Monitor Report 2000*, p. 865.

24 *Chechenskaya Pravda*, 2 January 2000.

25 *Segodnya*, NTV, 6 March 2000.

26 'Minefields Will Separate Russia from Georgia', *Moscow Kommersant*, 12 April 2000.

27 International Campaign to Ban Landmines, *Landmine Monitor Report 2000*, p. 864.

28 *Ibid.*

8: Desert Storms

1 International Campaign to Ban Landmines, *Landmine Monitor Report 2000*, p. 961.

2 Human Rights Watch & Physicians for Human Rights, *Landmines: A Deadly Legacy*, Human Rights Watch, New York, 1993, pp. 35–6.

3 Anthony H. Cordsman and Abraham R. Wagner, *The Lessons of Modern Warfare: Volume 4 The Gulf War* (Westview, Boulder, CO, 1996), p. 519.

4 Lieutenant-Colonel C. E. E. Sloan RE, *Mine Warfare on Land* (London, Brassey's, 1986), p. 9.

5 *Ibid.*

6 Bruce W. Watson, Bruce George MP, Peter Tsouras and B. L. Cyr, *Military Lessons of the Gulf War* (London, Greenhill Books, 1991), p. 103.

7 Rick Atkinson, *Crusdade* (London, HarperCollins, 1994), p. 375.

8 Watson *et al. Military Lessons of the Gulf War*, p. 117.

9 Human Rights Watch, *In Its Own Words: The US Army and Anti-Personnel Mines in the Korean and Vietnam Wars*, July 1997, p. 11.

10 General Sir Peter de la Billière, *Storm Command: A Personal Account of the Gulf War* (London, HarperCollins, 1992), p. 308.

11 Don Hubert, 'The Challenge of Humanitarian Mine Clearance', in *To Walk Without Fear: The Global Movement to Ban Landmines* (Ontario, Oxford University Press, Canada 1998), p. 321.

12 Hussain Arif, quoted in Rae McGrath, *Hidden Death: Land Mines and Civilian Casualties in Iraqi Kurdistan*, Human Rights Watch, 1992.

13 Human Rights Watch, *Hidden Death: Land Mines and Civilian Casualties in Iraqi Kurdistan*, Human Rights Watch, 1992, p. 53.

14 'Iraq Objects to Demining Groups in Kurdish North', Fox News On-line, 29 December 1998.

15 Owen Boycott, *Guardian*, 2 March 1999.

16 Human Rights Watch & Physicians for Human Rights, *Landmines: A Deadly Legacy*, Human Rights Watch, New York, 1993, p. 104.

17 United States State Department, *Hidden Killers 1998: The Global Landmine Crisis.*

18 Human Rights Watch, *Hidden Death*, p. 1.

Epilogue

1 US Defense Intelligence Agency and US Army Foreign Science and Technology Center (DIK/FSTC), 'Landmines Warfare – Trends and Projections', December 1992, DST–1160S–019, pp. 1–2.

Bibliography

Americas Watch, *Landmines in El Salvador and Nicaragua: The Civilian Victims*, The Americas Watch Committee, 1986.

Africa Watch, *Landmines in Angola,* Human Rights Watch, New York, 1993.

Asia Watch & Physicians for Human Rights, *Landmines in Cambodia: The Coward's War*, Human Rights Watch & Physicians for Human Rights, New York, 1991.

Brogan, Patrick, *World Conflicts*, Bloomsbury, London, 1998.

Calvocoressi, Peter, *World Politics Since 1945*, Longman, New York, 1991.

Cameron, Maxwell A., Lawson, Robert J., Tomlin, Brian W. (eds), *To Walk Without Fear: The Global Movement to Ban Landmines*, Oxford University Press, Ontario, Canada, 1998.

Carey, John (ed.), *The Faber Book of Reportage,* Faber and Faber, London, 1987.

Clark, Alan, *Barbarossa: The Russian–German Conflict 1941–45*, Phoenix Press, London, 2000.

Corell, Paul, *Hitler's War on Russia: The Story of the German Defeat in the East*, Harrap, London, 1964.

Cornish, Paul, *Anti-Personnel Mines: Controlling the Plague of 'Butterflies'*, The Royal Institute of International Affairs, London, 1994.

Coupland, Robin M., *Assistance for Victims of Anti-Personnel Mines: Needs, Constraints and Strategy*, International Committee of the Red Cross, 1 August 1997.

Croll, Mike, *The History of Landmines*, Leo Cooper, London, 1998.

De la Billière, General Sir Peter, *Storm Command: A Personal Account of the Gulf War*, HarperCollins, London, 1992.

Glenny, Misha, *The Balkans 1804–1999: Nationalism, War and the Great Powers*, Granta Books, London, 1999.

Gray, Bruce, 'Landmines: The Most Toxic and Widespread Pollution Facing Mankind', lecture at the colloquium 'Towards Ottawa and Beyond: De-mining the Region', International House, University of Sydney, 14–17 July 1997.

Grenville, J. A. S., *The Collins History of the World in the Twentieth Century*, HarperCollins, London, 1994.

Handford, G. A., *Diary of G. A. Handford*, Imperial War Museum, London.

Handicap International, *Anti-Personnel Landmines: For the Banning of Massacres of Civilians in Time of Peace, Facts and Chronologies* (2nd edition), Handicap International, 1997.

Handicap International, *Victim Assistance Thematic Report 2000*, Handicap International, September 2000.

Handicap International & Oxfam Hong Kong, *The Cowards' War: Landmines in Vietnam*, Handicap International Belgique, 1991.

Hastings, Max, *Going to the Wars*, Macmillan, London, 2000.

Hastings, Max and Jenkins, Simon, *The Battle for the Falklands*, Pan Books, London, 1997.

Heyman, Major Charles, *Trends in Land Mine Warfare*, Jane's Information Group, Coulsdon, Surrey, 1995.

Hobsbawm, Eric, *Age of Extremes, The Short Twentieth Century, 1914–1991*, Michael Joseph, London, 1994.

Human Rights Watch, *In Its Own Words: The US Army and Anti-Personnel Mines in the Korean and Vietnam Wars*, July 1997.

Human Rights Watch & Physicians for Human Rights, *Landmines: A Deadly Legacy*, Human Rights Watch, New York, October 1993.

Human Rights Watch Arms Project & Human Rights Watch Africa, *Landmines in Mozambique*, Human Rights Watch, New York, 1994.

Hutchings, R. J., *The Private Diary of a Young Campaigner*, Imperial War Museum, London.

Ignatieff, Michael, *The Warrior's Honor: Ethnic War and the Modern Conscience*, Vintage, London, 1999.

International Campaign to Ban Landmines, *Landmine Monitor Report 2000: Toward a Mine Free World*, Human Rights Watch, 2000.

International Committee of the Red Cross, *Banning Anti-Personnel Mines: The Ottawa Treaty Explained*, ICRC, 1 February 1998.

ICRC in collaboration with the Office of the UNHCR, *The Silent Menace: Landmines in Bosnia-Hercegovina*, Geneva, 1997.

Keegan, John, *The First World War*, Hutchinson, London, 1998.

King, Colin (ed.), *Jane's Mines and Mine Clearance*, Jane's Information Group Ltd, Surrey, 1996.

Lewis, Alfred William, *Wanderers in a Strange Land: The Story of Alfred William Lewis in the 1914–1918 War*. Local History Group of the Clevedon Civic Society.

McGrath, Rae, *Cluster Bombs: The Military Effectiveness and Impact on Civilians of Cluster Munitions*, UK Working Group on Landmines, August 2000.

——, *Landmines: Legacy of Conflict – A Manual for Development Workers*, Oxfam, 1994.

——, *Landmines and Unexploded Ordnance: A Resource Book*, Pluto Press, London, 2000.

Messenger, Charles, *The Century of Warfare: Worldwide Conflict from 1900 to the Present Day*, BCA, London, 1995.

Middle East Watch, *Hidden Death: Landmines and Civilian Casualties in Iraqi Kurdistan*, Human Rights Watch, New York, 1992.

——, *Genocide in Iraq: The Anfal Campaign Against the Kurds*, Human Rights Watch, New York, 1993.

Middlebrook, Martin, *The First Day on the Somme*, Penguin Books, London, 1971.

Minter, William, *Apartheid's Contras: An Inquiry into the Roots of War in Angola and Mozambique*, Zed Books, London, 1994.

Piekalkiewicz, Janusz, *Tank War: 1939–1945*, Blandford Press, Blandford, 1986.

Pilger, John, *Distant Voices*, Vintage, London, 1992.

Roberts, J. M., *History of the World*, BCA, London, 1993.

Roberts, Shawn and Williams, Jody, *After the Guns Fall Silent: The Enduring Legacy of Landmines*, Vietnam Veterans of America Foundation, Washington, 1995.

Sloan RE, Lieutenant-Colonel C. E. E., *Mine Warfare on Land*, Brassey's, London, 1986.

Smith, Dr Chris (ed.), *The Military Utility of Landmines*, Centre for Defence Studies, King's College, University of London, June 1996.

Sneden, Robert Knox, Bryan, Charles F., Jr and Lankford, Nelson D. (eds), *Eye of The Storm: A Civil War Odyssey*, The Free Press, New York, 2000.

Teed, Peter, *Dictionary of 20th-Century History 1914–1990*, BCA,

London, 1992.

Thompson, Leroy, *Ragged War: The Story of Unconventional and Counter-Revolutionary Warfare*, Arms and Armour Press, London, 1994.

Watson, Bruce W., George MP, Bruce, Tsouras, Peter, Cyr, B. L. and the International Analysis Group of the Gulf War, *Military Lessons of the Gulf War*, Greenhill Books, London, and Presidio Press, Novato, California, 1991.

Westwood, J. N., *Eastern Front: The Soviet–German War 1941–45*, Hamlyn, London, 1984.

Williams, Robin, *A Time In My Life*, Imperial War Museum, London.

Winslow, Philip C., *Sowing the Dragon's Teeth: Landmines and the Global Legacy of War*, Beacon Press, Boston, 1997.

Ziemke, Earl F., *Stalingrad to Berlin: The German Defeat in the East*, Office of the Chief of Military History, United States Army, Washington, DC, 1968.

Hidden Killers: The Global Landmine Crisis, Report released by the US Department of State, Bureau of Political-Military Affairs, Office of Humanitarian Demining Programs, Washington, DC, September 1998.

Index